DEGUNKING™ YOUR PERSONAL FINANCES

Quick D

The Degunking 12-Step Program

Here is the basic 12-step degunking process that you should follow to fully degunk your personal finances:

1. Get your financial life organized and set aside a place in your home to work on your finances (Chapter 3).
2. Create a clear picture of your current financial situation (Chapter 4).
3. Clean up your credit and debit cards (Chapter 5).
4. Get your consumer debt under control by paying it down. (Chapter 6).
5. Fine-tune your home mortgage, and put measures in place to lower your household and other living expenses (Chapters 7 and 8).
6. Put a program together to boost your savings and investments (Chapter 9).
7. Clean up your credit report and improve your FICO credit score (Chapter 10).
8. Fine-tune and optimize your budget and improve your spending habits for transportation, groceries, and other activities (Chapters 11 and 12).
9. Get your taxes, employee benefits, and insurance in better shape (Chapter 13).
10. Find hidden money you didn't know you had (Chapter 14).
11. Put your computer to work to help you automate managing and tracking your finances (Chapter 15).
12. Improve your financial security, avoid identity theft, and put a good back-up record-keeping system in place (Chapters 16 and 17).

Degunking with Time Limitations

To get the full benefits of degunking, we highly recommend that you complete all of the main degunking tasks in the order that they are presented. Performing all of these tasks will require a bit of time. If your time is limited, however, here are some suggestions for valuable degunking tasks you can perform in the time you *do* have—whether it's fifteen minutes, three hours, or a half day.

Fifteen-Minute Degunking

If you have a very short amount of time—less than half an hour, say—you should focus on the following

1. Find some ways to spend less money on entertainment (Page 263).
2. Review your utility bills and make some changes to save a little in this area (Page 138).
3. Find out if your debt level is too high (Page 93).

Thirty-Minute Degunking

If you only have thirty minutes or so, I recommend you perform the fifteen-minute degunking plan listed above and then the following tasks to get help you get a handle on your finances:

1. Get your credit report and check your credit score (Page 38).
2. Cancel all but one or two of your credit cards and close accounts you don't intend to use (Page 76).
3. Review the interest rates on the various loans and credit cards that you have (Page 97).
4. Learn how to choose which credit card balances to pay off first (Page 99).

One-Hour Degunking

If you have an hour to degunk your finances, you can fine-tune your budget and look for hidden money. Here are the tasks to focus on:

1. Perform the thirty-minute degunking plan.
2. Organize your bills by paycheck so that you'll know what you can pay each pay period (Page 58).
3. Learn how to save money on your basic living expenses—utilities, groceries, and packaged goods (Page 143).
4. Learn which financial documents to keep and which you can toss (Page 36).
5. Eliminate some of the gunk in your house by selling or donating these items (Page 259).

Three-Hour Degunking

Because you now have a little more time to degunk your finances, with this plan you'll be able to:

1. Perform the one-hour degunking tasks.
2. Review and fine-tune your current savings strategy so that you balance your priorities (Page 155).
3. Review your paycheck withholding to make sure the current amount is being deducted (Page 235).

4. Review your employee benefits (Page 243).
5. Make record-keeping a top priority and standardize it so you stay up-to-date (Page 198).

Half-Day Degunking

When you have limited time to degunk, your focus should be on saving some money, reviewing your consumer debt, and reviewing your credit report and correcting errors that you find. Having a half day to degunk allows you to:

1. Perform the three-hour degunking tasks.
2. Use electronic bill pay to better manage your budget (Page 277).
3. Asses whether you have the right home mortgage or if it's right to refinance your home (Page 119).
4. Review your credit report in a little more detail and report any errors you find (Page 193). This may improve your credit score, too.
5. Learn about which tax deductions you can take (Page 237).

Spare Moment Degunking

There may be times when you are doing something around the house and you discover that you have a few minutes to spare. To this end, here is my Top Twenty list of degunking tasks that you can perform. These tasks do not need to be performed in any specific order. Simply select a task and perform it to improve your financial picture.

Twenty Useful Degunking Tasks

1. Organize your bills by paycheck so that you'll know what you can pay each pay period (Page 58).
2. Get your credit report and check your credit score (Page 38).
3. Review the interest rates on the various loans and credit cards that you have (Page 97).
4. Determine the true cost of using your credit cards (Page 71).
5. Cancel all but one or two of your credit cards and close accounts you don't intend to use (Page 76).
6. Determine if you have the best mortgage or if it's right to refinance your home (Page 119).
7. Review your utility bills and make some changes to get a little more for your money (Page 138).
8. Create a savings plan and start paying yourself first (Page 150).
9. Review and fine-tune your retirement savings plan (Page 158).
10. Improve your credit score by following four simple steps—pay your bills on time, keep your credit card balances low, shop for credit, and have manageable credit limits (Page 191).

11. Review your credit report and report any errors that you find (Page 183).
12. Look at what you buy and what you pay, and vow to get the best price on what you purchase (Page 204).
13. Determine what documentation to save for tax purposes (Page 202).
14. Create a separate savings account for your big expenses (Page 207).
15. Set up a budget to fund your vacations or long weekends (Page 231).
16. Adjust your paycheck withholding and plan for your tax refund (Page 235).
17. Find some ways to spend less money on entertainment (Page 263).
18. Develop a plan to pay bills electronically, paying some automatically and some manually (Page 283).
19. Organize and secure your key documents appropriately (Page 290).
20. Know what to do if a catastrophe hits your home and all your financial records are destroyed (Page 317).

Shannon Plate

President
Keith Weiskamp

Editor-at-Large
Jeff Duntemann

Vice President, Sales, Marketing, and Distribution
Steve Sayre

Vice President, International Sales and Marketing
Cynthia Caldwell

Production Manager
Kim Eoff

Cover Designer
Kris Sotelo

Degunking™ Your Personal Finances

Paraglyph Press, Inc.
4015 N. 78th Street, #115
Scottsdale, Arizona 85251
Phone: 602-749-8787
www.paraglyphpress.com

Paraglyph Press ISBN: 1-933097-02-7

Printed in the United States of America
10 9 8 7 6 5 4 3 2 1

PARAGLYPH PRESS

The Paraglyph Mission

This book you've purchased is a collaborative creation involving the work of many hands, from authors to editors to designers to technical reviewers. At Paraglyph Press, we like to think that everything we create, develop, and publish is the result of one form creating another. And as this cycle continues on, we believe that your suggestions, ideas, feedback, and comments on how you've used our books is an important part of the process for us and our authors.

We've created Paraglyph Press with the sole mission of producing and publishing books that make a difference. The last thing we all need is yet another book on the same tired, old topic. So we ask our authors and all of the many creative hands who touch our publications to do a little extra, dig a little deeper, think a little harder, and create a better book. The founders of Paraglyph are dedicated to finding the best authors, developing the best books, and helping you find the solutions you need.

As you use this book, please take a moment to drop us a line at **feedback@paraglyphpress.com** and let us know how we are doing—and how we can keep producing and publishing the kinds of books that you can't live without.

Sincerely,

Keith Weiskamp & Jeff Duntemann
Paraglyph Press Founders
4015 N. 78th Street, #115
Scottsdale, Arizona 85251
email: **feedback@paraglyphpress.com**
Web: **www.paraglyphpress.com**

Recently Published by Paraglyph Press:

Degunking Your PC
By Joli Ballew
and Jeff Dunteman

Degunking eBay
By Greg Holden

Degunking Your Email, Spam, and Viruses
By Jeff Duntemann

Degunking Windows
By Joli Ballew
and Jeff Duntemann

Degunking Your Mac
By Joli Ballew

There are some debts that cannot be repaid. I owe a great deal to Dick Towner and the Good Sense Ministry of Willow Creek Community Church. Without their trust, teaching, and encouragement, my life would be very different, and not nearly as exciting.

My deep thanks also to my husband, who unwaveringly supports my endeavors, but reins me in on occasion. I need both.

❧

About the Author

Shannon Plate is the president of Everyday Money, a budget counseling practice in Palatine, Illinois. She has an associate's degree from Harper College (Palatine, Illinois), a bachelor's degree in Psychology and Public Speaking from Roosevelt University (Chicago, Illinois), and a master's degree in Counseling Psychology from Trinity Evangelical Divinity School (Deerfield, Illinois). In her business, Shannon has seen the entire range of "gunked-up" personal finances. Her clients include individuals who are in serious financial difficulty, facing the loss of a house or personal bankruptcy. They also include those who are reeling from the death of a breadwinning spouse, enormous medical bills, or crushing credit card debt. Her firm helps individuals untangle their financial messes, take control of their debts, learn how to live on a manageable and realistic budget, and rebuild their financial health.

Shannon's career in financial counseling began when she volunteered at Willow Creek Community Church (South Barrington, Illinois) in their Good $ense program, helping people in financial distress learn how to budget their money, get out of debt, and develop long-term savings. As a previous single mother of two—who in the past has had to work several jobs just to make ends meet—Shannon was intimately aware of the challenges that single parents face in managing their money and keeping control of their indebtedness. After seeing the number of people with seriously gunked-up finances and recognizing her ability to help them out of their financial crises, Shannon was inspired to pursue the field of financial counseling as a career.

Shannon says, "Money touches all parts of our existence. You can't have money trouble and confine it to one little area of your life. It affects your relationships, your job, your lifestyle, and your self-image." Shannon found that people would talk with her about these issues, and she recognized quickly that it wasn't just money that was being discussed. It was because of this that she decided, with encouragement from people who knew her well, to get a degree in counseling. Shannon owns a small manufacturing business, runs her financial counseling firm, and continues to volunteer at her church. She has developed programs and seminars to help individuals degunk their finances and hopes this book will be a useful resource to those who are looking for help in this area. Shannon is also doing a graduate internship at Fellowship Housing, which provides low-cost housing, counseling, and care to single mothers and their children.

Acknowledgments

I owe great thanks to a variety of people for the writing of this book. To Keith Weiskamp, Steve Sayre, and the rest of the Paraglyph family, I am grateful for this opportunity, and for the gracious help and encouragement along the journey. My thanks as well to Keith Cantrell, Hugh Masterson, Mike Ryan, Carol Douglas, Tom MacCarthy, David Gaare, and Pam Jackson, all of whom answered questions at inconvenient times, and let me bother them with picky details. My continued thanks to Dr. Barbara Butler, who fed my writing bug early, and supports the habit even now.

To the clients I have worked with over the years, my profound thanks for letting me be a part of your process and your lives. You have my undying respect. To my patient friends, small group, and family, one of the truths of life is that mine would a barren wasteland without you. I am grateful.

My final thanks to America West Airlines, who sat me next to Keith Weiskamp on a flight from Arizona to Chicago, and started the process that ended with the publishing of this book. Never discount the seemingly serendipitous details of your life. You never know what may come of them.

Contents at a Glance

Contents

Introduction

Dealing with money is a necessary part of all of our lives. Seldom does a day go by when we are not expected to buy a $5 cup of coffee, pay a bill, or make a decision on future earning or spending. Within the framework of how money works in our culture, there is good news and bad news. The good news is that if you take the time to manage the resources you accumulate, your financial life can be a paved road to tremendous freedom. The bad news is that if you ignore this aspect of your life or you manage it poorly, it will only get worse. Bad financial choices, compounded over time, lead to fewer resources to work with and the good possibility of endlessly scratching to make ends meet.

There is a good solution. Positive changes you make on a daily basis will compound and bring you enormous benefits. By making some of these changes to your spending patterns permanent, you can rearrange the stars of your financial life. These changes are within your control and need only a little time and attention to produce noticeable results. That's what *Degunking Your Personal Finances* is about.

Managing your personal finances, no matter what you have to work with, can be a messy business. Unless you have done it flawlessly from the start—which is unlikely, since few of us receive any type of training to manage our money—it's quite possible that there are areas of your financial world that have become gunked up over time. Whether you haven't found time to balance your checkbook for a few months (or years), use the ATM card like it's attached to Bill Gates' account, can't remember where your investments are, or haven't seen your credit report for eons (and wouldn't understand it if you did), cleaning up your financial doings can free up time and money.

Degunking your personal finances will benefit areas of your life other than the financial. Money issues don't stay contained in your checkbook. It's very possible that your gunked-up finances are causing you worry, making you irritable, and are having a negative impact on your close relationships. If you successfully degunk your financial situation, it can improve not only your own general outlook but the way in which you deal with your friends, family, and business associates. Imagine that as a result of reducing your debt and improving your money-management skills, you have a lower stress level, a sunnier outlook, and better communication with family members. Wouldn't it be worth some time and effort on your part to improve your knowledge and understand how your money actually works in order to earn these benefits?

Why You Need This Book

Degunking Your Personal Finances is practical, easy to use, and deserving of your time. This book will give you useful instructions on what you can do *immediately* to begin cleaning up your financial situation. It will also show you how you can keep your finances degunked in the future. No matter how gunked up your finances may be, I am confident that if you read this book and use these tested methods for improving your financial picture, you will see immediate and lasting effects on your finances.

No one is born knowing how to manage money. Most of us learn these skills by watching how our parents did it. Some of us might learn a little by taking a fairly useless one-semester class in high school. Mostly, however, we learn on our own. We stumble along and get influenced by the culture we live in, and we make all kinds of mistakes. If we take on too much debt when we're young, it starts us down the very rocky road of long-term debt and can end up with the bill collectors and credit card companies having our phone number on speed dial.

Once your finances are gunked up, you might feel overwhelmed in trying to come up with a process to clean them up, especially if you're not exactly sure how they got that way in the first place. The goal of this book is to give you clear, specific ways to degunk your money issues that will have a lasting effect on your finances and your life. Here's a list of the unique features of this book:

- √ A 12-step degunking process, to be followed one step at a time, that will help you identify and degunk different areas of your financial life
- √ Ways to recognize how your finances got degunked, and how to prevent it in the future
- √ Instructions on how to physically organize your financial information
- √ GunkBuster's Notebooks in every chapter—tips that will help you improve your understanding of money and its role in your life
- √ Step-by-step instructions on how to lower and eliminate that nagging consumer debt, such as credit card balances, installment loans, and vehicle loans
- √ Degunking instructions on how to match your lifestyle choices with your financial realities

- √ Techniques for developing short- and long-term savings plans
- √ Tips on how to degunk everyday spending habits to improve your finances and make future degunking unnecessary

How to Use This Book

This book is written in the order that it should be used. Chapters 1–4 deal with the more basic degunking needs, such as how you can organize your documents and get a clear picture of how gunked up your finances are. Chapters 5–17 will then help you fine-tune the degunking process that's described at the beginning. Each of those later chapters covers a key piece of your financial picture, including credit cards, living expenses, and your personal spending habits. Once you've worked through the entire degunking process the first time, you can continue to degunk in whatever area needs special attention. For all of our good intentions, re-gunking is always a possibility. The goal with this book is to degunk your finances and keep them that way.

The Degunking Mindset

Managing money is not just following a concrete set of rules. The way we make decisions on how to earn and spend our money is a highly individualized process. *Degunking Your Personal Finances* will encourage you to have and teach you about a more knowledgeable process by which to make those decisions. If you follow the steps in this book, not only will your finances be degunked but, I hope, your life will change for the better.

Throughout this book, I talk about the mindset of degunking. *Degunking Your Personal Finances* is often more about psychology than simply having a set of money-management skills. Before you clean up your finances, it's important to understand how your finances got gunked up to begin with and what psychological triggers cause you to overspend or mismanage your money. Once you understand the roots of how you view money, you can address the behaviors associated with it. In this book, I'll show you why going to the mall "just to browse" is usually a colossally bad idea, how our sense of entitlement can ruin our finances, and why charging weekend getaways on a credit card is to be avoided at all costs. There are reasons why you should never *ever* enter a car dealership unless you've budgeted yourself for a new car purchase and why establishing financial goals as a family is essential if you are to keep your finances under control. Most bad money-management decisions can be traced to a poor understanding of why we spend. Once you understand your own view of money and why you personally spend, you'll be able to recognize those impulses that get you into financial trouble and have the tools to avoid them.

Ready for Degunking?

We are busy people. The world we live in moves quickly, and it may seem that paying stricter attention to our finances takes time that we really need for something else. As our financial gunk gets worse, though, it likely floats back toward the top of the priority list because our money problems touch so many other parts of our lives. Degunking your financial picture will take time, but it will be time well spent. If you read this book carefully, you'll develop practical techniques you can use now and in the future, and you can pass these skills on to the people in your life who are watching and learning from your money-management habits (good and bad).

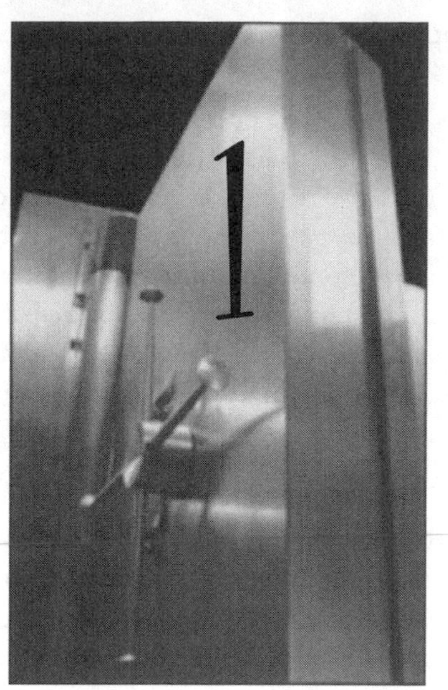

Why Are My Finances All Gunked Up?

Degunking Checklist:

√ Make sure you understand the four basic processes involved in degunking your finances.

√ Learn how (and why) your finances have gotten so gunked up in the first place.

√ Learn about the consequences of overspending and the shortfalls of underearning.

√ Understand that your finances can get gunked up from "living large" and mismanaging your credit cards.

√ Learn how important it is to have a safety net and learn to plan for emergencies and large purchases.

No one ever intends to gunk up their finances. It just happens. One time, the bills all get paid within a couple days of their arrival, and the next time you're sending the phone bill check to the gas company to create confusion and buy you some time. Late charges accumulate on accounts, interest builds, and before you realize it, 95 percent of the payment you're making is going to interest and 5 percent to principal. Paying the minimums on your credit cards gets to be a challenge in itself, and on really bad days, you might even be thinking about moving to some foreign country or donating blood to raise some quick cash. The mountain of debt suddenly gets very high and seems insurmountable.

What changed? What steps led to your finances getting out of control and becoming so gunked up? Even with circumstances somewhat less dramatic than these, financial dealings have a way of getting away from all of us, and what takes the place of good decision making is the nebulous thought that everything will somehow work out.

Our finances are like everything else in our lives—neglect leads to problems that in turn seem impossible to solve. Through a combination of poor planning, procrastination, not knowing where your money goes, and mishaps that are just part of life, your finances can get really gunked up. Your checkbook becomes impossible to read, your credit report is undecipherable, you're paying more late fees and interest than you'll divulge even to your closest friends, and your paycheck is already spent before it gets into your hand.

Fortunately, there are simple, practical ways for you to get your personal finances in order and gain more control of your life. You don't have to live in a cloud of worry, and you certainly don't have to spend your little free time dodging bothersome creditors. In this chapter, I'll explain how and why your finances have likely gotten gunked up in the first place. Whatever the state of your finances now, the first step is to know how you got in the weeds. Without this information, it's nearly impossible not to end up back there again, and the work you do in the interim can simply be a pause in the chaos, as opposed to a more permanent fix.

The Degunking Difference

As a financial counselor, I have been helping individuals and couples get out of financial trouble for a number of years. After helping lots of folks take back control of their financial situations and get rid of the gunk and clutter that holds them hostage, I've noticed some basic patterns that seem to get people into trouble. There are practical solutions and procedures to help solve these problems. What makes this book different from others on the "personal finances" shelf is that it will present problem-solving techniques to you in a manner that you can readily use to help change your situation.

What I'm about to share with you isn't difficult and doesn't take as much time as you might think. You don't need a degree in math; in fact, you don't even have to like math. Much of it is based on common sense and applying simple organizational skills. By following these steps in order, you can keep your personal finances in good shape and get rid of the confusing clutter that's making a mess of your financial organization:

1. *Basic financial housekeeping.* Here I'll focus on how to get your finances set up properly and rid yourself of the clutter you don't need. You'll learn how to get all of your financial data organized and how to create a clear picture of your current financial situation. My goal is to help you quickly create a budget that is a realistic tool in your financial life. You'll also learn how to start paying down any costly consumer debt and learn how to degunk your credit and debit cards. After you complete this first set of tasks, you'll feel as good as you do when you finish cleaning out that icky corner of the basement you've ignored for years.
2. *Building a more solid financial foundation.* Once you've gotten your debt under control, it's time to start building more financial resources for your future. We'll start by looking at how you can improve your home mortgage situation (if you have one) and your housing and living expenses. These expenses can often be loaded with hidden charges and fees and can cause you to waste money that could be used in other areas. It's probable that you're spending a bit more money than you should, and that can stop, much to your benefit. You'll also learn how to degunk your savings and investments, and be able to develop an investment strategy that you can understand and put into practice. Won't it be great to finally begin saving?
3. *Repairing less-than-perfect financial issues and fine-tuning your finances.* Everyone should be fully aware of what is on their credit report. Your credit report is like your financial passport, and if you maintain it well, it can help get you into places you want to go. If you neglect it, on the other hand, you'll pay a higher price for any credit you might obtain. We'll start by looking at how credit reports really work, and you'll learn how to get yours in much better shape. We'll also spend time fine-tuning and optimizing your budget, as well as degunking your other spending habits for areas such as transportation, grocery shopping, and clothing purchases.
4. *Improving your financial security.* You can think of these tasks as the icing on the cake of your financial degunking process. Here, you'll learn how to find hidden money and use your computer to help you automate important

financial tasks (such as paying your bills online). You'll learn how to deal with financial security issues like identity theft and how to set up a system for safe record-keeping. I'll also give you some tips on what to do when things go wrong with your finances. Unfortunate things do happen, but having a good financial plan in place will help you to better ride out the storm.

Understand How Your Personal Finances Got So Gunked Up

To see the unfortunate (and sometimes hidden) effect of gunk, take a moment and think back to when your finances weren't so gunked up. Spend some real time thinking back to when your finances seemed in control, the bills got paid on time, and money was regularly going into a savings account.

When did you first notice things had changed? There was probably a time when things were running more smoothly than they are now. What were the differences? Was it before children, before the new house purchase, before changing jobs? Did a wedding incur new financial challenges, or did the marriage partners bring gunk with them? Was a move to a new area, a new hobby, or a new relationship the beginning of financial gunking? For some, addictions have played a huge role, and dealing with gambling, drug abuse, or alcoholism have had major effects on their finances, along with the rest of their lives. Pinpoint when things started to go wrong.

Reality Check: The point of reviewing your financial missteps is to reflect back on how your financial circumstances have changed. We often get overwhelmed with gunk over the years, only to find ourselves in a situation we don't know how to fix. For right now, I simply want you to do a quick review of how you got to the position you are in currently. At this stage, it's very important for you to be honest with yourself. Get out a pad of paper and list the things you think have really gunked up your finances. Think about it chronologically—what has happened recently to contribute to your situation and what problems have been around messing things up from an earlier time frame? Once you compile your list of gunk contributors, take a look at the list I've provided to see if, perhaps, there's something you may have forgotten to include.

The Consequences of Overspending

Consistent overspending is a guaranteed gunker for your finances. The culture in the U.S. provides us with a huge selection of credit opportunities designed to keep us well in debt. Without self-discipline, we can spend more than we earn for the rest of our natural born days. The consequence of this behavior is that the money you do earn is never really yours—it is already promised to pay for the meal you had last month, the tires you bought last year, or the shoes you bought for your friend's wedding and wore only once. There is no freedom there, and no joy in spending the money you have. Make a commitment now, starting today, to *spend less than you earn*.

The Shortfalls of Underearning

You'll likely experience a time in your work life when you take a cut in pay. This is painful on many fronts. For a variety of reasons, in the current economy, a job change could mean you'll receive less pay instead of a raise. Economic downturns can drastically affect the availability of jobs in general, and it is often necessary to take a lower-paying job. In the early 2000s, many professionals had to quickly downsize and reduce their lifestyles for just this reason. I've worked with many clients who, at the height of their earning potential, took cuts of up to 50 percent in their pay and had to cut their lifestyles by the same amount. In these cases, in order to restrict the strain to your finances that earning less can cause, you'll need to immediately change your budget and lifestyle to fit your new economic limitations. You might need to take actions as considerable as downsizing your home or take somewhat less drastic ones, such as reducing the number of times you eat out, cutting back on your spending for entertainment, and reducing extracurricular activities for your children.

Lifestyle Enlargement

A common way for finances to get gunked up is from "living large." It's possible you have piled on too many lifestyle enhancements. There are always new toys to be had, new gadgets that will make your life easier, and a new way to get even more than the standard 150 channels on your TV. Savvy marketers are happy to provide unlimited ways to make your lifestyle more expensive, and it is imperative to draw a personal line as to what is reasonable and affordable and what is, for you, bordering on the ridiculous. Comparing your situation to others can be a huge detriment in this area. Everyone's income, priorities, and needs are different, and so will their lifestyles differ. Don't use someone else's lifestyle to determine your own. When it becomes possible or necessary to upgrade or add a lifestyle enhancement to your life (a new TV or a different car), be reasonable in your choice and plan for your purchase. Save up, pay cash, and don't let the 42-inch plasma model peeking out through your neighbor's curtains have anything to do with what you decide to buy.

Credit Card Mismanagement

A common misconception concerning credit cards is that they are good sources of personal credit. In reality, they shouldn't be used for credit except for emergency situations. If your car dies on the interstate outside of Kalamazoo on a holiday weekend, you may need to have it towed and get a hotel room overnight while you try to talk someone into fixing it (yes, this did happen to me; not much to do in Kalamazoo over Labor Day weekend). Credit cards should be used for convenience. Nothing should be charged on a credit card that is not budgeted for, and all cards should be paid off every month. The credit card companies dislike this approach because it reduces their profits by millions. Interest charges that can go up to 30 percent will not only gunk up your finances but are a sure way of keeping you far from your financial goals. To keep from mismanaging your credit cards, you'll need to practice self-discipline. You'll also need to set up a budget and an emergency fund that you can draw on in times of need, or in times of the most amazing shoe sale ever.

Unexpected but Necessary Expenses—Lack of a Safety Net

Financial gunk can occur when the unexpected happens and you don't have a safety net. If the refrigerator suddenly stops working or something falls out of the innards of the car, your only choice seems to be to dig out the credit card and get the problem fixed. After a few of these instances, the strain on your finances is evident. A long-term solution for unexpected expenses is to build up an emergency fund, worked into your budget as an expense. A short-term solution is to carefully decide what needs fixing and what doesn't. You may need the car to get to work, but a broken DVD player isn't an emergency in anybody's book except Blockbuster's.

Financial life can be dangerous, and a safety net is so very necessary. Savings are important for both emergency short-term use (fixing the aforementioned car to get another 10,000 miles out of the old mare) and long-term use (saving for college, retirement, and that wire cart to hold your groceries). If you don't have a solid emergency fund, you can get further into debt for expenses that can't be avoided. An expense like college for your infant children may seem far away now; think of how much easier it would be to start saving $150 per month now, as opposed to coming up with $60,000 overnight. The only way to formulate savings is to have it as a line item on your budget. If you wait until you have "enough" to save, the piggy bank will get little use.

Not Planning for Large Expenditures

Cars die. They are designed to run for only so long, and even if you try to take good care of your car and do everything you are supposed to do, it will, at some point, sputter, gasp, and quit. Major and minor appliances work the same way, as do roofs and gutters, your heating system, and your microwave. The only way to stay ahead of all the time-saving, comfort-giving, money-eating devices in your life is to set money aside to replace them when the dreaded time comes. Although it may seem that all of your money would be needed to fulfill this requirement, it is not the case. The key is, for example, to start saving for your next car when you drive the one you just purchased off the lot.

Sense of Entitlement

Every culture has its norms. In the American culture, it seems that everyone 12 and older has a cell phone, everyone 16 and older has a car, and the amount we spend on clothing is equal to the defense budget for some small countries. Buying into what you think you have to have because everyone else seems to and you certainly deserve it can be a sure way to add gunk to your finances. What you attain should be decided by what you can reasonably afford, divided by what you need and want. Tell the Joneses they win, and get entitlement out of your mind.

Planned but Ill-Financed Life Changes

We often take on major life-changing activities, such as getting married, buying a new home, having a child, and starting a new business, without really thinking through the financial requirements. Leaping head-first into financial decisions without careful thought is a dangerous way to handle your money, and it can be financially disastrous if you overextend and then a catastrophic life change occurs (see the next section). Whenever you think about making a major life change, stop and put some thought into how you are going to pay for everything. Don't let yourself get into a situation without first reviewing how your decision will impact your finances.

Catastrophic Life Changes

The only thing you can count on in life is its unpredictability. Unfortunate and unwanted changes can be draining on your finances, and the emotional upheaval that comes with them can make managing your affairs very difficult. Death, divorce, job loss, illness, natural disaster—any of these events can make mincemeat out of your budget. Having your finances in order can help, but if the worst happens and the sky falls in, you'll likely have some major gunk to clean up when the dust settles. Be aware that any catastrophe will cause more changes in its wake, and be ready to make allowances when necessary.

Co-signing and Common Debt

Co-signing is very risky and usually not advisable. In going into a co-signing situation, the litmus test is whether you can afford to make 100 percent of the arranged payments for the life of the loan, as that is what you are promising to do if the primary signer defaults. Most co-signers who get burned were brought into the deal with heartfelt promises and good intentions, and many a friendship or family has been torn apart when promised payments are missed and the credit rating of the co-signer suffers alongside that of the primary. Consider how having two car or mortgage payments could gunk up your finances. Common debt, such as buying a home together or sharing a boat, can be unpleasant as well, and it is imperative to discuss and prepare for all such transactions with a lawyer so that all parties fully understand the terms of the deal.

Bad Investment or a Failing Business

A contributor to financial gunk, and one that few like to talk about, is bad investments or a failing business. If you make poor investment or get involved in a business that is going south, it's difficult to know when to throw in the towel and admit defeat. As human beings, we're somewhat wired to think the best and hope things will turn out well if we just keep working at it. The "My luck is about to change" song plays in our heads, and it seems certain that the situation will get better momentarily. The truth is that a bad investment or a failing business doesn't have anything to do with luck. When defeat is clear, chalk up your experience (and loss) as an investment in your education, and learn how to make better choices. A bad investment or failing business can gunk up your finances for years, but the sooner you get out of a bad situation, the less damage it will do (and the less gunk you'll need to clean up).

Overgiving to Charitable Organizations without a Plan

Finding a charitable organization you believe in and donating what you can helps keep them alive and able to do their important work. Gunk can occur, however, when you make gifts without first understanding the impact they will have on the rest of your budget. It can be easy to get carried away by the emotion of the moment and sign a monthly automatic withdrawal that makes paying the electric bill impossible. Charitable giving must be worked out in the context of your budget. Prioritizing giving as you do saving (give and save first, and work the budget around what's left) may help you decide how much and what to give. As with saving, if you don't make giving a priority, it probably won't happen, so if it is important to you, get it in your budget and treat it as you would a budget line item, as opposed to writing checks on a whim and hoping the money will magically appear.

This will also help you keep from getting caught up in scams disguised as religious, environmental, or child-saving advertisements that want your money but have little to show for what you give. When giving to any organization, first check into what they stand for, what happens to the money given (the organization's financial statements can be requested), and who specifically benefits from your hard-earned money.

Technological Pitfalls

In this golden age of technology, convenience can sometimes add to your pile of gunk. Signing up for automatic withdrawals can make certain your bills are paid on time, but if your account is running short, overdraft fees can add a quick $30 to a transaction, making that free service quite expensive. Before electing to allow automatic withdrawals, you must have organization in place to make sure the money gets there before that automatic hand reaches in to take it. Before using an ATM card on a regular basis, you must have a system by which to track what is leaving your account. By first getting your finances in order, using technology can be an asset instead of yet another area of your financial life that is confusing and unclear.

Ready for Degunking?

We are busy people. The world we live in moves quickly, and it may have seemed that paying more strict attention to your finances took time you really needed for something else. As the financial gunk gets worse, however, it floats back toward the top of the priority list because how we deal with our money touches so many other parts of our lives. Degunking will take time, but it will be time well spent and it will be information you can use now and in the future and pass on to the people in your life who are watching you do this and learning from your habits, good or bad. This will become individualized, like a recipe for really good deviled eggs. Everybody makes them, but you really like yours the best. Get out the pot, and start degunking!

In the next chapter, I'm going to share advice on getting your finances degunked and back in order. There is a practical 12-step financial degunking program that, if followed step-by-step, will help you clean up your financial situation in a regulated and timely manner. By sticking to the program, you can work toward a financial future that will be gunk-free and stress-free, helping to create a better life for you and your family. Sound good to you? My guess is that it may be just what your finances (and your family) need.

Where Do I Start Degunking My Finances?

Degunking Checklist:

- √ Learn why taking control of your finances is a critical part of degunking them.
- √ Decide on your own financial goals, and see how managing your money and spending your money are interrelated.
- √ Discover the #1 most important lesson in managing your money.
- √ Learn how to develop self-control when you shop.
- √ If you're part of a couple, learn why communication is important when discussing gunked-up finances.
- √ Get a reality check on your actual financial situation.
- √ Find out if your sense of entitlement is gunking up your personal finances.
- √ Learn that degunking your finances can help reduce your stress—immediately!
- √ Learn the degunking 12-step program and put it into practice.

Take control of your finances! As you sit there reading, the thought of your gunked-up finances may seem overwhelming. Fortunately, the good news is that you can learn how to put your finances in order and maintain them as you continue to work, earn, and spend money. If you approach this problem with the right mindset, you'll be amazed at what you can accomplish. Even if you have limited time (as most of us do), any step you perform will help you take control.

You may never have had control of your finances, or you did until an unforeseen event occurred that changed your financial picture. Whatever the case, take control now. Remember that you will have to deal with money for the rest of your life. Money management is a skill like any other. Unlike your short foray into racquetball, money management is a skill you will need and use long after your fancy racquet ends up in the garage, gathering dust.

This chapter will show you how to immediately start the process of taking control of your finances. This is Degunking 101. In Chapter 1, you learned how your finances can get gunked up in the first place. Now it's time roll up your sleeves and create a plan that really works to help your situation .The 12-step degunking plan is designed to greatly improve your financial situation and, in turn, your life. Working through this chapter will help you get into the important mindset of degunking, and in the following chapters, you will learn how to complete the 12 essential steps of the degunking program. As you read on, an important thing to understand about the degunking program is that you'll get the best results if you follow the process outlined in this book in the order that it is presented.

Taking Charge of Your Finances Is the Key

Lack of money management skills can make your life seem unpredictable—and sometimes downright miserable. The constant worry of not having enough money to pay bills, save for college, or buy clothing for growing children creates tremendous stress, and in this culture, most of us are already frazzled by the pace of life. In a household with financial worries, usually everyone who can work does, and family relationships can suffer from neglect and lack of communication. As working carries with it certain expenses (such as transportation, child care, and clothing needs), the money you make doesn't go nearly as far as it seems it should. Although everyone may be working as hard as they can, this doesn't guarantee that your family has *control* over its finances.

Whatever your situation, and whatever depth of gunk you're swimming in, establishing the habit of keeping your personal finances degunked is imperative.

Ignoring a bad financial situation is like ignoring your lawn—not paying attention to your grass doesn't mean it stops growing. The longer you don't mow, the harder it is to manage when you finally get the mower out and the more time and work it will take to get the lawn looking good again.

Take the time and effort to get a handle on your financial situation now. This book is about taking control of your financial life, eliminating stress, and achieving your goals—in short, it's about you taking the reins of your financial life. If you make the 12-step degunking program a part of your routine, these simple steps will make money management forever easier, automatic, and less stressful. You and your money will be dance partners forever. The key is to make sure you're always the one leading.

Focus on the Future!

Although it's important to know how you got into this situation, it's not usually helpful to spend much more time whaling on yourself, or your partner, for the current situation. You've probably spent enough time worrying and blaming, so now let's do something about it. Remorse is fine, to a point, but the focus now needs to be on making changes and forming a better future. My job, as I see it, is to help you clean up the mess and get you headed on to a better path! Over the years, I've worked with people who have gotten into many different types of financially difficult situations. Most of this was the result of not having a good system in place for managing finances and of making some poor choices. What's important now is that you take an honest look at your current situation and work on developing solutions for the issues at hand. Throughout this book, I'll provide tips and suggestions to help you degunk your situation and achieve success.

Understand the Benefits of Financial Freedom

When your finances are gunked up, you may feel as if you're stuck in the corner with no way out—you completely lose your sense of freedom. Every dollar earned is promised to someone else and is, in essence, already spent. Somehow, money is scraped together for Christmas, new clothes, or an occasional evening out, but there is no joy in these purchases because you know the money should be going to pay for something else. Guilt abounds, and lethargy can set in that encourages negativity. "Why bother trying to fix it?" the Bad Voice says. "It's never going to get better."

The Bad Voice is lying because there is hope for anyone with gunked-up personal finances. Right now, you probably can't see the benefits that can come from taking what you have and creating a budget that not only allows, but encourages, spending for the things you want and need. How would it feel to know there is money available for clothing, gifts, and even an unexpected weekend away? In terms of saving, any money stashed away will grow, and it is never too late to begin contributing to accounts for college or retirement. The fact that you might not have all you need when that time arrives is no excuse to not save now.

Financial freedom can mean many things. Although it can mean that money is freed up for you to spend, it can also mean there is money for you to give. Chances are there have been causes or charities you have wanted to support but felt that you couldn't afford to pull money from other sources for that use. Giving of your time is often a good contribution, but these organizations still have electric bills and staff to pay. Managing your finances well can free up money to give, and the personal satisfaction (and tax benefits) from these gifts can make your effort and sacrifices even more real.

Another plus to financial freedom is the effect it will have on any children in your home. Children watch how you manage and spend your money and will, to some extent, emulate you when they are on their own. Are you providing a good example? If you have been challenged financially, you will inspire and teach your children if you change how you handle money and develop the self-discipline to make your household less stressful and money less of an issue.

At the end of the day, you get to choose. Developing financial freedom will take work, but with a little vision, the benefits will be obvious. The longer your finances have been gunked up, the longer it will take to degunk them. The good news is the benefits will steadily build over time. As your budget gets in place, money will be better spent and your consumer debt will decrease. That will free up more money to pay off other debt more quickly, freeing up money to spend, save, or give in other areas. As the process continues, more benefits will present themselves, and you get to make more decisions concerning your money.

Hmm. That sounds like freedom, doesn't it?

Decide on Specific Financial Goals

The first step in your new financial life is deciding on intentional goals. If you are part of a couple, this needs to be done together. Without specific goals to work toward, your personal financial situation will continue to attract gunk, and any efforts you undertake will be fragmented and counterproductive. A good way to decide on your goals is to write them all down and then prioritize them in the order they need to be addressed. Here are three possible goals:

1. Incur no further debt.
2. Take a cruise for an upcoming anniversary.
3. Pay off your credit cards.

To incur no further debt, paying off the credit cards needs to come before the cruise. It's probable the cruise may have to wait, but how much more enjoyable will it be if you know it is paid for and you're not using resources that should be channeled toward other debt reduction? The fun you have on the cruise will not end the moment you leave the ship and come home to the bills you left, plus the bills for the cruise. Imagine what a difference that would make!

Financial goals come in two flavors. Some goals have to do with managing money, and some have to do with spending it. Write down your goals, and separate them into those two categories. You might have some of the following financial goals:

Managing Your Money	Spending Your Money
Incur no further consumer debt.	Buy new or used car for cash.
Pay all bills on time.	Pay down credit cards.
Develop an emergency fund.	Save for college.
Pay off school loans early.	Buy a larger house.
Save for retirement.	Send the kids to music camp this summer.
Pay into 401k plan at work.	Give to church building fund.
Don't bounce checks.	Help Mom with expenses.
Don't use overdraft protection.	Take a vacation once a year.
Balance bank accounts each month.	Buy vacation property.

Before you spend any money, it's important that you think about how that purchase will align with the items in the "Managing Your Money" category. Thinking about buying a new suit? Perhaps not. This expense probably conflicts with several items in the "Managing Your Money" category, such as "incur no further consumer debt" or "don't bounce checks."

Both of these lists should include short-term and long-term goals. While not bouncing checks is something you can work at today, developing an emergency fund is a longer-term project. Helping your mom with her expenses may happen more quickly than saving up enough cash for a new car.

TIP: At the top of every "Managing Your Money" list should be "Incur No Further Consumer Debt." For your goals to be realized, this hole in your financial dam must be plugged up. The accumulation of consumer debt (such as credit cards, overdraft protection, payday loans, car loans, and buying furniture with an installment loan) is a deal-breaker when it comes to financial goals. Adding to consumer debt will cripple your plans for the future and remove any hope for the financial freedom you are working toward. With my apologies to Nike: Just Don't Do It.

Take Control of Your Money

None of your goals will be met without a plan. Really wanting them to happen isn't enough. Armed with this book, you will learn how to be actively involved with how your money is spent and how you want the rest of your financial life to look. Even before you get down to developing a budget, you can help your situation greatly by putting some basic controls in place. These may seem picky at first, but they are all good habits for the purpose of achieving your financial goals.

So much of managing anything has to do with making decisions and taking some action instead of getting carried away by the moment. To that end, take away the opportunities to spend money impulsively:

- √ *Don't go shopping unless you have a purchase you must make.* Wandering the mall as entertainment is a financial accident waiting to happen. You will certainly run across an unbudgeted item that is either so cheap you can't believe it or so perfect you can't live without it. Don't put yourself in that position.
- √ *Before grocery shopping, make a list and stick to it.* There are companies that make a very nice living by getting you to buy things in grocery stores that you don't want or need. The next time you are in a store, take notice of the items that are stacked at the end of aisles. The companies that produce these products pay huge money to place their products right in your face, and they put lots of effort into making them look attractive to you. Don't fall for this marketing strategy and buy items not on your list because of their location in the store. Another important shopping tip is that, although it will take some time to get used to, try not to buy anything at the grocery store that is not on sale. It all gets cheaper on a regular basis, and buying your Cheerios at $2.00 a box instead of $3.50 can save you a chunk of money every week. Join your grocery store's "club" program to take advantage of all price breaks. Coupons are good, if you have the patience, and putting a coupon toward an item that's already on sale will net you even larger savings.

- √ *Don't step foot on a car lot unless you have a car purchase budgeted.* This is a dangerous place to be without the intention of buying a car. I have a friend who was at the dealership for a repair, and instead of spending her time in the dingy waiting room, waited in the new car showroom for her car to be fixed. What stunned her was that the salesmen, when there were no actual customers present, took turns pretending to be customers, giving each other the opportunity to try out new sales techniques. Car salesmen are trained in inflaming your vision of having a new car even though you can't afford one. Keep in mind that their concern is making a living, not managing your money, and their consideration for you ends as soon as you sign the papers for the vehicle. Stay away from the shiny cars that look so very much better than yours. Stay far, far away. If you feel tempted to get a new car, consider having yours detailed instead. It's amazing how good a nice clean car can make you feel.
- √ *Do not attend sales presentations for time-shares, cruises, lake property, or anything else with the thought that you will just win the car they're giving away and go home.* These salespeople are trained to not let you leave the room without signing something. It is simply not worth the crummy nylon carry-on bag that will be your consolation prize (instead of the car they practically promised you), and you may end up tied into a 25-year contract for a time-share you didn't plan for and can't afford.

These are only a few action steps you can take to control the spending of your money. You probably know what your particular weak spots are, so use that knowledge for your benefit and avoid the danger areas that can do damage to your financial plan. And, yes, that includes the unbudgeted trips to the flea market and the golf shop tent sale.

Know What Is Happening with Your Finances

One of the main goals behind the strategy of degunking your finances is finding out what you're working with. Once your finances get gunked up, it may seem easier to ignore them and wait to see if it all works itself out. That's like waiting for the drip under the sink to fix itself. Not only will it continue dripping, it will just get messier (and costlier) if you don't pay attention to it now.

In order for degunking to work, you need to dig into all areas of your financial life. There can't be any black holes concerning your money, and as knowledge is power, you will be much better equipped to degunk if you fully know what is gunked up in the first place.

GunkBuster's Notebook: Advice for Couples

An important word is necessary here concerning couples or other partners or friends sharing their money. For you, dividing the financial duties probably derived from convenience. One person may be better at it than the other, or one had more access to the checkbook, computer, and drive-in at the bank. In the hustle of life, financial information is often not shared between partners, and if the discussion could prove to be unpleasant, it can be easily avoided like the plague. For a couple whose finances are getting more gunked up by the day, not talking about financial challenges or spending habits can make matters much worse. Resentments can build for the partner who must deal with the entire mess, and the person not in the know can be oblivious to their behaviors or may get good and mad about not being in the loop when the nasty truth finally reveals itself. Although it may be easy to pile fault on one party, it is counterproductive to add a mound of guilt to the mix. Here are some immediate steps you can take:

- √ Make an agreement to open up communication in this issue, with no fingers pointed, so both of you can be on the same page and get to degunking your joint finances together.
- √ Decide what needs to be changed, make an agreement on what needs to be done, and be accountable to each other for the results.
- √ Schedule some time to follow up with each other and review how you are doing. Going over the monthly finances is a great way of facilitating follow-up conversations about how things are going and what you need to change or improve in your degunking plans.

No matter how your finances got gunked up in the first place, it is a problem for you to solve together. When I meet with couples, it is often the case that there seems to be one person who is (or is perceived to be) more responsible than the other. If this situation feels familiar, it's important to work together to solve these issues. Pointing fingers will likely get you further into trouble and won't do a single good thing for your communication. The best thing you can do is develop a strategy together so that you can change your behaviors as a couple. It's natural that one of you might be better at financial activities—like planning, budgeting, and paying the bills—than the other. If this is the case, develop a plan so that each person can do the activities that fit best with their strengths and interests.

For any degunking step, having as much information as possible can never hurt the process. If you have never balanced your checkbook and don't know how, ask someone who does. Many banks have online services that make balancing your monthly statement much easier than it used to be. Even bank statements are easier to decipher than before. If you don't want to ask a friend, get a book from the library. If your investment statements make as much sense to you as a French menu, ask your broker to explain them. If they can't find the time, take your business elsewhere. If there are strange charges on your phone bill or credit card statement, or if the budgeted amount on your gas bill changes, make a phone call. You are the consumer, and you are paying the bills. Get all of the information you need, and use it to your benefit.

Reality Check: Your personal finances can get gunked up when you make decisions based on what you think will happen, or what you wish would happen, instead of what is really happening. Optimism, for all of its good qualities, can end up steering you away from reality if you don't keep a good eye on it. Sometimes, plans are made presuming what will happen in the future, and when the future doesn't cooperate, gunk happens. Counting on the raise or bonus you were promised, the sale of your car, or the increase in stock prices before you actually have the money can cause terrific problems if you spend it prematurely. Deals fall through and decisions change. It's not really yours until you have it in your hand, and spending it before then can cause a huge mess.

Education Loans

It is a common fallacy that more education will automatically get you a better job making more money. Many people take out student loans under the assumption that getting a degree will instantly make them the money to easily pay back the loans and keep them in bonbons forever. Although education may well get you where you want to go, be very careful about the level of debt you accumulate to that end. Student loans are like any other debt. There are a great number of people walking around with tens of thousands of dollars in student loans who are not using their degree—which they will still be paying for 15 years from now. I am not downplaying the value of getting a good education. I've had a fair bit of it myself. It is important, however, to find ways to fund it responsibly.

Some people seem to have the attitude that a student loan is a debt that they don't have to pay back. This is simply not true. Being in default on your student loan can hurt your credit record like any other defaulted loan and can keep you from being able to get credit or good rates when you apply for a home mortgage. An education loan is like any other type of a loan. You must pay it back on time or you will be charged penalties and points on your credit score.

College Credit Card Debt

Even more harmful for students is racking up credit card debt while in college. Opportunities to apply for credit cards are everywhere on campus (a fact I find infuriating), from applications in your textbooks to tables set up in the cafeteria giving you a free T-shirt in exchange for your credit card application. What a great racket for the credit card companies—offer credit to college students with little or no income, give them a limit of a few hundred dollars, give them a few different cards to max out before they leave school, and the pattern of being in debt feels normal to them. The interest piles, the payments go up, and between credit card payments and student loans, this 22 year-old won't see a full paycheck for 10 years or more.

Good Intentions

Gunk can also accumulate as a result of really good intentions. When in financial trouble, people in the heat of the moment will decide that now is the time to do something that they have wanted to do for years and that will also benefit their finances: quit smoking, stay off of eBay, stop going to the gambling boat, or stay away from garage sales. Although their hearts are good, often these habits are not quite so easy to break, and the result on their finances is double spending—once on the forbidden carton of cigarettes and another on the electric bill that the money saved from quitting smoking was to pay.

Although the habit still took her life, when my mother quit smoking, she put all the money she saved in the back of her wallet and bought things she wouldn't have been able to purchase before, like beautiful sable paintbrushes and a new couch. She bought gifts for her children and grandchildren, and she lamented all the money she spent on cigarettes the 50 years she smoked. Although she had tried several times in the past to quit, the money didn't get to the back of her wallet until she actually did quit.

Another mine field of good intentions is helping out relatives or close friends who are in financial need. You may be tempted to help poor old Aunt Agnes or the neighbor who is going through a nasty divorce. It may be your parents who always seem to need something, or perhaps a child that just can't seem to get it together. While help to family members is sometimes required, your own financial well-being needs to be a top priority for you and those in your life. Consider very carefully whether you can provide financial assistance (and, if it is truly in their best interests) to those who ask for it.

Work with Real Information

When making financial decisions, work with your current information. As your income or expenses change, decide then what to alter. If you get a raise, decide whether to save it, use it to pay off credit card debt, or put it away for your children's education. The only exception to this rule is when you think your income may be going down. If you think you might be laid off, or if you are having a baby and not returning to work or taking time off, change your spending patterns immediately, even before the change takes place. Lower all of your variable spending to accommodate the lowest possible income for the changing season. Your checkbook (and your mortgage company) will thank you.

Eliminate Entitlement

A strong sense of entitlement is common in many cultures, and the more luxuries available, the more common a sense of entitlement becomes. Feeling you deserve something because so many others around you have it can spell death for your financial life. Many advertisers encourage us to buy by telling us we "owe ourselves" this car, or vacation, or house, or diamond. Making purchases with entitlement as your deciding factor is a perfect way to make a mess of your money. Now is your chance to decide if your own sense of entitlement is out of control. Has it gunked up your finances?

To get degunked and stay gunk-free, your decisions about what to buy must be made as a result of careful consideration of your needs and resources. Envy and coveting don't get a line in your budget. The truth is that there will always be someone who has more money and stuff than you do, and many people who will have less. For your mental and financial health, be thankful for what you can afford and take your eyes away from what you can't.

There are several mythological entitlements capable of gunking up your finances. Let's look at some of the biggest ones.

Everyone Needs a Cell Phone to Be Safe

Not. Cell phones are a very recent invention. The world survived a good long time without them, and although they may make life more convenient, your ultimate safety doesn't count on having one. There are benefits to having a cell phone with you in case of emergency (and how often do emergencies happen, really?), and if you feel the need for that security, there are various cell phone plans to fit your need and budget. Check with the major carriers on their offerings, but keep in mind that charges for excess minutes can rapidly add up. If you have had previous financial trouble with a cell phone or are concerned about going over on your minutes, consider a prepaid cell phone. You buy the cell phone, purchase phone card minutes separately, and transfer them to the phone. When you use them up, you buy another card. It can go a long way to restricting your use of the phone and keeping you from getting an unexpected $300 cell phone bill.

Every 16-Year-Old Needs a Car

From the insurance statistics alone, this may not be a good idea. Teens are four times as likely to be involved in a fatal crash than people in their 30s. Until a teenager has the time and chaperoned opportunity to get to know what a car can and cannot do, having one for full-time use may not be wise. Although it might make parents' lives easier to give the teenager a car, financially it can be detrimental as well.

From the cost of the car itself to the gas, repairs, licenses, and stickers, another car in the family can be a huge drain on resources. Insurance alone is very costly. For a female driver insured on her parents' policy, the price of insurance can go up 35 percent to 50 percent, and for a male, it will raise 50 percent to 100 percent. These numbers are leveling out, actually, as teenage female drivers are proving themselves worthy of lower rates. If there is a car for each licensed driver, the teen is the primary driver on one of the cars. Then, insurance can double once again. It is possible that your teen has offered to pay all of the expenses associated with owning a car. What must be considered at that point is the time needed to work to pay those costs. Will working negate the opportunity to be involved in school activities, or will grades suffer as a result of working enough hours to pay for car payments, insurance, and gas? To everything there is a cost, and a determination needs to be made on the liability of tying the teen to the responsibility of owning a car.

You Need New Clothes

Take a good look in your closet. Count the number of items you rarely or never wear. Estimate how much you spent on those items. Imagine what you could have done with that money instead. No matter who you are, chances are that you own more clothing than you need. Not only will the sheer amount of clothing you may buy be hard on finances, but where you buy may be costing you as well. Designer labels keep the designers happily ensconced in their Malibu beach houses, but in reality they buy you little more than the see-through status of wearing DKNY, even though no one knows that but you. Shop where you never thought you'd shop for clothing, and if you still have a favorite designer (or you just love the Gap no matter what I say), look for better prices at outlet stores or whatever poses for T.J. Maxx where you live.

You Need the Latest Gadgets

The world is full of companies and marketers that are masters at convincing us that we need the latest new toy. Pick up a magazine at the newsstand, scan through a few pages, and you'll see the ads. Every year, manufacturers come out with more and "better" versions of what we already have—DVD players, home theaters, iPods, computers, televisions, and cappuccino makers. Do we really need all this stuff? Of course not. Most of us have gadgets now that we don't use. They fill up our counters and closets and gunk up our homes. The mere thought of "upgrading" to the next model should put us into gadget-shock.

When it comes to gadgets, think through what you really want and how you plan to use it, and buy the best one you can afford (assuming you really need it). If you buy a good-quality product, it will last for years and you'll likely not outgrow it. Gadgets are fun and can make our lives better. They can also be very addicting. If you're spending too much of your money on gadgets, stop letting yourself get carried away with the latest and greatest "thing." Even if you're not adding to your debt, you're adding to your "stuff," and most of us need that about as much as we need a new set of Ginsu knives.

Get a Grip on Your Sense of Entitlement

If you eliminated designer clothes, a new iPod, and that fancy camera phone from your budget this year, how much would you save? Total it up and see what your sense of entitlement can really cost you. These items are but a few of the products that we may think we deserve. Other entitlements may include yearly raises, a bigger house, a paid-for college education, newer cars, satellite TV, and eating out. The truth is, we deserve what we can reasonably afford, and anything we purchase on top of that will keep us from achieving our long-term goals. What is more important—a bigger house now or financial security when you're in your late 60s and your earning power is virtually gone? Get entitlement out of your brain, and replace it with the goals you are working toward. As you come closer to reaching your goals, entitlement will lose its grip, you'll be saving $75 a month on your cell phone bill, and you'll feel great about your work and discipline. Win-win-win.

Reduce Harmful Stress in Your Life

The largest benefit from degunking your finances may not be what you financially gain from the process, but what you lose. Money problems have a tendency to follow you around all day. They're like a hungry cat—every time you turn around, they're meowing and nagging at your ankles. Although the degunking process may be difficult at first, try to imagine a life without financial worries and the constant stress that comes with them. Imagine knowing that the rent or mortgage will be paid, you can go out to dinner occasionally, and you have money set aside for your next car. And, when your daughter comes home with a $100 invoice to join cheerleading, you don't feel asthmatic.

This could be you. Really.

Stress can cause physical, emotional, and spiritual problems. Stress has been linked to heart problems, sleep disturbances, depression, drug and alcohol use, sexual dysfunction, overeating, undereating, and a sudden urge to change your name and go live in Mexico on $12 a day. Life can be difficult enough without having to worry about money daily, or hourly. Degunk your finances now, and live longer with less stress. It will be much easier than leaving the country.

Don't misunderstand. Your financial life may never be seamless. There may forever be money issues that come up from behind and startle you, but having your financial ducks in a row will make those situations ever so much easier to manage. You don't have to be rich for this to work. You have to understand your boundaries and manage well what you have.

Stress less, starting now. Grab control of your money, and get to work. It will be well worth the trouble.

The Degunking 12-Step Program

Here is the basic 12-step degunking process you'll follow in this book:

1. Get your financial life organized and set aside a place in your home to work on your finances (Chapter 3).
2. Create a clear picture of your current financial situation (Chapter 4).
3. Clean up your credit and debit cards (Chapter 5).
4. Get your consumer debt under control by paying it down. (Chapter 6).
5. Fine-tune your home mortgage, and put measures in place to lower your household and other living expenses (Chapters 7 and 8).
6. Put a program together to boost your savings and investments (Chapter 9).
7. Clean up your credit report and improve your FICO credit score (Chapter 10).
8. Fine-tune and optimize your budget and improve your spending habits for transportation, groceries, and other activities (Chapters 11 and 12).
9. Get your taxes, benefits, and insurance in better shape (Chapter 13).
10. Find hidden money you didn't know you had (Chapter 14).
11. Put your computer to work to help you automate managing and tracking your finances (Chapter 15).
12. Improve your financial security and put a good record-keeping system in place (Chapters 16 and 17).

These steps are straightforward and easy to follow. Take the time to do them, and you'll begin to get your finances on track and save yourself boatloads of money and a great deal of aggravation in the long run of your financial life.

Summing Up

In this chapter, we discussed why taking control of your finances is a critical part of the degunking process. Although specific actions will improve your financial position, having empowerment over your financial destiny is hugely important. The benefits of financial freedom, and how you can choose to pursue this goal, are attainable for everyone. We discussed how you can decide on your own financial goals and how managing your money and spending your money are interrelated. You also learned that the most important lesson in managing your money is not to incur additional consumer debt and how you should remember this principle and exercise self-control when you shop. I discussed how many people's sense of entitlement gets them into financial trouble and how marketers are trained to prey on our wants as opposed to our needs. You also learned that degunking your finances can help reduce your stress—immediately!

This chapter finished with the important 12-step degunking program. This is the process that will be in place for the rest of this book. If you follow the degunking process in the way that I've described and perform certain tasks on a regular basis, you'll be surprised at how quickly you can gain control of your financial life. Even though you may feel that your current financial situation is amazingly gunked up, there are many steps you can do right away to improve your situation.

Aren't you glad you chose to address this situation? Don't you feel more hopeful already? Stick around. We haven't even gotten to the best part yet.

Organizing Your Financial Life

Degunking Checklist:

- √ Choose (or create) a spot in your house to work.
- √ Organize your documents.
- √ Learn which documents to keep and which documents you can toss.
- √ Develop a master list of all your accounts.
- √ Get your credit report.

We can find lots of reasons to delay the process of cleaning up personal finances. We tell ourselves we need a new desk, a free Saturday, or a fancier computer program. And, really, wouldn't it be better to wait until we renovate the extra bedroom so we'll have an office? It's easy to put off activities that are very important but not necessarily a ton of fun. You may put organizing your finances into this category now, but just you wait—when you're done taking charge of your financial situation, it will be satisfying enough to be labeled as "fun." We'll start with simple steps that will improve your financial situation immediately and will make doing the rest of what I have planned for you even more fun!

The goal of this chapter is to get you set up so that you have a system in place for degunking your personal finances. If you do nothing else, there are four crucial steps to getting your financial life degunked:

1. Set up a personal work space.
2. Create an organizational system for your documents.
3. List all your accounts and bills.
4. Get your credit report.

By tackling these four items in the order listed here, you'll be well on your way to having a gunk-free financial life. I know it sounds really basic, but if you have a dedicated work space and an easy system in place for paying all your bills, then writing checks and paying bills won't be nearly as painful as it may be now.

Time is a precious commodity, so this system is designed to help you work as efficiently as possible. The more efficiently your work, the less suffering you'll go through every month when it comes time to pay your bills and do your monthly reconciliations. Having an efficient system and regularly scheduled times for paying your bills will also keep you from making mistakes and wasting money on late fees and finance charges. When you have a system in place, bill paying will be smooth and (almost) painless. Remember that it will be much more difficult to degunk your financial situation if you have to scurry around finding the files, bills and statements you need, so organizing your paperwork is essential.

If you have a system, you won't have to reinvent the wheel every month when it comes to paying bills. You know which bills come at about the same time in the month. They will probably all be paid with the same paycheck at the same time every month. Once you get a system set up, you'll be amazed at how smoothly it works. Although you will need to customize your organizational system to your specific needs, it should be simple, effective, and consistent. Here are some guidelines for you to follow. If you get these four pieces of the process together, it will make a huge difference in how you view your finances and will set you up for a successful degunking process overall. Ready? Let's go!

Choose a Place to Work

Most of us, with the possible exception of Bill Gates and perhaps your grandmother, don't have an unused, dusty portion of their house just waiting to be converted into an office. Lucky for you, that's not necessary to start degunking. You will, however, need to find a corner somewhere to lay claim to for your personal space. This is critical. You may have children and a dog and a spouse and some hobbies all crowded into your house or apartment and feel there's not an inch left to spare. It's time to make some, even if it's just a small desk in the corner of your bedroom and a cardboard file box. You need a spot in your home where you can work. If possible, it should be out of the major traffic areas, and it should have the potential of being quiet (even if that means simply closing the door). This will be the place where you will file paperwork, gather and pay bills, fill in your budget sheet every month, and think about and plan your financial future. If you pay bills online, store financial information on the computer, or need to do investment research, it would be helpful to have your personal work area near the computer. Because I'm trying to help you degunk your finances, keep in mind that this isn't an excuse to go out and get that computer unit with the built-in bookcase and recessed lighting you've had your eye on. Sorry.

A filing system will be essential. A filing cabinet would be good, but an accordion-pleated paper or plastic holder with at least 10 to 15 sections will do. Any of the office supply stores or your local low-cost retailer will have these for $10 or less. Have a section for every bill you need to pay, as well as sections for your various statements. You will need a container in which to keep current unpaid bills. Keep in mind, again, that your work space doesn't have to look like it belongs in *House Beautiful.* If you want this to be a nicer space, you can save up and get something better later on. For now, a card table will work just fine. Get yourself a couple of pens, a calculator, and a pad of paper. A calendar or planner is helpful as well. You're ready to go! Let's call this space "The Office," and whatever surface you're writing on is "The Desk." Now, when any piece of mail comes into the house concerning finances, it goes directly onto The Desk in The Office. Even if it doesn't get dealt with immediately, it's in the right place, and it will be easy to locate when the time comes. For those of you with children (especially small ones), it's important to make clear that *no one* gets to put anything on The Desk, or remove anything from it, except you. This will eliminate the "Where did the gas bill go?" discussion that can occur toward the end of the month. It also declares that this is your personal space for doing important work, and degunking your finances is *very* important work. For you, for your spouse, and for your children, the steps you're taking now will lead you to a better financial future. It is well worth making the space and protecting it from little (or big) peanut-butter-covered fingers.

GunkBuster's Notebook: Creating a Personal Space

We tend to use up all the space we're given. It's possible you can't think of an empty spot anywhere to put a desk and are right now deciding to do the bills at the dining room table where you've always done them. I would ask you to run through your home again in your mind. Isn't there a corner in your room, at the top of the stairs, or even by the washer that you could commandeer? It makes a ton of difference to have this area in which to work, and the benefits of having a space will far outweigh whatever you have to move to make it happen. I should specify, I guess, that I'm not suggesting you get rid of one of the kids to make space. Boundaries are good in these matters. But, for your financial and emotional health, find your space and do your work there. In my experience, it can make or break your system. It is nearly always true that my clients who have a specific place to work are more successful than those who keep their bills in various piles around the house and dig them out from under old permission slips and expired coupons when the time comes to pay them.

Separate Your Documents

Probably the scariest thing about organizing your documents is finally seeing them in a big mountainous pile on your desk (in your office, in your private space). Some of my clients' reaction when we gather their bills together for the first time is a momentary panic attack. This passes quickly, though, because I have a system for putting these documents into smaller, much less-threatening piles. This will make sense of your reams of paperwork and stop scaring you in the process.

There are two basic types of documents: bills and statements. Anything asking you for money is a bill, and anything telling you how much money you have (or don't have) is a statement. Make two piles. If you have limited time, focus on your bill pile first. Statements rarely ask for action from you, but paying a bill late can cost you fees and heartache—neither of which you need.

Most people find that they do better if they designate a specific time to organize and pay their bills. There will be some bills to pay with almost every paycheck, so choose a time very close to when you get paid. If you get paid on Friday, pay bills Saturday morning. Put it on your calendar, and it starts to become a habit to get these bills paid and off of your desk and mind. Because our lives are so busy with work, family activities, and everything else that fills up our days, it's important to develop a system that allows you to get things done in short bursts of time. If you are waiting until you have the entire day free to get your bills organized and paid, you're setting yourself up to pay some late charges and fees that will make bill-paying even more painful than usual. Pick a time within a day or two (at the most) from when you get paid, and get the job done. Think how freeing it will be to have that task completed, and your bills out on time consistently! You're going to like how this feels.

The Bill Pile

I know this is scary, but it's time to look at the Bill Pile. It may be high. There may be multiple copies of some bills. Some of the envelopes may have nasty stamps on them like "Past Due" or "Final Notice." Don't worry! I'll help you sort through this pile, prioritize your bills, and figure out a way of getting that nasty pile under control.

If your finances have gotten out of hand, it's possible that you have more than one copy of certain bills. It is also possible that many of the envelopes have never been opened. The first thing to do is open all the bills and sort them by payee. While you're at it, throw out all the advertisements and offers for free credit cards and free gifts. Companies love to send you this stuff because they make bundles of money selling you things that you weren't even shopping for, and certainly don't need. Keep only the complete bill itself and the envelope that comes with it.

If you have duplicate bills that give you identical information, keep the most current copy, and shred or recycle the rest. For credit card statements, keep all copies that give you new information of any kind (new purchases, cash advances, or payment information), and shred the doubles.

***CAUTION:** Shredding sensitive information is good protection. Your credit card account can be abused by someone finding and using your account number. Protect yourself by destroying any documents that contain your credit card numbers or other important information such as your Social Security number or bank account information. Thieves are very successful (though smelly) at rummaging through the garbage and piecing together financial profiles using the information that people just toss in the trash.*

Back to work. You should have one copy of every bill that is due. Depending on where you are in your financial month, you will have more bills coming. Make a list of the bills that have not yet arrived, and estimate what the amounts due will be. (If you don't know, you don't know. But making an estimate would be a good start.) Sort the ones you have by due date. Make a full list of which bills are due on what date, including your mortgage or rent and those bills that haven't arrived yet. Keep in mind that these due dates will be roughly the same every month, so this list will help you plan which bills to pay with which paycheck (see Chapter 4 for more on this topic). It is important to decide when you will be paying your bills. I suggest doing it as close to when you get your paycheck as possible. If you get paid every other Friday, make a set time to pay your bills on Saturday morning. That way, you get into a schedule, and there isn't money spent before the bills get paid.

TIP: One of the things I do to keep my bills organized is to use a bill keeper on my desk. Whenever I get a bill in the mail and it's not yet time to make the payment, I put it in the bill holder so that the bill is obvious every time I go to my desk. That is where the bills live until my paycheck comes. That way, a bill never gets lost. This is a very visual reminder to me what is due and what else needs to be paid. I find that if bills are out of sight, they can also be out of mind. Keep them in the open, and there's no hunting for them when the time comes to send them off.

There is one very important goal you should probably set for yourself right now: *Pay your bills on time.* If you have trouble motivating yourself to get your bills organized and paid on time, you might try coming up with an incentive to reward yourself for performing these activities. This can help take the sting away. Your reward doesn't have to be something that costs money. For example, you could schedule your bill time so that you get to watch your favorite TV show afterward or you get to eat your favorite meal that day. Feeling organized is a good reward, but a little (low or no-cost) "sugar" on top never hurts.

Get Current and Stay There

At this point, you may have some old bills that need to be cleaned up. Once you get everything current, however, make it a point to stay there. Whether you pay bills by mail or online, allow at least seven days for the money to get where it needs to go. Late payments may hit your credit report and lower your score, which you want to avoid. Also, late charges can quickly eat up buckets of money that could be used for much more fun purposes, like debt repayment or saving for a car or vacation.

Many companies charge a significant amount for a late fee. For example, you might receive a $20 gas bill during the summer and if you pay it late, the gas company can charge you a late fee that is greater than the bill itself. This can certainly make a mess of your monthly budget. In short, paying bills on time is a great step in degunking your financial situation.

Jot down on your calendar or planner when you need to mail or pay your bills online in order to keep them all current and on time. Put bills that need to be paid in the bill keeper, and file the paid bills as you pay them, complete with date paid and check number (if applicable), in your new file. Paying your bills on time will put you well on your way toward degunking your finances. Although you may have to work a bit to get to the point where this is possible and consistent, it is a major step in the degunking process and will benefit you in ways you haven't even thought of yet.

I bet you feel more organized already, but we're far from done. Keep reading!

Credit Card Statements

I encourage my clients to always pay close attention to their credit card statements. As soon as these statements come in, you should do the following as a quick review:

- √ Note the date the bill is due so that you won't incur late charges or finance fees. Remember that you must allow enough time to pay the bill so that your payment is received by the due date.
- √ Scan the statement to make sure that there are no charges that you didn't make. Later, you will learn a system that will ensure that your statement is correct, but for now, spend some time looking it over for accuracy.
- √ Review the charge amounts to make sure they look correct to the best of your recollection. If you have receipts, check the statement against the receipts.

This early quick review is important because if you spot something that is incorrect in a statement, you'll have a better chance of getting the problem taken care of if you act quickly. In Chapter 6, I'll be showing you how to degunk your credit cards in much more detail, but for now, put a process in place to quickly review your credit card statements. Theft has increased dramatically over the past few years, and you need to be very diligent about reviewing your statements to make sure that someone else isn't using your credit card number. It's also easy for vendors to make mistakes, and the more diligent you get at reviewing your statements, the more mistakes you can find and the more money you can possibly save.

The Statement Pile

As I mentioned earlier, I'm using the word *statement* for any document that represents your assets, such as checking, savings, and brokerage accounts. You may also receive statements from your company's retirement or 401(k) plan or from some other pension plans or investment accounts you have.

Every month, you should receive a statement for every checking and savings account you have. (If you don't get monthly bank statements, call your bank *right now* and find out why.) Some investment statements will come monthly, some quarterly, and there may be municipal fund statements you get only twice a year. Some pension plan statements are issued only annually, as are Social Security statements. Bank statements and investment statements should be dealt with differently (see the following sections).

Bank Statements

This may be a radical concept for many readers, but you should start reconciling (balancing) your bank statements every month. It's important to keep track of possible discrepancies as the result of your or the bank's error, as well as unexpected bank fees. As efficient as banks can be, mistakes can be made, and the sooner such errors are caught, the less trouble it will be for you later on.

CAUTION:* *One of your goals in degunking your finances is to take control of your money. An important reason to check your bank statements every month is to find out what kinds of fees the bank may be sneaking into your statement. Remember that when it comes to bank fees, I'm talking about your money going directly to a bank's bottom line. Even though you may think that a $2 service fee or a $5 charge isn't much, keep in mind that this is pure profit for the bank—and it's usually the result of a situation that, in reality, doesn't cost the bank anything at all. Think about it: If the bank charges you an $8 monthly fee for your checking account, that's $96 a year of your money that you could spend on something else. Many banks offer "no fee" checking as long as you have your paycheck direct-deposited into your account, and no minimum balance may be required. One little phone call could save you over $100 or more a year in bank fees!

Investment Statements

Investment statements are a different kettle of fish. Some are long term (stocks, municipal funds, IRAs, brokerage accounts) and some are more short term (money markets, CDs). Most helpful for the organization of these statements is to three-hole-punch them and put them in a binder. These statements will then be accessible when you want to look more closely at them or to compare one month's activity to another. Keep in mind that this information doesn't need to be scrutinized every month in the same manner as your bank statements. Although investment statements should be looked at every time they come in, the point is more to double-check any recent activity as opposed to analyze all the information. (See more on degunking your savings and investments in Chapter 9.) If you send a certain amount to your brokerage account every month, it is very important to know that the money arrived. It should be noted on your account, along with withdrawals. It's important to make sure that, for example, you actually withdrew the money or that the company didn't make a one-digit error.

The very nature of investing is changeability. Unlike your bank statements, the balance in your investment accounts change constantly with no help from you. To understand every line of your investment statement, plan on spending some quality time with your broker to analyze your situation, and the statement itself, more thoroughly. It is important information to have, and this process will take you out of the queasy realm of trusting your broker implicitly about what's happening in your account. Until then, make certain that the deposits and withdrawals match your records and that your broker is available to answer questions about anything else that concerns you.

***TIP:* Your bank and investment statements need to be kept for three years after the date that you filed taxes concerning them. If you file taxes on February 10, 2005, then statements need to be kept until February 10, 2008. I actually recommend retaining these records longer because the statute of limitations for some states is four years. Keeping them in folders by calendar year can make finding one particular piece of paper much easier. In this day of data overload, the information will still be available from the account holder, but getting a statement from two years ago will certainly cost you if you have to get it from your investment company.**

Computerize Your Financial Data

If you have access to a computer, putting all of your accounts on Quicken (or another money management product) will make this procedure much less painful. One thing to remember, however, is that your financial information doesn't float on to Quicken by itself. It will take time and effort to get it up and running, but it will be time well spent. (See more about using technology in Chapter 15.) Once you get used to entering your information on a daily or weekly basis, you will be amazed at how much data you have at your fingertips. How much you spent on food last year or how much you paid in interest will be immediately accessible, and knowing exactly how much you paid in medical bills will be very helpful when filing this year's taxes.

GunkBuster's Notebook: What to Keep and What to Toss

In Chapter 17 I'll be showing you how to keep good records of all of your financial information. This will help you stay organized and keep track of everything that is important for activities like paying taxes, dealing with insurance companies, and so on. For now, here's a simple checklist that you can use as you gather your financial information. There are some pieces of information you don't have to keep forever. When it comes to documents and bills, a good rule of thumb is to keep them for a year after they were current. The way I do it is to make the switch around New Year's Day. It's a bit of a ceremony. I clean out my files of that year's utility bills, bank statements, credit card statements, and bank receipts. I put them all in a manilla envelope, and store them in the basement. When I put this one away, I toss the one I put there last year. Though it may seem silly to keep your old utility bills for a year, I have found it useful to have them when you're trying to figure out why your gas bill doubled, and you have last year's bill, with all the therm use (what exactly is a therm, anyway?) and payment information handy. If you don't keep your financial information on the computer, you should keep this paperwork for a couple of years. Here are some other guidelines to consider:

- √ Items to toss after one year of being stored:

  There are records you can toss after one year if you don't need them for tax and/or business purposes. These would include your utility bills, credit card statements, ATM and bank receipts, insurance policy declaration pages, and bank statements. One thing to make certain you remember, however, is if you are going to toss your last year's manilla envelope, shred the contents first. This puppy contains almost all of your important financial numbers, and could be a very nicely packaged bonanza for a thief.
- √ Items that you need to keep for a much longer period:
  - √ Real estate documents should be kept as long as you own the property plus a minimum of four years. These documents include home improvement records, yearly mortgage statements, loan documents, and receipts for purchases whose replacement cost exceeds the deductible on your insurance.

- √ W-2s, 1099s, and year-end credit card and bank statements should be kept for seven years.
- √ Annual tax returns should be kept indefinitely.
- √ Year-end statements from financial service companies should be kept indefinitely.

Make a Master List

Now that you've assembled all your documentation and have a list of all your bills and statements, it's time to put all that information into one master list. This may seem time-consuming, but it is another major step in degunking your finances. Once you have a complete picture of your financial situation, you'll be able to better manage your finances going forward. This master list will be crucial in your future financial planning.

By now you have most of the information you need to make a master list of all your accounts (bank, investment, and credit card), utilities, loans, and rent or mortgage information. Make a list of all the names, addresses, phone numbers, and account numbers for every account or payee. Table 3-1 shows an example of what your list should look like.

Table 3-1 Creating a master list of your accounts and statements.

Description	Institution	Address	City/State/ZIP	Account #	Phone #
Mortgage	Bank One	1 Arizona Plaza	Phoenix, AZ 85001	123-123-123	800-555-1212
Car payment	Chase	2 Federal Way	New York, NY 10001	888-1234-123	877-555-1212
Visa	Wells Fargo	3 Banking Road	San Diego, CA 92001	xxx-456-789	800-222-2222
Gas bill	Nicor	4 Gas Line Ave.	Aurora, IL 69701	1478-9632	623-555-4545
Electricity	Com Ed	5 Shortage Road	Barrington, IL 60010	987-987-987	800-987-9877
Dept store	Big Lots	6 Layaway Drive	Fresno, CA 92222	258-2588	800-456-4566

This list will be invaluable when it comes to contacting any of these accounts for a missing bill, incorrect charge, or lost or stolen credit card. Keep this list in a different place than your files so the flood that soaks your filing cabinet doesn't also soak and destroy your list of bills and statements. (Don't do as my grandmother did, which was to keep the spare key to her safety deposit box in her safety deposit box.) If you have a safe, that's a good place to keep your list. Your undie drawer is a fine second, and it would be good to also keep it somewhere on your computer, accessible only by password. Keep in mind, though, that misuse of these numbers can cause you a great deal of trouble and paperwork, so protect this information closely.

Get Your Credit Report

For most people, their credit report is a mystery. Consumers commonly have a lot of questions—and even more misconceptions—about this area of their personal finances. What does a credit report really mean? Will I be able to understand what's on it? What happens if there's erroneous information in this report? Will requesting a credit report hurt my credit score? Will it cost me anything? The topic of credit reports is covered extensively in Chapter 10, "Degunking Your Credit Report," but for now, we just want you to get the report itself. How can you do this? Read on.

There are three major credit reporting bureaus in the United States: Equifax, Experian, and TransUnion. Any of the three will sell you a credit report. Your credit report will list any credit you have currently, or on which you have defaulted, credit you have applied for, and who has checked into your credit. Each credit bureau will also give you a credit score. These scores will not necessarily match because the different bureaus do not share information. Your credit score will help determine if you get credit, how much credit you are eligible for, and what your interest rate will be for the credit you receive. Once you get your credit report, add it to your statements in its own file.

The three websites from which to obtain a credit report are as follows:

√ **www.equifax.com 1-800-685-1111**

√ **www.experian.com 1-888-397-3742**

√ **www.transunion.com 1-800-916-8800**

Each company offers different incentives and services. Be careful about what you sign up for, and remember that these firms are in business to make money. Don't buy more than you need.

***TIP:** Since this book is about getting control of your finances, I recommend that you spend as little as possible on your credit report. By September of 2005, everyone will be able to request a free credit report from each of the three reporting agencies per year. This service is available at **www.annualcreditreport.com**. This will be the report only, with no accompanying score. The score is available for purchase from this site, and from the individual credit reporting agency sites. If you want to see all three reports and scores, each of the credit reporting agencies sells a 3-in-1 report, giving you information and credit scores from all three services. Be sure you are purchasing only what you need—a credit report with an accompanying score. You don't need investment advice, weekly updates, or a new Visa, all of which they will try to sell you. I'd like to add some additional reassuring words here. Requesting your own credit report will not hurt your credit score, as long as you do it no more than once per year. In addition, I will show you how to read your credit report, assess your credit score, correct credit-reporting errors, and contact individual credit-reporting agencies in Chapter 10.*

GunkBuster's Notebook: Misconceptions about Credit Reports and Scores

Your credit report isn't an evil entity, designed to keep you from getting what you want. It is simply a record of your credit history with a number attached. The credit report will state what you have borrowed, if you have paid it back on time, and any late payments or judgments that have happened in your credit history. Then, it gives you a number (your credit score) by which creditors can decide whether or not to offer you more credit, and at what rate. Here's the good news: If there are negative aspects to your credit report, you can do something about it. Hardly anyone goes through their entire financial life without a mistake, but having the information is the first step to fixing it. You can't manage what you don't know. There will be much more about credit reports in Chapter 10, but be reassured—this is just a report, just a piece in the puzzle of your financial life. Get the report, look it over for huge errors, such as loans you never had or accounts you don't recognize, and when you get to Chapter 10, I'll show you what to do with it.

Summing Up

Before you begin degunking your personal finances in earnest, there are four essential things you need to do:

- √ Create a private work space in your residence
- √ Organize your documents
- √ Develop a master list of all accounts (bills and statements)
- √ Get your credit report

By simply doing these things, you will have gone a long way in taking control of your finances. Having a plan on what to do with all of these documents will come next, but take a moment to enjoy the good feeling that having everything at your fingertips will provide. You are now on your way to having a gunk-free financial life! For the next step—creating a clear picture of your financial situation—proceed to the next chapter. And don't worry: any questions you have will be answered as you continue to read. Let's keep going!

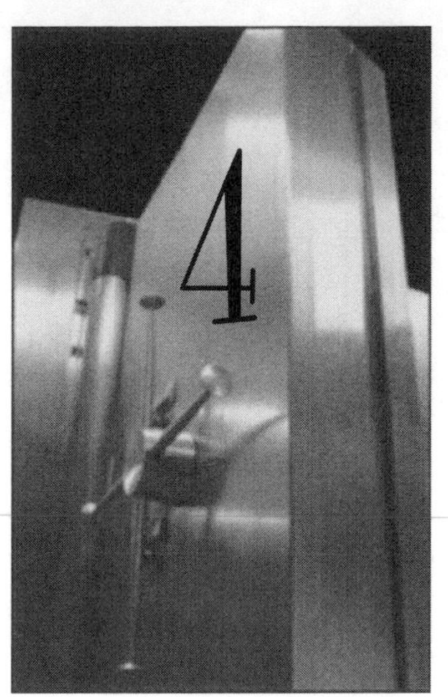

Creating a Clear Picture of Your Financial Situation

Degunking Checklist:

√ Keep track of all income and expenses.

√ Find out what you have, what you owe, and what you spend.

√ Decide what to change.

√ Organize your bills by paycheck.

√ Learn how to manage unspent money.

In the previous chapter, you got your financial life organized. You now have a place to work and a system for paying and filing your bills. You know what all of your bills are and when they're due. You even have a little routine set up for yourself on how and when to pay your bills—the point being that you now have a system for managing your money. Whew!

Now that you have a system, the time has come to look at the unvarnished truth and see exactly where you stand with your finances. I know it's scary, but once this task is done, you can put a financial plan in place to get degunked and stay degunked!

This chapter will provide the tools to paint a picture of what your finances look like today and what you need to do to improve your financial situation. Gone are the days of not knowing what happened to the $20 you had in your wallet yesterday or why you seem to be visiting the ATM machine several times a week. Even though some of what you discover might be a bit painful to see, it will only stay painful if you continue to ignore it. Once you begin to deal with the reality of your situation, it will then be easier to plan for the future and decide how best to manage your individual situation. Putting your financial gunk on paper doesn't create the problem—it just exposes it to the light of day. After completing the assessment of where you stand, it will be much easier to get to where you want to go. As the saying goes, you can't map out where you want to go until you know where you're starting. In this chapter, we'll create a good map, and then you'll be ready to degunk your credit cards in Chapter 5.

***NOTE:** In this chapter we'll be filling out three main forms: the Income and Assets form, the Big D (Debt) form, and the Monthly Expenditures form. All three of these forms are provided in Appendix A. I'll also provide you with two forms in this chapter—Gift List Form and Dividing Bill by Paycheck Form—that we will be filling out as we go along to help you fill out the main forms presented in the appendix.*

Keep Track of All Expenditures and Income

I know that this sounds tough, but keeping track of your expenses and income is an essential part of degunking your finances. One reason your finances may be out of control is that you don't know where your money is going. Although this process will be difficult to start, you will be amazed at how much you will learn once you begin keeping track of every dollar. Who knew a newspaper and coffee every day could add up to $728 per year? (And that's not even fancy coffee!) Who knew that lunches out cost you'*thousands* a year? And did you know that the amount you spend on dry cleaning every year could possibly finance an annual vacation instead? Money gets spent in so many different ways that, without knowing where it's going, there is no way to decide what to change.

***TIP:* Commit now to finding out where all of your money goes and deciding how to spend it instead of giving it a mind of its own.**

Carry with you a notebook of some kind to write down expenditures, or for PDA fans, keep track there. Mark down everything to begin with, even cans of pop or a bag of pretzels. If you have a FranklinCovey daily planner, this is a perfect place to document your expenditures. Just set aside a little time at the end of the day to write down what you bought, regardless of how trivial or small the cost. Jot down each and every expense. Everything you mark down will be put into a budget category, so make sure you can decipher your scribbles. "16.50-Tom" might not mean much a week after you paid your friend the balance you owed him for football tickets, so be specific as to how the money is spent. Filling out the Monthly Expenditures form later in this chapter will help in deciding what categories are appropriate for your individual situation. If you buy several items at once, note which items go into which category. The trip to the grocery store will net food, but it may also be the place you get your toilet paper when it's on sale, and although you may buy yarn at Wal-Mart, you may also get a part for the car. The point is to make a dedicated effort to track what's being spent on which items.

Keep Track of Credit/Debit Card Purchases

Many people use a credit card to make most of their purchases. For you, the best way to keep track is to keep a separate check register for all credit card transactions. Each entry should include the date, the store, the amount of purchase, and the category for each item. A big source of financial gunk is created by credit card debt (see more on this in Chapter 5), so if you begin to track your credit card purchases now, you will quickly get a very real picture of how much of a problem your use of credit cards actually poses to your financial health. But as you'll learn in Chapter 5, it's important to track not only your credit card purchases but your hidden credit card costs as well, including late fees and finance charges. These expenses can add up quickly and take a huge bite out of your monthly budget.

If you use a separate credit card register, when the credit card bill comes in, it will be much easier to check your purchases against the statement. Credit card companies make mistakes too, and after a month you may be hard-pressed to remember if the Ace Hardware purchase was really about $20.00, as your spouse remembered, or the $78.42 that has shown up on your statement. I don't know about you, but my husband will always tell me it was a lesser amount, just so I let him go back. The joke in our house is that he can't go to Ace Hardware without a chaperone.

It only takes a few seconds during any purchase to jot down this information. This method works well for categorizing expenses, too and is certainly more efficient than digging out your receipt later and figuring out how much of the bill was food and how much was flannel sheets and paper towels.

For people who use a debit card, the same principle holds true. Carry your credit or debit card in a checkbook (some have pockets on the outside for ID that fit a credit card perfectly), and write down your expenditures as you go.

TIP: A quick note on receipts is warranted here: Save your receipts for everything you may, for any reason, need to take back. Returning anything is a pain without them, and putting them in the same place in your purse or wallet and emptying them into an envelope every few days can save you from headaches, arguments at the service desk, and store credits at places you may not want to shop.

I'm not suggesting that you have to record every penny for the rest of your life—just for a couple of months. After two months of tracking all your expenses, you should have a good picture of where you spend your money. You can revisit your tracking needs then. The mere act of documenting your expenditures might actually get you to think twice before making rash purchases. This could save you from buying that pair of $200 sunglasses that you're sure make you look like Johnny Depp. Impulse purchases don't fit well into your degunking program, and the truth is, you're still not going to look like Johnny Depp. Keep your money and stay on your very useful, life-changing program.

Document All Income Sources

Income is important to track as well. Although the all-cash side jobs or banquet catering you do on the weekends doesn't seem to add up to much, you might be surprised at what it comes out to in a year's time. The garage sale money or selling your shot glass collection on eBay is income, too, and needs to be noted as such. Don't forget the occasional dividends that you get from your stocks or other investments.

If you put all your income transactions on your computer in a check register form, be sure to split out the amounts of your various taxes, IRA contributions, and insurance costs. This will make tax time a bit less of a hair-pulling event, and you can track during the year what you have put into the different funds. The payroll department that issues your checks might be filled with lovely people, but mistakes are still made, and having your numbers at the ready can lower your stress when it's near highest—April 15th at 9:00 P.M.

Getting Used to the Process

You're probably slowly getting used to the idea of tracking your expenses and income. It may be a little odd at first, taking time out a couple of times a day to write down that you bought a pack of gum, filled up your car, bought lunch for you and a friend, and ordered a spiral-cut ham at your local butcher, but you'll get used to it. At the end of the day, you probably have an interesting little list of expenses. And, at the end of the first week, you might be shocked at how much "stuff" you seem to be buying. I had a client recently tell me that now she understands why she's gaining weight—she had no idea she was spending so much on groceries. This is just part of the process of degunking your finances, but it is a fundamental and important part. Keep at it. By the end of this chapter, your record-keeping will be a key part of your financial picture!

Fill Out Your Forms

The next step in creating your financial picture is to start filling out some forms that will show you what you have, what you owe, what you spend, and what the bottom line looks like. But do not despair—again, it's all part of the process.

In Appendix A, you'll find these forms:

- √ Income and Assets form
- √ The Big D (Debt) form
- √ Monthly Expenditures form

You're going to use all three of these forms to help you get a sense of your true financial picture.

Income and Assets Form

The first of the forms is the Income and Assets form. You'll need to gather what you need to fill out this form as completely and accurately as possible. If all your statements and check stubs are filed and available, it should be an easy task to pull out the most current ones. If you followed the recommendations in the previous chapter, that information will be in your files.

For the income section, you should use your net income to fill in the spaces of how much you make and on what schedule you are paid. Make a note next to each income entry of how much in voluntary contributions to retirement, IRA accounts, or profit sharing is being taken out of your check. If your income is variable, average out the last 12 months' earnings and use that number for now. If you have been on public assistance, unemployment, or disability, be sure to include that income as well. In short, any check or cash that you received for your services should be included in this list. Keep in mind, we're not reporting this to the IRS—it's just for your own use!

If you receive tips as part of your job, make sure you include them as income. You might be surprised at how quickly they add up. It's easy to overlook this income because it comes in as cash, but it needs to be included and not used as "fun" money.

As for your assets, you should try to come as close as possible when you estimate the value of what you own. If you don't know what your car is worth, go online to **www.kbb.com** (Kelley Blue Book) to get a good idea, or just look in the paper (or online to your local paper) at the Used Cars section to see prices on comparable makes and models. Make sure to include other assets when listing what you own—motorcycles, jewelry, coins, artwork, or your shot glass collection (if you chose not to sell it on eBay after all). Try to be realistic about what you have. Although a particular baseball card may be "worth" $2000, it's really only worth what someone will give you for it today.

The point of this exercise is not an attempt to value everything you own. What we're trying to do with the Income and Assets form is to get a sense of the actual money you have, and items of worth that have marketable value should you choose to sell them. If you've filled out this form thoroughly, you should now have a good picture of what you own and what kind of income is regularly coming in.

The Big D Form

For most people, this is going to be one of the toughest parts of degunking their finances—listing all the debt. This section will be uncomfortable for you if your finances are gunked up, so my guess is that most people reading this section are going to be squirming in the beginning. Keep in mind, though, that knowledge is power, and getting this information down is the first step to making it go away. Take a couple of deep breaths, and let's move ahead.

In the interest of accuracy, put down every person and every institution to which you owe money. Include any debts that have been defaulted on in the past, as well as current, active debt. When making this list, make sure to include interest rates for each debt. Later on, we'll look at ways to save you money on interest, but it's important for now to know which accounts are killing you with their interest rates. Again, if you've done the work of organizing your financial situation as discussed in Chapter 3, you should have all of this information at your fingertips. Make sure that you include any personal loans that you have outstanding with a friend or family member.

Don't be discouraged if this list seems very long or if the numbers seem surprisingly large. This is what the form will look like for great numbers of people, so you're not alone. The good news is, you've had the courage to get this far. This is probably the single hardest step in degunking your finances—listing your debt—and you've gotten through it! Congratulations! When you're done, take another couple of deep breaths.

Figuring Out Your Net Worth

Your net worth is determined by figuring out your financial worth and then subtracting your debt, or liabilities. The equation is as follows: assets minus liabilities equals net worth. Your assets are the amount in dollars (or local currency) that you have in savings, investments, real estate, personal property, and anything else you can trade for money. Your assets don't include great ideas that you may some day patent, future inheritances, or the pension plan you pay into now. These are things that may or may not end up in your hand, and may represent cash flow at some point, but are not included in your asset list. Assets represent resources you may some day draw upon in order to satisfy needs.

Liabilities are debt and represent obligations that detract from your net worth. Say your only asset is your house. It's worth $250,000, but your mortgage is $240,000. You are "obligated" to pay that money (a liability), and your net worth would not be the $250,000 that your house would sell for but $250,000 minus your obligation ($240,000), leaving you with a net worth of $10,000.

There is a goal when it comes to net worth. Not everyone wants or needs the same amount of money when they retire, but something to shoot for would be to have your assets as close to your net worth as possible. What that means in degunking terms is that you have no liability (debt) to detract from your net worth and make your pool of resources smaller. Having a million dollars in the bank when you retire is no big deal if you have debt totaling $990,000. It doesn't leave much of a resource pool.

The way to accomplish this goal is to consistently raise your net worth throughout your working years. Starting out, a college student at graduation will have a net worth of $0 or might very possibly be in the hole with student loans and credit card debt. Throughout the years, the standard is to make the asset list bigger and keep the liability list small. A key in the process is to not add anything that is heavier on the liability side than it is on the asset side. Buying a house should net you more asset than liability over time, but buying a new car with nothing down is a liability that will never be higher in asset level than it will be in debt level. Your new car is worth less the minute you drive it off the lot than it was when you signed the papers, and it is a "depreciating asset," meaning that it will decrease in value the longer you own it. The fact that you're paying interest for several years makes that equation even worse. Instead, save up for a used car and pay cash. This will lower your asset side by the amount you pay for the car, but it will not add to your liabilities with payments or interest, and someone else will have taken the first, and largest, hunk of depreciation on your purchase.

There is no magic number when it comes to net worth. Someone paying into a nice pension actually needs less net worth than someone who will have no promised income other than Social Security (and that seems an insecure promise at best) when they retire. Because those in the latter category will have to support their needs completely on their own, more resources have to be available from which to draw.

The delineation between "good" debt and "bad" debt can be stated in terms of what it does to your net worth. Good debt will raise your net worth, and bad debt will lower it. Buying a new wardrobe (quite a depreciating asset) and charging it will lower your net worth. Buying a home should, over time, raise it. Of course, any debt can be bad if you don't have the budgeted funds to cover it, but after, "Can I afford this?," the next question to ask is what this purchase will do to your net worth.

To figure out your net worth, make two lists. Put down everything you listed as an asset on your Income and Assets form. Add up the dollar amounts to get a total. Next to that, list all of your debt, including mortgage balances, credit card balances, and the $200 you owe Aunt Norma. Add up those amounts. Next, subtract the amount you figured for debt (liabilities) from the amount you figured for your assets. That, my friend, is your net worth. It's not your worth as a person, or how much you're loved. It's the amount of money you could draw upon if need be. If you are happy with it, good for you. If not, you can change it. Keep reading. More help is coming.

Understand Your Debt and Payment Priorities

When it comes to paying your debt and expenses, especially if you are having any financial difficulties, it's important for you to be able to prioritize. Generally, the top priority is to pay for your shelter (mortgage or rent). Then, you need to pay for your transportation (car loan), especially if you need it to get to work. This would be followed by your basic housing expenses (food, utilities, phone bill). Finally, you need to pay your consumer debt—credit cards and other personal loans. There may be times when this order gets a bit confused. If you get a shut-off notice for your heat, it's hard to pay your car payment first. It may be necessary to work with your utilities and other debtors if you are in financial trouble. All they really want is their money, and if, together, you can work out a reasonable way to pay them, they are usually understanding of occasional cash-flow issues. Now we're going to tackle your monthly expenditures. Ready for another dose of reality?

Monthly Expenditures Form

That helpful little exercise you started performing earlier in the chapter—tracking your income and expenses—is now going to be documented on the Monthly Expenditures form. On this form, we're going to summarize where you spend your money each month. This will be the most time-consuming form to fill out, and it will also give the most information on where your money is going. This will be a record of what you are spending now, not what you *want* to spend or what you *think* you're spending. What we're doing is getting a current picture of where your finances sit. Let's look at some of the particular line items by section. Most are self-explanatory, but the ones I'll highlight are those whose meaning may not be completely clear on first sight.

Total Income

Take the numbers from your income and assets sheet to figure your total monthly income. Mark down what you are saving or giving. You'll come to a bottom line of spendable income.

Housing

The "other" line in this section could be for lawn mowing, your invaluable cleaning person, having water delivered to the house, or the tree trimmer you need twice a year for that overgrown willow in your front yard.

Auto/Transportation

You can figure your maintenance costs for a particular car by adding together what you have spent on repairs and maintenance in the previous year and dividing by 12. Work out your insurance, license plate, and city sticker costs in the same fashion; add them up and divide by 12. The "other" line in this section could be for car washes or the occasional detailing.

Household/Personal

The line that causes the most surprise in this section is "gifts." I would guess few people reading this can accurately state what they spent during last year's holiday season. In that way, your gift-giving costs are much like giving birth—it hurts for a while, but you tend to forget what it feels like until you go through it again. Very few people realize how much money they spend on gifts. This is a category that can be tweaked later if need be, but for now, you should list everything you buy for everyone—it will be a true eye-opener. To help you determine your list of gifts and what you've spent on these gifts, I've included a form in Figure 4-1 called the Gift List. You can use this form to collect the following information:

- √ Birthdays. To begin, list everyone for whom you buy a birthday gift, and make a column of about how much you spend. Don't forget to fill in an average number of children's birthday parties your kids attend (if applicable to your situation) and gifts you might chip in for at work or school.
- √ Religious Holidays. If you celebrate religious holidays, make another column of how much you spend on those same people for those occasions. Add people for whom you might buy a gift for Christmas but not for their birthday.
- √ Other Holidays. Fill in the list for other holidays that include gift-giving, such as Mother's and Father's days, Valentine's Day, and Easter. Put down an amount for each holiday or per person on that holiday.
- √ Attending Special Events. Depending on your season in life, friends and family may be marrying and having children, and invitations to showers and weddings come with the expectation of bringing a gift. Budget for an average number of weddings and showers per year, depending on information you already have and from what you can guess may be in the works. Decide on a reasonable amount to spend for these occasions, and add them to the list.

Gift List

Religious Holidays and Birthdays

Name	Holiday $ Amt.	Birthday $ Amt.

Grab Bags -
Kids' parties -
Work Gifts -

Valentine's Day	Easter	Mother's Day, Father's Day
Halloween	Weddings and Showers	Hostess Gifts
Teachers and Coaches	Churches or Charities	Misc.

Figure 4-1

Use the Gift List Form to track your gift spending.

√ Participating in Special Events. You might incur expenses by being a part of a special event. Weddings are notorious for costing bundles to those involved. Between a bridesmaid's dress, a couple of shower gifts, a wedding gift, and getting your hair done the day of the wedding (and did I mention dyed shoes?), this event can cost hundreds to the unsuspecting friend. It is a bit less expensive for the men participating, but there is a lesson here for future brides: be considerate about what you are asking of your dearest friends, and remember this is a one-day event. If you're married at the end of it, it was a success.

√ Unexpected Events. There will be unexpected gifts during the year. Flowers to a friend in the hospital or a memorial donation aren't necessarily in the budget, but working a bit extra into the gift budget for these purposes is a very wise move. Also add anything not mentioned earlier that you do on a regular basis.

This is your current gift list. Add up *all* the amounts, divide by 12, and that's what you spend on gifts per month. Are you surprised it's that much? Most people are shocked at how much is spent on gifts in the course of a year.

Personal Maintenance

"Personal maintenance" would include haircuts, nails, massages, and vitamins—anything for the personal care of you and your family. "Books/magazines" includes subscriptions, as well as what you pick up at the store or news-stand. The "education" line in this section is for current education—private school for the children or grandchildren and continuing education for adults, for example. This would not include student loans. Your "other" could be anything not listed.

Insurance

When figuring your insurance costs, don't include anything taken automatically out of your check. As you are working from your net income amount, it will distort your bottom line (not in your favor!) if it is taken out again. Also, don't include your homeowners insurance if it's part of your mortgage payment, as that is already listed in the Housing section. Include only that insurance for which you pay out of pocket.

Loan Payments

For your loan payments, list what you have historically been paying, not what you would like to be paying. At some point in the future you may make those numbers bigger, but for now, an accurate representation of reality is paramount.

Pets

If you buy your pet's food at the grocery store and you've already counted it in your "groceries" line, don't mark it again. "Food" here would denote money spent in a different place or broken out of your grocery budget. Calling your vet will give you a good idea what is spent on visits, and don't forget to include preventative medications, like Heartgard and rabies shots. Items such as clothing for your pets (I actually saw three little dogs in cowboy hats recently), overnight stays in kennels while you're traveling, grooming, and emergency medical services should also be included.

TIP:* *Consider making a special file to keep track of your pet's expenses. These expenses can add up and it's easy to forget certain items. This will also be helpful in tracking when shots and visits are due so planning for them is possible. Your vet should be able to give you a copy of the record of each visit.

Professional Services

It may be difficult to decide on a number for "medical/dental/prescriptions," but do your best by coming up with an average dollar amount of doctor visits and co-pays, cavities and orthodontia, and prescriptions that fit your family's historical pattern. If your child ends up in the emergency room a couple of times per year, add it in. If a medical emergency arises unlike anything you have experienced, however, that money would come out of your emergency fund and wouldn't be part of your budgeted expense. This section is for the expenses you can reasonably assume are coming. Don't forget to include expenses for special services such as a gym membership, sessions with a personal trainer, or fees or dues for diet programs. More people are joining these programs to improve their health and well-being and they are typically not covered by insurance.

Entertainment

Unless they have been diligent about tracking their entertainment expenses, most people don't know exactly what they spend in this category. With your current habit of writing down everything you spend, though, you may have a clearer idea. For now, estimate how often you eat out and what that runs; how many movies, shows, or events you might attend in a month; and any travel or vacation you're planning. Be honest. I need to warn you right now, though, that since entertainment is an item over which you have complete control, it may soon change! Getting an accurate view of what you have been spending is very important, however, so don't try to fudge this number.

Total Expenses

Add up all the totals of each category to come up with your total expenses. Subtract your spendable income, and get a number that is either positive (you have money left at the end of the month) or negative (you are in the red every month).

When you're finished, you will have a fairly accurate view of where you money goes and what you think is left after all your spending. If you show a positive amount but know you have nothing left at the end of the month, take another look at your expenses. You must be spending more somewhere.

TIP:* *Many banks and credit cards offer, as part of their services, an expense summary feature. One bank (Wells Fargo) asks you to categorize various transactions and bill-paying accounts as part of its online banking services and then provides monthly expense summaries for you. Some credit cards offer year-end summaries on what your expenditures were for the year, all categorized for your convenience. These are terrific tools for helping you to degunk your spending patterns. If you can get these statements for the past few years, they can give you a great view of how you have been spending recently. Call your credit card companies and see what they can provide.

As you track your expenses and categorize them, your financial picture will get even clearer, and the missing money will turn up in something like expressway tolls or dues for Weight Watchers. If you are consistently in the red at the end of every month, figure out where the money is coming from to pay the difference. Is that why your credit card balances are steadily rising? Is that why your savings are steadily dwindling? Are you borrowing from retirement accounts or your parents to cover your shortfalls? The answer is in there somewhere, and it's important for you to uncover it.

Commit to Making a Change

If you've gotten this far in the chapter, give yourself a large pat on the back. Looking at how you spend money, how much of it you spend, what you earn, and what you owe isn't easy—especially if you have gunked-up finances. It takes a lot of courage and desire for change to do this analysis. You've gotten this far, though, so I have to believe that you're ready to make a change in order to improve your financial situation. You're on your way to degunking your finances once and for all. The big truth here is that once your finances are degunked, you'll never want to go back to a gunked-up financial situation again!

So, what do you see as the result of all this analysis? Were you shocked at how much you owe? Are you surprised at how your money is spent? Are you content with how much you are giving or saving? Is your debt load where you want it to be? Chances are there is something you want to change as a result of getting a fuller picture of your financial situation. You may want to lower your debt or increase your savings, or you may resolve to buy a new home or put away some funds for a family vacation. Regardless of what you've learned from this exercise, I'm hoping that you now want to make some resolutions about your financial future.

Most people make financial decisions (even important ones) based on an incomplete picture of their real situation. This is a dangerous habit. Once you know where you stand, you'll sleep better at night and have the confidence and information to make decisions and continue to improve your financial situation.

What Can I Change?

With the numbers in black and white, your financial picture may not be the lovely landscape you hoped for. But don't despair. You have the opportunity to redesign your financial picture and to paint the landscape you want to see. You didn't get in this financial shape overnight, and you won't be able to change it overnight either, but with attention, commitment, and resolve, you can make your finances work for you. It's time to make positive changes in your situation that will benefit your forever.

Look at Monthly Expenditures

If you're consistently in the red at the end of each month, look over your Monthly Expenditures form. If you are under in your income-to-spending ratio, look for places to cut. The numbers have to balance so your Over/Under number is zero. Any money left should be put toward savings, debt repayment, or other responsible spending. Any amount under needs to disappear by cutting spending or increasing income.

GunkBuster's Notebook: Include Your Family in Your Planning

It's essential for you to include all household members—spouse, partner, children, roommates, and other family members—if you make major changes to the household budget. Young children may not fully grasp the importance of these changes, but it's perfectly reasonable to say to a young child that the entire family will be cutting back on expenses. One way of getting the children to participate is to say that they can choose to go to a movie or go out to dinner, but not both. This will be a lesson in responsible financial management for the children as well. It's important to enlist cooperation from all members of the household who earn and spend money. If credit card purchases are being curtailed, then *all* use of credit cards must be restricted. If food budgets are to be consolidated, then everyone, even if they don't necessarily agree, must be aware of how and why the changes are being made. It is a lot to expect that your children will be completely on board with the new plan immediately, but they will see the benefits in the lessening of tension and strife in the household. In short, the more "buy in" you get from your household, the easier it will be to fight the battle of financial gunk!

Try to make the work of financial planning a positive experience for everyone you need to involve. It is common for people to feel uncomfortable talking about money, even with close relatives and good friends. We've all heard stories about families in which one person makes all of the financial decisions and then one day unexpectedly passes away. A situation like that can leave a spouse or other family members in a state of panic, with no idea how to manage the family's finances. Imagine the stress that would cause to the family, already reeling from the loss of a loved one. It's imperative to share your financial process with your spouse or partner and get the rest of the family involved to an appropriate level for their age. This is great training for your kids, and working together as a family can reduce the stress associated with a difficult financial situation.

There is always the possibility that no matter how you present it, someone may not agree to the new plan. I have worked with clients over the years who desperately want to resolve their financial issues and met with great resistance from their spouse, who didn't see any need or have any intention of changing their habits to help the situation. I had one client whose wife continued to spend in her previous patterns even though there had been a job change that lowered their income significantly. It made a screaming mess of their already challenged finances, and talking to her was like trying to move a stone wall. Over time, she did change her behaviors, but it was a very frustrating and draining period for this family in terms of money and harmony. Although this is obviously not the optimal situation, you can still work the program from your end, even with little shared cooperation. If you follow degunking principles, even with no help from a resistant partner, things can still improve. It won't happen as quickly, and it will feel lonely and unfair that you're the one doing all the work, but if you keep your goals in mind, you can make a positive difference in your situation. As well, there is a great possibility that your actions and the ensuing results will have some effect on your difficult family member and will help move them in the degunking direction. One can only hope. For you, however, stay the course. It will help, and there will be improvement, even if the pace is slower than you might like.

Once the household has begun curtailing certain expenses, fill out a new Monthly Expenditures form with the changes you have decided on—keeping in mind that the goal is to balance your budget. It may be difficult to decide what to change. Take time to play around with the numbers. Once you've agreed on where the cuts are to be made, it will be important for everyone to understand that this will be your new spending plan. And although it may feel very odd at first, everyone will adjust to the new plan as it continues.

For example, by moving $100 of what you may spend on dinners out to your debt repayment, you may be able to pay off that credit card in 18 months. Or, by making coffee at home, you can save $84 per month that can go to pay the electric bill. By changing your cable plan to the most basic of all plans (often around $10, though the companies don't publish this rate), you can save the $35 a month, that will make up the shortfall in the cost for your daughter's ballet lessons. Move the money around. See what you can do without. Change what you expect from your lifestyle. And, most importantly, *don't forget your goal.* Paying down your debt or saving for a down payment on a home can be much more important than yet another first-run movie. Wait a month, and rent it for a 10th of the price of all four of you going to the theater—and even that doesn't even include the savings on the amazingly overpriced popcorn.

Do You Need to Increase Income?

Making the decision to increase your income can be a difficult one. Perhaps all the adults in the household are already working full-time jobs. Some of them may have more than one job, and the teenagers may be contributing through part-time jobs after school. Maybe you, as a single mother, simply can't take on another job and care for your children as well.

But, if after making all the cuts you can you are still showing a deficit, it may be necessary to increase what is coming in. Increasing your income can be a huge help in this process, but keep in mind the costs associated with working more. Child care, clothing needs, time away from family, and higher taxes need to be subtracted from what will be gained by a second (or third) job or by working more hours at your first job.

The question to ask is whether this is a short- or long-term solution. Are you willing or able to work more for the rest of your days or just until the credit cards are paid off? Perhaps working a second job is a season of your life, instead of drudgery forever. It is possible, also, that it is more advantageous to make drastic changes to your lifestyle—by reducing your spending habits, possibly significantly—so that you can work less and be home more. What is the use of working more to pay for a big house if the family is never there together? Is your second car a necessity or a luxury?

Think and talk about these issues with your family, and decide on what changes are appropriate for your situation. Fill out a new Monthly Expenditures sheet with your decisions, and commit to working within that spending plan. It may help to write your financial goals in big letters across the top.

Having a Workable Budget

Once you have made financial decisions that get you in the black every month, you finally have a budget to work from. Congratulations! This is a monstrous step in the reaching of your goals and a healthy process through which to go. Your money is no longer in charge—you are! You control your money, as opposed to your money controlling you. Look at this as a hose that's turned on full blast, whipping around, spraying money in all different directions. Once you grab the hose, you direct the money where you want it to go. Much better, isn't it? Keep in mind that you need to keep your resolve firm and your commitment clear, and your finances will be degunked steadily and consistently.

Divide Your Expenditures by Paycheck

For most people, getting paid is a weekly, biweekly, or monthly affair. The goal of the following sections is to decide what to pay with each paycheck. Once you get into a schedule of when to pay what, there will be no more guessing on how the mortgage will be paid or where the money will come from for groceries or, worse yet, running out of money midmonth and having to use credit cards to meet expenses.

Create a Chart

On a piece of paper, make as many sections as you get paychecks per month. If you and your spouse get paid at the same time, include that in one section. If you get paid at different times, make different sections. List the total amount of money available (the net) in each section. I've included a form to help you put in this information (see Figure 4-2).

Using your bill due dates as a guide (refer to the master list you created in Chapter 3), decide which paychecks will cover which bills. For example, if you get paid every two weeks, there will usually be two sections on your piece of paper. Coming off the top of every check is savings and giving. What is left is your spendable income. Since most rents and mortgages are due on the first of the month, they will be paid by the second paycheck in the month before the due date. The mortgage for October will paid by the second check in September. Subtract that amount from the second check. The electric bill and the phone bill are due in the middle of the month. They will be paid by the first check. Subtract those amounts. Once all the bills are paid in that fashion, you can see where the other expenditures fit in. Groceries may be split up from both paychecks or may come completely out of one. The same is true for any

Dividing Your Bills by Paycheck

Paycheck 1 amt. ________	Paycheck 2 amt. ________
Paycheck 3 amt. ________	Paycheck 4 amt. ________
Paycheck 5 amt. ________	Paycheck 6 amt. ________
Side Jobs amt. ________	Extra Income amt. ________

Figure 4-2
Form to help you divide your bills by paycheck.

expense without a due date. Figure 4-3 shows an example of what a couple's budget might look like. Notice that I am using the Monthly Expenditures Form presented in Appendix A and the Dividing Your Bills by Paycheck Form that was presented in this chapter.

GunkBuster's Notebook: Try to Live Below Your Means for a Month

If after looking at your income and expenses you determine that you are operating without much of a cushion, you can try an experiment with your family for a month. On paper, it might be difficult to simply decrease your expenses or find ways to increase your income. Before you make any drastic plans, take a month and try to live below your means. Decide on some things to forgo for the month, and simply do without. At the end of the month you can discuss the things that you sacrificed and take a hard look to see if eliminating them really made a difference in your lifestyle. For example, skip your regular Saturday night out and have the family make homemade pizza together. Cut the number of times you play golf in half. Use the scrapbooking materials you have in the house instead of buying more. You can make a bit of a game out of this and have some fun in the process. Here are some items to look at as you try to live below your means for a month:

- √ Are there things around the house you can fix yourself instead of paying the handyman?
- √ Could you carpool for a month or take public transportation and save on your gas and auto maintenance charges?
- √ Are there some coupons you could be using to save money when you purchase items that are in the budget?
- √ Can you find less-expensive ways to handle your dry cleaning or haircuts and color? Is it time to start doing your own nails?
- √ Can you skip going to the coffee shop or your favorite bagel place in the morning or the deli at lunch and prepare your own coffee and food?
- √ Can you rent movies (or get them from the library) and make your own popcorn instead of forking out a pile at the theater?
- √ Can you discontinue features in your phone package to save some money?
- √ If you are overusing your cell phone (and spending extra money outside of the plan you currently have), can you cut back for a month?
- √ Can you limit the amount of money you give to your children for entertainment?
- √ Can you bathe the dog yourself?
- √ If you have a cleaning person, could you have them come less often?
- √ Could you get books and magazines from the library instead of purchasing them?

Managing Unspent Money

Money that is not spent within the month should stay in the bank. You may not spend all of your budgeted gift money in one month, but the extra amount will be needed when the holidays come around. The situation with unspent money can be handled in two ways:

Dividing Your Bills by Paycheck

Paycheck 1 amt. 1584

Car payment	210
Car gas	155
Loan payments	270
Child care	250
Cell phones	60
Car maintenance	75
Home repairs	75
Savings	150
Giving	150
Gifts	106
Dinners out	80
	1581 $3.00 left

Paycheck 2 amt. 1584

Mortgage	1245
Gas bill	120
Phone/Internet	82
Electric bill	88
Water	22
Trash	10
License/sticker	16
	1583 $1.00 left

Paycheck 3 amt. 450

Groceries	137
Clothing	55
Household items	35
Car insurance	120
Travel/vacation	100
	447 $3.00 left

Paycheck 4 amt. 450

Groceries	138
Medical	50
Counseling	60
Lunches	40
Movies	25
Babysitting	20
Pets	40
Activities	40
Kickboxing	20
Cable TV	15
	448 $2.00 left

Paycheck 5 amt. ________

Paycheck 6 amt. ________

Side Jobs amt. 103 + 9 left from above

Car washes	15
Personal maintenance	25
Books	10
Fitness	20
Hobbies	30
Media rental	12
	112

Extra Income amt. ________

Figure 4-3

Creating a budget for our couple.

1. If you have self-control and don't see money in your checkbook as money to spend, leave it there. Before you exercise this option, however, *be honest with yourself.* Do you have a history of exercising self-control when it comes to unspent money? If not, proceed to Option #2.
2. If you're like most people, you'll need some help in handling that unspent cash. I recommend that you open a savings account and, on a monthly basis, transfer the extra money from individual categories into that account as soon as your bills are paid. That way, the cash isn't just sitting there, tempting you to buy that cute flat-screen TV for the kitchen.

Reality Check: In order for a savings account to work for you, you must tell yourself that the money in your savings account is *not* to be accessed under any circumstances other than to pay the bills it is holding the money to pay. This is the only way this account will help you achieve the goal of saving money for your future budgeted expenses, and the only way you'll have the money you need when your quarterly insurance premium comes due.

Regardless of where your savings are held, you should keep a record of how much in the account is gift money and how much is savings to pay for car repairs when they become necessary. An easy way to gunk up your finances is to spend money you have put away for particular expenses on other things and, when those expenses come due (such as your annual neighborhood association dues), to rob from Peter to pay Paul. This will develop a pattern of always being a couple of steps (and dollars) behind and will keep you from being able to reach your important financial goals.

Another way to handle certain categories is to take money out in cash and keep it in individual envelopes. It is a very physical, visual thing to have $85 in cash for monthly entertainment. It stays in the Entertainment envelope until you need it, and when it's gone, it's gone. This works well for other line items as well, including groceries, clothing, personal maintenance, books/magazines, babysitting, and hobbies. Even doing this for a short time can make spending money a much more definitive thing. Using credit and debit cards takes the intentionality out of spending money, and studies have proven that using plastic can increase spending by as much as 30 percent. It just doesn't seem very real. If you are having trouble restricting spending in some areas, use the envelope system until you have mastered some self-control. For some people, this may forever be the best solution. This doesn't attest to their eternal lack of self-control, but to finding what works and sticking with it.

GunkBuster's Notebook: Put the Credit Cards Away

Living a "cash only" life is a great way to help you stick to your budget. Use the envelope system for a month to see what a difference it makes in your financial life to go without using credit. I have found myself walking away from the grocery store after charging my purchases, unable to remember how much I spent until I look in my register. That rarely happens when I use cash. Try this, and see what a difference it makes. Leave your credit cards at home, and work with cash only for purchases. You will be amazed at how much more attention you will pay to what you buy and how much you're paying for it.

When you have worked through all the categories, all your expenditures will be designated to a paycheck. You know how every bill will be paid, and the money for Fluffy's vet visit is being set aside. Of course, nothing goes completely according to plan. You may be saving $100 per month for car repairs, but two months into this program, the timing chain goes on the car and the repair bill is $385. You use the $200 you have in that account and need $185 more. Early on in your degunking program, these types of unplanned-for expenses will have to come from relegating money from other categories from which you have control (such as entertainment, clothing, vacation, or personal maintenance) or from dipping into your emergency fund. For the next month, though, you should start saving for the next unanticipated repair. The plan is that by the time you need tires—and you know you'll need them in a year or two—there will be enough in your maintenance fund to cover such expenses.

Summing Up

In this chapter, we took a hard look at what you earn, what you spend, what you owe, and how to organize your monthly bills into a budget. This is a difficult task for most people because it's hard to face how gunked up our finances are. But, once this task is done, we have a clear picture of what our finances really look like. This picture doesn't represent what we *think* is going on or what we *wish* was going on—it's what's actually going on.

By using the three worksheets in Appendix A—the Income and Assets form, the Big D (Debt) form, and the Monthly Expenditures form—you now have documents that show you where your finances stand. Again, this may not be pretty, but at least you know what your situation is. Having this knowledge, you can now proceed with an action plan to tidy things up and degunk your finances for the long haul.

The process of managing your budget won't be seamless, but if you are dedicated, it will help you achieve your financial goals. You may need to change some of your line item amounts as the months pass, but the imperative thing is to stay focused on your goals and get your budget balanced. You may decide you need more in your clothing budget, but you don't get to add more to this area until you take money out of another category. As you start to live with your new budget, what may surprise you is what you decide you don't need or enjoy enough to pay the price to have it. Many people who thought they couldn't live without cable are finding that after canceling this service, the money saved and the free time created (by not watching so much TV) has opened up new opportunities: spending more one-on-one time with their kids, having time to read, or having more time to work on that side business (which will be fun and can generate some extra income).

Life is all about trade-offs. Decide what is most important, and live like you mean it.

Degunking Your Credit and Debit Cards

Degunking Checklist:

√ Determine the true cost of using your credit cards.

√ Use credit cards for budgeted purchases only.

√ Learn why paying off your balance each month is important.

√ Cancel all but one or two cards and close accounts you don't intend to use.

√ Learn how transferring balances can save you money.

√ Learn why overdraft protection doesn't protect you.

√ Put in place a record-keeping system that helps you track and improve your credit card spending habits.

When dealing with your personal finances, it may seem that your credit cards have developed a life of their own, throwing themselves on the counter of Marshall Field's during a big sale or sneaking out of your purse or wallet to buy that new riding lawn mower you recently saw advertised. How evil! Credit must indeed be a horrible thing to get you in so much trouble. It is, of course, more accurate to think that perhaps there is some improvement you can make in how you manage your credit cards and that credit can be a very good tool if it's used properly. Taking your credit cards to the mall when you know you shouldn't increase the balances is like visiting the Godiva Chocolate factory when you're on a diet. I, for one, am positive that I could manufacture some reason that eating a pound or so of truffles was not only acceptable, but in some way good for me, and I bet you could rationalize why using your credit cards for unbudgeted purchases is good for you.

In this chapter, I'll help you work through your credit card gunk. I'll show you how to better manage your credit cards, and then in Chapter 6, I'll show you how you can put a solid plan together to pay down your consumer debt. It's imperative in this process to understand what went wrong, but don't spend a lot of time beating yourself up for your past mistakes. Use that energy to make things better. Many people abuse credit cards at one time or another, and the important step is to stop. Your improvement will come with understanding what you did and moving forward with a comprehensive plan to make your situation better. As you'll learn in this chapter, the important first step with credit and debit cards is that you get them under control and then develop a plan for using them that furthers your long-term goals. We'll focus on determining what credit cards really cost you, learning how to use them wisely, getting rid of the cards you don't need, and keeping better records of what you spend.

Avoid the Credit Card Trap

Credit cards make purchasing nearly anything easy. A quick swipe, and you walk away from the gas pump, the grocery store, or the car rental desk with what you need. In a grocery store line, you can feel frustration when someone pulls out a checkbook to make a purchase (they will have to provide ID, numbers have to be written down—how time consuming and inconvenient). In our fast-paced lifestyle, even cash is growing to be a much less common way to pay than pulling out the plastic.

Then, to make matters worse, the credit card companies keep coming up with new ways to entice us. They offer us cards that will help us accumulate free miles, get discounts on purchasing new cars, and save up points that we can use to purchase more stuff. Your credit card company has probably offered you "checks" that can be used to pay off other debt—which only increases the debt on your current card! Some credit card companies are even trying to make it easier for us to use our credit cards to buy things even more quickly (have you seen the latest "mini" credit cards that fit on your key chain?) so that we don't even have to pull out our wallet to make a purchase. The more aggressive companies have mastered the art of marketing credit cards to our kids so that they become "credit junkies" even before they graduate from college. Credit is a big and highly profitable business, and one that can rip your budget to shreds if you're not careful.

The first thing to keep in mind about using your credit cards is that you don't *have* to use a credit card for a purchase. Although they may be required for reservation purposes in cases of car rentals, hotel reservations, or booking a vacation, the actual payment can always be made in cash (or check, in some cases) if you prefer. Don't forget, you are the customer. If you want to pay by check or cash, don't let anyone influence you otherwise—even that person standing impatiently in line behind you, waiting for you to get out your ID. Ignore them. It will give them more time to finish the conversation they're having on their cell phone.

Most of us don't care to carry huge bundles of cash around with us, so credit cards seem like a safe, convenient way to purchase everything from food to baubles to our health club membership. It is a choice, though, and one you should make after looking at your history and making changes, if necessary, in the way you think of credit. Paying by cash is an approach you should consider, however, especially if you are having trouble paying off your credit bills every month in full and you're still tempted to use your credit cards.

Why Are Credit Cards So Encouraged?

Merchants encourage the use of credit cards for a couple of reasons. Most importantly, it ensures that they get paid. The money comes to the merchant from the credit card companies, and even though the merchant pays a fee for this service, at least they are assured of getting their money. If you don't pay the credit card company, that's their problem, not the merchant's. As for the 3.5-percent fee, the merchant can pass that cost directly on to the consumer through higher prices. Another plus is the speed by which the transaction can be made and the ease in tracking transactions after the sale. Making a return to a store when you've used a credit card can be as easy as scanning the bar code on the receipt (which of course, you kept in an envelope for this very use) and crediting the amount back to your card. No muss, no fuss, and little paperwork.

Banks, credit card companies, and even large vendors love credit cards because they are huge moneymakers. Think about it: what other business could you go into that offers a return on investment of 12 percent, 16 percent, 19 percent, or more per year? The business of lending money at these rates is *hugely* profitable. This is why so much money is spent on telemarketing and direct mail. In 2003 alone, banks mailed out 5.2 billion offers for credit cards. Banks and credit card companies are constantly hunting for new customers. In recent years, merchants have gotten into the credit business as well by introducing their own credit cards. Today, you can get credit cards from the likes of Amazon.com, your favorite airline, your alma mater—you name it. Some companies will do anything to make a new credit card (that works the same as all the others but has a pretty picture on the front) more attractive to you.

GunkBuster's Notebook: Give Charity Credit Cards the Boot

In some credit card offers, a tricky detail to get you hooked is that the company promises to give a tiny percentage of your purchase amounts to your alma mater or a charity. If you want to support an organization, do yourself, and them, a favor. Put your intentions to give to them in your budget, write them a check, and avoid paying 21-percent interest in hopes of a few dollars being funneled to the entity you want to support. The same is true of telemarketers who call and ask you to buy particular products whose makers will then donate money to specific charities. Buy your product on sale somewhere, and send a check to the charity. That way, there's nothing taken out of your donation to pay for the middleman that made the call and your charity receives what you intend it to get. These are marketing ploys, and nothing else. Don't fall for them.

What's Gone Wrong?

The problem with credit cards comes not with the use of them, but the misuse of them. As with a slingshot, it's not when you have one that's dangerous, it's when it's badly used. Some people should never have a credit card, and many of us obtain credit cards when we are far too young, long before we understand the basic concepts of how to manage our personal finances. I have clients for whom credit cards are a disaster. There is something in them that does not associate charging on a card as money they will have to someday pay.

I worked with a wonderful woman who showed up at my office with 30+ credit cards, and she had reasons why she needed every one. She was about $40,000 in debt on cards, and there seemed to be no end in sight. Through all that spending, she simply ignored that there would be a reckoning for what she was doing. Talk about denial being more than a river in Egypt! After some work, she shook herself out of her fog, tearfully but happily cut up all of her cards but one, and started a new financial life with the envelope system. She still has all of her cut-up cards in a bag to remind herself not to ever get in that position again.

If you are stuck in the mindset of not tying your spending to the big bills you get every month, throughout this book I'll try to help you learn how to change this way of thinking. For now, it's likely that using your credit cards will only cause problems and pain. Instead of further gunking up your finances with credit cards, you should think about sticking to cash and organize your spending habits around not having access to little pieces of rectangular plastic.

Reality Check: Look at your credit card history and decide if you have used credit responsibly in the past. It may be best, in the beginning stages of degunking, to discontinue all use of credit cards until you develop self-discipline and a better pattern of budgeting and spending. It won't be the end of Western Civilization, and it probably won't be forever, but decide now whether continued credit card use will get you closer or farther away from your financial goals.

GunkBuster's Notebook: Pay by Cash or Credit?

I've already introduced the notion that it may be preferable for you to make your purchases by cash and skip the credit card. There are times, though, when using your credit cards instead of cash makes very good sense. I've provided a checklist in this section to help you determine if you should use cash (check) or credit in making a purchase. You might want to review a few of your credit card bills and see how these guidelines relate to your own credit card spending habits.

- √ Purchasing items online. If you are purchasing goods or services online, using a credit card is a plus because it gives you an extra level of protection. If you purchase something that you never receive or something that is not represented properly, your credit card company will help you get a refund and save you from being fleeced by a dishonest merchant.
- √ Tracking business expenses or other important expenses. If you make purchases for business or other critical expenses that you need to track, using a credit card may work well because the bank will provide you a more detailed level of record-keeping than you would have by using cash or

checks. Some credit card companies will even provide you with an end-of-year statement that shows all of your major purchases categorized into areas such as medical expenses, travel, auto, and so on. This can really benefit you in preparing for your taxes.

- √ Purchasing from merchants you don't fully trust. Occasionally, you might find yourself in the position of having to make a significant purchase from a merchant that you don't fully know or of whom you are unsure. For example, you might find the perfect sofa at a brand-new furniture store. Using your credit card will provide you with a backup plan in case the vendor doesn't provide you with the item you've purchased.
- √ Purchasing items on which you need to make down payments. Some products must be special-ordered and aren't delivered for months. Often, merchants take orders and then proceed to have an item made. To protect themselves, they might ask for a deposit or down payment. But to get the protection you need so that you have recourse if the merchant doesn't come through, you should consider using a credit card. Paying a deposit by cash or check gives you no recourse other than to hound the merchant (if you can find them) or call an attorney, which can get very expensive.
- √ Travel-related expenses. If you travel frequently for business or pleasure, you'll likely need a credit card to make reservations and possibly to pay for some of your expenses. The travel industry utilizes a reservation system that usually requires you to make reservations in advance for airline tickets, car rentals, hotel rooms, and even some restaurants. When you make these reservations, you'll need a credit card. Paying by credit card for some travel services, such as car rentals, can offer you an advantage. Some credit card companies will provide basic insurance when you rent a car and save you from paying for the insurance the car rental company tries to sell you.

Keep in mind, these suggestions only hold true if you are paying your card off in full every month. If not, save up your money, make the purchase on your card at that time, and pay off the amount immediately with what you have saved. At that point, you aren't building debt with the excuse of needing the extra protection a credit card offers.

Reality Check: Avoid using your credit card to pay your federal or state taxes. I know people who think this is a great idea because they have a credit card that offers them incentives, such as airline miles or cash back. You wouldn't even consider this if you were carrying a balance on your credit cards because the only thing more painful than paying taxes would be paying interest for a couple of years on your taxes. Even if you pay your cards off every month, it's still not a good move. The kicker here is that your credit card will be charging you an extra "service fee" for the joy of paying your taxes. All Visa cards, for instance, charge 2.49 percent of the tax amount over and above any other charges you incur to make the payment. The usual rate of return in goods or services from credit card incentives is around 1.00 percent. That makes the fee that you will pay over twice as much as the incentives you would receive. That's a bad deal no matter how you look at it.

Determine the True Cost of Using Your Credit Cards

It's easy to think that using credit cards is basically free. After all, most credit card companies now offer cards that don't have a yearly fee. The reality is that there are costs to using credit that you may not be considering because they are not being tracked. For our first credit card degunking task, I'll try to help you uncover these costs.

Start by selecting two of your most frequently used credit cards. (If you only have one active credit card, good for you. One card will be fine.) Gather up the credit card statements that I had you set aside in Chapter 3. For each card, review the year of statements and jot down the following:

- √ Any annual fees—Most cards with good incentives (airline miles or travel benefits) charge a yearly fee. Though it still may be well worth keeping the card, be sure you know which cards are charging you a fee and which are without a yearly hit.
- √ Any late fees that have been accessed—You probably had a reason for making this payment late, but the company is still happy to charge you around $30 anyway. If you went over your limit, that's another $30.
- √ Any finance charges—There is a section on your statement that will list your finance charges for the current month and for the year to date.

Total these three items up for the year. Then, think about all of the other things that you could have done with the money you've spent on fees and finance charges. This is the real cost of using your credit cards. If you compare this cost to what you've likely spent on bank fees for writing checks or ATM fees for withdrawing cash, you might decide that your credit cards are simply not worth the convenience that they provide.

Tracking the hidden costs for credit isn't fun, but if you set up a system to do this on a regular basis, such as once a quarter, it will help keep you from abusing your credit cards. Once you realize that the real cost of buying those great new shoes was the original price ($40) plus finance charges over several months ($20 in compounded interest), a late fee ($30), and an over-your-limit fee as the cherry on top of the sundae ($30), you may think twice (or three times or four!) about paying $120 for a pair of shoes that were on sale for $40. Chances are, with this kind of information, you'll show more restraint the next time you're tempted to use your credit card, or if this is a budgeted item, you'll use your checkbook instead.

Use Credit Cards Wisely

With all the possible problems of using credit cards come some benefits, *if* you learn how to use your cards wisely and degunk your purchasing activities. In the following sections, I'll show you how to take advantage of the credit card system by using the "buy now, pay now" technique, getting rid of cards you don't need, and maximizing the use of incentive cards.

Adopt the "Buy Now, Pay Now" Technique

There is only one way to use credit cards completely for your benefit: use them only for budgeted purchases, and pay off your balances every month. The point of this is to pay absolutely no interest or late fees. This will only work if you are starting with a zero balance. It's cheating to add purchases to a card with a previous balance, pay off your new purchases every month, and leave what was there. The credit card companies are smarter than that. You will be charged interest on the new purchases, and what you pay will go to previous interest and principal. These companies aren't outsmarted easily. They're in the business to make money, and they've been doing it a lot longer than you've had a pretty credit card.

So, starting at a zero balance, if you have purchases you need to make in a month and the money is budgeted for that month, feel free to charge the jeans or food or piano lessons on your credit card. When the bill comes in, pay it in full and smile. You have now used the credit card company's money for a month or so for free. Even better is when a credit card company has incentives for you to use its card and you still pay it off every month. Now, you are using its money and getting free air travel or cash back at the expense of the company.

GunkBuster's Notebook: Avoid Sneaky Finance Charges

Some credit card companies have started levying interest charges within 21 days of a purchase. What this can mean is, if you normally get your statement on the 10th of the month and you make a purchase on the 9th using your credit card (which doesn't show up on that month's statement), when your next bill appears, you will see a finance charge for that purchase. The lesson here is to scrutinize your credit card statements every month to see which fees are being charged to you. Make appropriate and complete monthly payments as necessary to avoid these charges. Here's what I do: My credit card balance and all recent transactions are available online. Every time we get paid, I go online, check the purchases against my checkbook register, and pay the full amount. Using that system will keep you from ever being levied finance charges or late charges. You aren't using the company's money for as long, but that is small potatoes when compared to peace of mind.

No need to shed any tears for the credit card companies. There are millions of people in the U.S. alone who pay billions of dollars in interest for the honor of using their cards, and even those who default don't worry the companies much. There are always those college students to entice for new business.

Don't Sign Up When They Call You

It's 6:00 P.M. and you are just sitting down to dinner. The phone rings and some telemarketer on the other end of the line has this incredible offer just for you. If you sign up now, you'll get credit cards for your entire family, no monthly fees, and a bucket of ice cream for each member of your family every month. What a deal! Sign me up.

Instead, count to five and come to your senses. The card you are about to get charges nearly 22-percent interest and you already have cards in your wallet that you are planning to shred. Signing up for anything over the phone is a poor idea anyway, and credit cards are near the top of the list for future regrets. If you need a credit card, do the research yourself and go shopping on your own to find the one that meets your needs and will benefit you the most.

Credit card marketing people are very smart and darned persistent. Keep in mind, you're the one holding the phone. Hang up, and get back to dinner.

Credit card marketing has increased tremendously, and the gunk we receive from credit card companies can be overwhelming. This gunk is stuffed into our bank statements, letters from alumni associations, and our e-mail. You can't make a purchase anywhere without the clerk asking you if are putting it on the store's card, and if not, whether you would like (for a 10-percent reduction in today's purchase cost) to apply for one right this minute. The irony is that the credit card companies are especially proficient at bugging you to sign up, but if you miss a few payments, they'll equally harangue you to pay up.

I had a friend who recently called up his investment broker at a discount brokerage firm to obtain a form so that he could transfer over some IRA funds. The associate who answered the phone, on hearing that the caller wanted to open up an account, proceeded to pitch the caller on the benefits of getting a brokerage credit card (and what exactly does a credit card have to do with opening a retirement account?). My friend kept saying he just wanted to open an IRA account to set up a savings plan, but the associate wouldn't let up for the next five minutes. I guess there is a time and a place to be sold a credit card, but a situation like this is not either. I told him to write a letter to the company's management and complain, which he did. I hope it makes a difference in the way they do business.

Don't let salespeople push you around. It's your money and your good credit that's at stake, and a bucket of Moose Tracks, as good as that can be, isn't worth putting that at risk.

GunkBuster's Notebook: Credit and Your Kids

Credit cards have become like cell phones—everyone, including your kids, thinks that they must have one. The credit card companies have learned over the past decade that the youth market has become a bonanza for them, and they've stepped up their marketing to entice college kids and even high school kids to become comfortable using credit cards. It's not uncommon for young people to pick up bad credit habits at an early age and build up thousands of dollars of debt by the time they graduate from college. To keep your kids from becoming caught in the credit card trap, there are some practical things that you can do:

√ Instead of simply ignoring the situation, try to teach your kids about responsible credit from an early age. Teach them, and show them with your actions, how credit should be used. When you're using your credit card, remind your kids that the money for this purchase is already in your account, or it will be there by the time the bill arrives. To make this real to them, if they want something at a store that they have to pay for out of their own money and ask to borrow from you, gently refuse. Talk about the bondage of owing someone money and how much more they will appreciate this purchase when they have saved up their money and bought it themselves. They won't believe you, of course, but it is true. Tell them if they had the money at home waiting to be spent, you would be happy to front them what they needed until they got home, but you won't lend it to them over a period of time. As difficult as this sounds, it is a very good practice and will help them develop good credit habits early. It also makes shopping with children easier for parents, and the constant begging for money or stuff can be thwarted before it has a chance to flourish.

√ Your kids will, at some point, need or want credit. A good way to start them on a responsible credit system is to get one of your cards with their name on it. If there is a purchase they need to make with a credit card (something online, or that set of *Disco Forever!* CDs on TV for your birthday gift), *and they have the money in their hand to pay for it,* give them the card and help them to make the transaction. They pay you immediately for the purchase, and you send the money in to the credit card company. If they have shown responsibility in money matters generally, you may want to help them establish credit for themselves. This is appropriate for college-age kids. There is no reason in the world for a high school student to need their own credit card. Together, choose a card that fits their needs. It will, by design, have a very low limit (usually under $500), but you can specify an even lower one if you like. Although their name will be on the card, have the bills sent to your house so you can monitor its use. The day the bill comes in, request payment for it. The first time payment is not made in full by the due date, the card gets taken away. If payment is made on time for a year, have the bills sent to the child, but keep abreast of the account online. If they go south on their payments or overspend, take the card. Although you can't keep your children from getting credit cards on their own, teaching them about the responsible use of credit from a young age will make them much more ready to accept that responsibility well when they're ready to take it on themselves.

√ Let them know about your mistakes. For parents with less than immaculate credit histories, some of the lessons you can teach are what you did wrong. Children can sense tension in their homes, and money issues cause trouble that they can easily see. As you change your habits, explain to them, at appropriate ages, what went wrong and what you had to do to fix it. Knowing what their parents went through is one way for children to learn what not to do with their finances.

Choose Which Cards to Keep

The days of having 22 different credit cards are over. When credit cards first became available, there were few cards accepted everywhere, and every department store and retail chain pushed the use of its own card. Although now even tiny stores offer specialty credit cards (with your account information tied into incentives), the interest rates are universally high, and they provide you with little more than more color and bulk to your wallet.

If you have decided to use credit cards wisely, it is time to choose which to keep and which to shred. Here are some quick guidelines to help you start the process of degunking your credit cards:

√ If you only want to keep one credit card active, choose a Visa or a MasterCard. These cards are accepted almost everywhere credit cards are accepted throughout the world. Some people who travel a great deal prefer to use American Express.

√ American Express isn't accepted as universally, but it has gotten more universal in the past five years. In some European countries, AmEx is as commonly accepted as Visa and MasterCard. One of the benefits of certain American Express cards is that they provide excellent year-end statements to help you track your charged expenses. Also, the AmEx "green card" doesn't have a preset spending limit, which allows you to make large purchases on the card, but it does require repayment every month. If you don't fit into this customer profile for AmEx, then consider dropping this card.

- √ Get rid of any department store credit cards that you have. These cards typically have the highest interest rates. Don't be enticed into signing up for one of these cards just because the new store where you're shopping over the holiday weekend is offering a special. This is how you end up with a huge collection of cards that, if used poorly, can totally gunk up your credit report.
- √ Get rid of any cards that require an annual fee. The exception to this would be a credit card that you're using because you get valuable incentives. Make sure, however, that if you keep this type of card you are actually using the incentives.

TIP:* *Many credit card companies will waive the annual fee if you ask them to. Give them a call and ask them to credit you back your annual fee. When they ask why, tell them that you're thinking about transferring your balance to another no-fee card. In order to keep your business, your credit card company will probably make a "special exception" to its policies and waive this fee. The catch is, be sure to watch your monthly statements because they may try to charge you this annual fee in the future! Another request to make of your credit card company is to waive an occasional late fee or over-the-limit fee. They have policies concerning this, and if your account has been in good standing for a certain amount of time, they have the authority to credit those fees back to your account. It's certainly worth a call to find out.

- √ Keep the cards that offer the lowest interest rates and late fees. Although I really want you to get into the habit of paying off your credit card balances every month, there are times when emergencies do occur and you might have to keep a balance. If this occurs, you'll be grateful for a low-interest card.
- √ If you can get a good interest rate, consider keeping the cards with which you have the longest history. These cards can help you build your credit history. One account with good, long-standing score is worth more on your credit report than several shorter-term cards. Keep this in mind when you are deciding what to keep and what to cancel. In Chapter 10, I'll show you how to make wise decisions about which credit cards to keep so that you can improve your credit score.

Now that you're armed with the basics, it's time to look closely at the properties of the cards you have.

Look at Interest Rates, Fees, and Credit Limits

Before we look at the interest rates, fees, and credit limits associated with all your credit cards, it will be helpful to get all your cards out in front of you. Some people are surprised to see how many cards they have accumulated over the years. Although it's not necessary to arrange them by color, get them on the table with their accompanying statements. Your credit report will also list all the credit card accounts you have open; this report will help remind you of credit card accounts you may have opened for the free Thermos and never used, and it will be handy if you no longer have the card associated with the account. Some accounts may have been open so long without activity that you've forgotten all about them. Gather all the cards, statements, and credit report information. You're now going to examine each and every account you have.

First, look at the interest rates. Although you hope to never pay interest, if a payment gets caught up in the mail or cyberspace, it is wise to keep the interest rate as low as possible. The interest rates on your credit cards are directly tied to you credit rating. If you have poor credit, the card companies consider you a larger risk and will charge you higher interest. Good credit will yield lower rates. The interest rate, by law, has to be printed on every statement you receive. See which of your major cards has the lowest interest and put those aside.

TIP:* *As with annual fees, interest rates can be negotiated with some credit card companies. Although I don't recommend them, if you have a variable-rate card and you notice an extremely high interest rate on your latest statement, call up the company and ask them to lower the rate. Tell them that you have another lower-interest-rate card and you're considering doing a balance transfer. I know you've used this story before, but, hey, it works. Again, your credit card company might make a "special exception" just for you and lower your interest rate a few points. Your new rate will probably be good for only six months, so make a note on your calendar when the special rate is up. When the rate is about to change back, call them again. If they won't extend the good rate, consider doing a balance transfer to another card.

Next, look for yearly fees. A no-fee card with great incentives would be best, but it's not always realistic. Some of the incentive-based cards carry a fee, and it might still make good sense to keep that one if it is worth what it costs you. The credit card I use has a $35 yearly fee, but because I get at least two very low-cost airline tickets every year as the result of my purchases, the fee is worth the benefit. But, if there is a fee and you don't charge enough to take advantage of the benefits, it's not worth it to you, and you should eliminate this card from your wallet. Put aside those whose cost aligns well with the benefits they provide.

Chain and department store cards are rarely a good deal. Although they try to rope you in with "special sales opportunities" and " member-only" ads, their point is to get you to spend more, rack up balances on their cards, and happily pay the 20-percent interest common to most of them. Add these to your shred pile.

Now, take a look at your credit limits. If your credit is good, the companies will routinely raise your limits without any help or permission from you. You may have enough credit to buy a small city if your credit rating is in the "excellent" range. If you were in the biggest bind imaginable, how much credit would you need? If there was an emergency across the country and you had to purchase airline tickets immediately for your family, what would it cost? If your house fell down, what would it cost to live in a hotel for a couple of months? Decide how much credit you need, and see which two cards will provide you with that number. If you have poor history with credit cards but still want to keep one or two for making car rental reservations, keep your limits low, just enough to cover the reservation fees the companies require, but don't use them to charge anything else.

What to Keep, What to Shred

You now have enough information to decide which cards to keep and which to shred. Since the number of cards to keep is down to one or two, when you use them, make sure it is to your biggest benefit. Here are some guidelines to help you:

- √ If both cards are at a zero balance and one has better incentives, use that one.
- √ If there is a balance on one and not the other, use the one with no balance and pay it off every month, incurring no further interest charges.
- √ If both cards have balances, keep them, but don't use them for anything until the past balances are paid off. Chapter 6 will show you, step-by-step, how to pay off your credit card debt in the most efficient way possible. Until then, use cash or checks.

GunkBuster's Notebook: Look for a Credit Card That Really Benefits You

Instead of just signing up for a credit card because you received a "once in a lifetime" solicitation in the mail or a nagging call from a telemarketer, go on your own credit card hunt and look for a card that really fits your needs. In particular, try to find one that offers not only low fees but incentives that you can really use as well.

If you master the discipline of paying off your credit card balance in full each month, you can truly benefit from a card that offers valuable incentives. Here are some examples of the many types of incentives available today:

√ Cash back for a percentage of your yearly purchases

√ Airline miles than can be redeemed for free flights

√ Other travel needs, such as rental cars and hotel stays

√ Free gas

√ Cash back on a car purchase

√ Points that you can use to obtain free goods and services.

The trick to benefiting from a card that offers incentives is threefold:

1. You should always pay off your monthly balance in full, as I've said previously.
2. You should pick a card that offers incentives that match your lifestyle. If you fly a lot, then picking a card that offers you airline miles is a smart idea, for example. Just remember to select a card that offers miles for the airline that you fly most often.
3. Make sure that you don't overpay for the privilege of receiving an incentive. Be cautious because some incentive cards charge very high fees. If that is the case, check to see if you can negotiate these annual fees to a minimum. It never hurts to ask.

One mistake that consumers make is that they sign up for incentive cards, use them to rack up "points," and then never use the incentives, all the while paying high yearly fees and interest. Many people may also use too many of these cards, splitting up their purchases so that accumulating enough points for the incentives takes much longer than it would were they only using a single card. My advice is to pick the best card you possibly can and use it as much as you can, *if, and only if, you pay it off each month.* Even if you have a great card, be on the lookout for special incentive periods. Some of the airline incentive cards offer special deals that double or triple the miles you'll receive for some of your purchases. For example, American Express provides a card that offers airline miles for Delta Airlines and provides double miles for purchases at the grocery store and gas station. It often runs specials in the summer months when you can get double miles for all of your purchases. The trick, though, with many of these incentives is that you have to sign up in advance. It is important to watch your credit card statement each month for details and be very aware that a good deal becomes a bad deal if you are getting yourself in debt to do it. Taking advantage of special promotions that put you in the hole, and make it more difficult (or impossible) to pay off your cards every month, ends up taking advantage of you.

At our house, we put all of our budget purchases on one card, which gets paid off each month. With all that we spend on food, gas, repairs, and everything else in our budget, the points add up quickly. We have taken vacations, rented cars, gotten a thousand dollars off a Paris trip, and given away plane tickets. It's a great deal for us for $35 per year, but it would be a terrible idea if we didn't pay off the card each and every month. As it is, we win.

Before the Shredding Party

Simply shredding your credit cards and wallpapering the bathroom with them doesn't close the account. It can feel great to pay off a balance on a card you've been paying interest on for years, but there is more to closing the account than picking up the phone and calling. Although the credit card companies make it easy for you to sign up, they certainly don't want to make it easy for you to leave! Here is a surefire procedure to follow to get rid of the credit cards you no longer need:

1. Call the credit card company to ensure that you fully understand what it needs to get the account closed.
2. Expect to send in a signed letter to cancel the card. A standard letter would most likely include your name and account number and a request to close the account.
3. Some companies might like you to send one-half of the cut-up card in the envelope, but I have reservations about that. Tell them you're shredding it and making a nice mosaic to hang on your wall. If they insist, fax them a picture or Xerox copy of the cut-up card.

TIP:* *Before cancelling credit cards, be sure to read Chapter 10. Cancelling too many cards could be detrimental to your credit score.

---

4. If you are canceling a few cards, make sure that you later follow up and check on your credit report to make sure that the cards really did get canceled. Part of this is to clear your credit report of any paid-off cards, and part is to protect you in case someone is running around with your account number. I'll show you how to check and degunk your credit report in Chapter 10.

Don't be surprised if the person on the phone does handsprings to try to keep you from canceling their card. You don't have to give them any details about why you are discontinuing your relationship with them, and unless they offer you a better deal than you are getting with one of the cards you plan on keeping, don't waver. You don't owe them an explanation. Just tell them that you don't want the card anymore. Be strong and persistent, because they will be aggressive to keep your business!

TIP: Accounts can be closed even if they have balances. You are still responsible for the balance, of course, but the account can be shut down to further use. As you are planning on paying off the balance, it doesn't hurt to ask the person on the phone for a lower interest rate during that process. All they can do is say no, and they might just lower it a point or two to try to get you to reopen the account after the balance is paid off. This technique is worth trying if you have a card that has a reasonably high balance and you are being charged an especially high interest rate. If you succeed, the savings you'll realize could be substantial.

Now, have some fun with the cards you are discontinuing. Cut them, shred them, make nice little shapes out of them. Get your kids in on this part, and explain what you're doing to them. Let them help. When you have a nice pile, mix them all up. If you're not planning on the mosaic idea, put the shreds in different garbage cans in your home. The point of this exercise is that if the big black garbage birds rip open your garbage as it sits on your curb, all of your cut-up credit cards won't be lying there like puzzle pieces to glue back together. This may seem picky, but there's no sense giving someone driving by such a great opportunity to cause you trouble.

You now know which of your accounts are open and closed, and you have closed all those you will no longer use. How does it feel to be on top of things? Feels organized, doesn't it? Keep reading. It just gets better.

Transfer Balances and Get the Best of Credit Card Companies

Chances are you have balances on either the credit cards you're keeping or the ones you just shredded. Part of your degunking procedure should include trying to beat the credit card companies at their own game. As you've probably guessed, I get hives when I think of how much hard-earned money is paid in interest to these conglomerates, and I think it's fair to take full advantage of the offers they make to encourage business. In that vein, if you have balances on credit cards, start checking your mailbox for the offers you get weekly to transfer balances. Keep in mind, even though an offer might say, "You're Pre-approved!" it doesn't really mean that. But, if it says, "0% for Six Months on Transferred Balances," it does mean that. If you transfer your $2500 balance from your 19-percent card to that one, in six months, you will have saved about $150 – more than 5 percent of your balance, all of which can go to pay off the total faster. After six months, if the interest rate is threatening to go up to 19.9 percent, transfer the balance again. One thing to look for on any card to which you are considering transferring a balance is if they carry a fee to make the transfer. In the very small print on the contract, it may say there is a 3.5 percent fee to do the very hard work of getting your balance from the other company. This is unacceptable. Give them a call. See if they will waive the transfer fee. If not, keep looking for a different card. If they agree to waive the fee, get something in writing, and get the name of the person you spoke to on the phone. No matter what they tell you, they are responsible only to do what's in writing.

This technique only works to pay off the balances faster if you don't add to the balance on your existing card. You will never win the game if you continue to add to your debt. This way, you get the lowest interest rate possible to pay off your debt, and you'll get closer every month to being debt-free.

Read the Tiny Print and Be Careful What You Sign

This is a good time to mention an important fact: *Never, never sign anything you haven't fully read.* Read the tiny print and the back of solicitations you get from credit card companies. If you are signing something that says you've been given some document and understand it, make sure you've read it and understand it. If not, ask questions. Everything you sign is sealed with your intent, and it is the law that you must abide by the rules that are stated. It's not like it doesn't count if you didn't read it—there is no defense in that.

If you are reading a document and something in it bothers you, or you disagree, change it. Draw a line through what is troubling, and add what you think should be there. When you sign, it is then up to the person requesting the signature whether they accept the changes to the contract. Credit card companies are not likely to renegotiate their customer agreements with you, but virtually every other contract (from an offer on a piece of real estate to a medical waiver) is negotiable.

Here's an example: Recently, I took my dog to the vet, and they asked me to sign a document saying they were in no way responsible if anything bad happened to my dog while he was in their care. I asked about that, and the woman told me they, of course, took every precaution to make sure nothing happened. It didn't say that on the contract, however, so I added that they were to take every precaution and that they were responsible for negligence of any kind. I signed it, and they accepted it.

Do not let anyone try to make you hurry through signing anything. Some people will give you a sentence summarizing what's in each paragraph and expect you to sign off on a document. Read it, and ask questions if you don't understand it. It will be your responsibility to carry out the contract, so you better know what's in it.

Be Wary of the Credit Card's Evil Twin—the Debit Card

A debit card looks like a credit card, and it may act like a credit card on the surface, but it is an imposter, so don't be fooled. In reality, it is just an extension of your checking account. Every time you use your debit card, picture a big hand instantly reaching in to your checking account and taking out wads of money. If you don't keep perfect track of how and when you use your debit card, then it's like the hand reaching in whenever it likes. If your spouse or child uses the debit card and doesn't tell you (I'll bet that's never happened to anyone reading this...), then it's like a hand reaching in when your back is turned.

There is only one way to use a debit card for your benefit: use it for budgeted items only, and keep track of where every dollar goes. (In the next section, I'll provide you with some degunking techniques so that you can better track how you use your debit card.) Just taking out cash a couple of times a week for unspecified purchases is the smooth road to disaster. Using the card at the bookstore or to buy stamps can get you a $30 overdraft fee if you didn't keep track of what you used it for last week. I've had clients who counted on calling the bank every couple of days to get their balances, but that is false security, at best. The bank doesn't know what checks are going to hit on a given day, so the $432 that was there this morning can be mostly gone by nightfall if a few withdrawals clear during that same day.

If debit cards are used properly, they can be a convenient way to make purchases. Used badly, they can eat up boatloads of money in overdraft fees and send your finances spinning out of control. Be careful with your debit card. Be very, very careful.

Reality Check: Don't be fooled into thinking that your debit card offers you the same level of protection that your credit card does. If you purchase something online or from a dishonest vendor, you won't be able to later call your bank and get any real satisfaction. Once you make a purchase with your debit card, the money is gone. If you need more protection, use your credit card instead of your debit card.

Overdraft Protection Doesn't Protect You

Though it may be very tempting to sign up for overdraft protection, look closely at your history before you do. If it has been common for you to use this in the past as a slush fund, now is the time to stop. The idea of overdraft protection is good—if you slip up and a check comes in without sufficient funds to cover it, the bank will cover the check for you. This isn't, however, simply out of the goodness of its heart. As a standard, banks charge 18 percent per year for this service. Some also charge a per-transaction fee of $20 or more. If you mess up once and pay the balance back immediately, it could very well be cheaper to pay a little interest rather than an overdraft fee. If this is a habit, it's the same as having yet another credit card at huge interest that gets more and more difficult to pay off, and not paying will cause the same trouble as any other debt: a lowered credit rating and more difficulty opening an account at another bank. You should manage your account so that you never need overdraft protection, and with most banks, if you are overdrawn once in five years, they will consider waiving your overdraft fee.

Set Up a Good Record-Keeping System

Recall that earlier in the chapter I assigned you the project of looking over your credit card statements for the past year to determine the fees you have been paying. In addition to looking into your past activities, it's important to set up a good tracking system so that you know how you're using your credit cards during the month. That way, you won't get blindsided when you receive your bill. I've heard from some of my clients that they are afraid to open their credit card bill when it comes in the mail because they have no idea what it will contain. If you find yourself feeling this way, then you need to immediately set up a tracking system and review it a few times throughout the month.

Using a check register for both debit and credit cards works very well. In my checkbook, I make a line down the middle of my check register. I use one side of the register for written checks and debit card transactions and the other side for credit card transactions. I have an up-to-date record of everything happening at my very fingertips, and I can easily check the transactions against each other when the statements come in. If you share a credit card account with your spouse, significant other, or children, you'll also need to make sure that they track their purchases and that the activity is recorded in the register that is being kept.

When you get the bill at the end of the month, you should compare the bill to the register that you've been keeping. Make sure that your bill is accurate and that there aren't any purchases that you didn't make. You should also make sure that the amounts for each purchase match up. The closer you track your activity, the better you become at finding mistakes—and catching these mistakes can save you money.

If you find a mistake, contact your credit card company immediately. Call and point out the issue and then be prepared to put the problem in writing. The company will send you a form to use, but it must be returned in a specified time period. Whenever you are disputing a credit card transaction, it is vitally important that you can create a written record in a timely manner.

Track Your Debit Cards

Always remember that the debit card is a plastic check. When you hand it over, have a check register ready to mark down the date, place, and amount of your purchase. If you're taking money from an ATM, mark it down as well, and categorize what the cash will be used for. Your check register becomes a record-keeping device by which to check your statements every month and to keep track of all spending out of this account.

There is a great way to avoid getting into trouble with the debit card. Since the ATM isn't really a magic machine that spits money, don't use it to get cash whenever you need it. Cash expenditures can be planned for like any other expense, so once a week, withdraw the cash you will need for the budgeted cash expenditures during that week. This may include parking fees, coffee, lunches out, or a glass of wine at the nice place on the corner. Use the money as it is supposed to be used, and when it's gone, it's gone. No running to the ATM for more.

If there is more than one of you using the debit card, it must be part of the deal that the withdrawal should be checked with the other partner before being made so you are both completely aware of what's happening in the account and that you record all of the transactions.

Summing Up

Credit and debit cards can make your financial life much easier, or much more difficult. As always, it's not the card that makes the difference, but how you use the card that draws that line. Finances are funny—you're not born knowing how to do this, and if you're not taught, it's hit or miss until you learn. Not being taught the proper way to use credit and debit cards is good for the credit card companies and bad for you. This chapter has shown you how to degunk your credit and debit cards and use them to your advantage. You learned how to close accounts you won't be using anymore and how to choose which to keep. You've learned how to do a close analysis of your credit card statements and watch items such as interest rates, fees, and credit limits. I hope you've also learned that you can call your credit card company and ask it to eliminate annual charges or lower your interest rates. This is another necessary step in the managing of your personal finances, and when you put it into practice, you will feel much more in control.

Degunking Your Consumer Debt

Degunking Checklist:

√ Commit to stop adding to your debt.

√ Avoid new and different types of debt.

√ Find out if your debt level is too high.

√ Review the interest rates on your various loans.

√ Make a chart of all current consumer (unsecured) debt.

√ Learn how to choose which balances to pay first.

√ Use windfalls for debt repayment.

√ Effectively deal with creditors who are harassing you for nonpayment.

√ Think about the ethics of bankruptcy.

For most people, having their finances gunked up involves some level of consumer debt. This is debt that is unsecured and not tied to a specific asset such as a home or a car. Credit in the U.S. is very easy to get initially, and when you don't have a plan in place for how to use it, it can quickly get out of control, leaving you with high-interest balances and a pounding headache. For things to improve, you must change your pattern of spending and develop a plan to pay off the debt you currently have. If not, you will forever be coughing up interest and late fees to your bank or credit card company. A good percentage of the money you work so hard to make—as much as 25 percent in some cases—will never see the light of day. Instead, it will be going to service these loans and support the companies who were nice enough to provide you with high-interest credit cards. Over the years, the clients I've had who were shining stars were the ones who put a firm lid on their credit card spending and other consumer debt and kept it there.

Now is your chance.

In the previous chapter I showed you how to degunk your credit cards and put better spending habits in place. In this chapter, the next step will be to create a sound, workable plan to pay off your credit card and other consumer debt. You'll learn how to pay down your debt in a way that will be motivating and encouraging. Imagine having five credit cards to pay off, then four, then three, then two, down to one, and then finished! This can be you, and you can do it sooner than you think. It's not magic, and it does require planning, hard work, and discipline. But within this process lies the formula to get you financially where you want to be—free of consumer debt.

This chapter contains the steps to help you create a very simple plan to pay off your debts one-by-one. I'll also give you some pointers on how to consolidate your debt in the way most beneficial to you, so that you pay down your debt in the most cost-efficient manner.

Stop Adding to Your Debt

Committing to stop the growth of your debt is the advice I give most often to clients of all backgrounds and socioeconomic groups. Without this commitment in place, everything else you do will only be bandaging the problem, not solving it. As good as this advice is, and as much as people agree with it, there are occasions where it seems next to impossible to follow. The car breaks down, a "once in a lifetime" sale occurs at your favorite store, and one of the kids needs braces. It seems that as soon as you get two steps ahead, some crisis or opportunity pops up to put you three steps behind. It's a vicious cycle and one that might almost seem impossible to break, but it can be done. You need to know where to start, how to direct your attention, and how to simply say "no" to unplanned and unbudgeted purchases.

To get out of debt using the degunking plan, you cannot continue to add to the balances on your credit cards or other consumer loans. It's like pouring water in a vase with a hole in the bottom. You can pour forever and that vase will never get full. At some point in this process, you want to be done paying off your debt. It will *never* happen if you continue to rack up charges. Your life will forever be one where you toil to scrape together money to pay for stuff that's already long gone, or even worse, stuff you never really needed or used in the first place.

Don't place yourself in that trap. Stop charging, and stop shopping for things that aren't part of your budget and that you can't afford. The carpeting can wait; I don't care who's coming for Thanksgiving. If the shabby carpet really bothers you that much, go to someone else's house for turkey. Don't feel obligated to spend more on that wedding gift than you have in your gift fund. Don't go out to dinner if your entertainment budget has already been depleted. Don't waste money buying things you don't need just because they are on sale. Paying $50 for a sweater that was originally $150 doesn't save you $100—it costs you $50. Keep your eye on the goal—having a gunk-free life—and the prize will be yours. And, when you pay off your last balance, you will know it was all worth it. Until then, I ask you to believe me, and believe all the people that have done it before you. It will be very, very worth it.

I knew a man who amassed some decent sized debt while in college, totaling more than $15,000 on credit cards and another $20,000 in student loans. When he got out of school, the trend continued. He added another $10,000 to his consumer debt in his first year of working, and bought himself a sporty new car and rented an expensive place to live. One night, while sitting in his pricey apartment with no food in the fridge, and after having to put off yet another creditor, he finally realized the gravity and the ridiculousness of his situation. He drove a great car but couldn't afford to put gas in it. He dressed like GQ but couldn't pay his credit card bills. He resolved to change whatever he needed to change in order to dig out of the massive hole he had made for himself. It took four years to become consumer debt-free, and he is still paying off student loans, but by selling the car, moving, tracking his expenses, and adding nothing to his existing debt, by the time he got married, he was clean of all his encumbrances and was able to enter into marriage as a responsible and financially savvy partner. What a gift for his wife, and what a great way to start that relationship!

Avoid New and Different Consumer Debt

I am constantly amazed at the sheer volume of different credit offers that come in the mail. An important point is that although they may come in different colors and styles, they all equal possible debt, and almost none are a good idea. Credit card advertisers spend their entire careers finding enticing ways to get you to accept their offers so you will owe their companies money for a very long time. Beware of *all* new offers to take on more debt. It's probably like shoes—you already have more now than you know what to do with, even if those pink ones are incredibly cool.

The "Pay No Interest Until..." Scam

My favorite credit offer in recent years is the "Pay No Interest Until Your Children Are in College" line. Just looking at that, it seems they're telling you that you don't have to pay interest until little Logan turns 18, and then you will pay interest on the unpaid balance. Oh, no. What they are actually saying is that unless the entire balance is paid when you pack Logan off to university, you will then owe *all* of the interest accrued over the life of the loan. Along those same lines, the "Make No Payments Until 2006" sounds like everything starts on New Year's Day 2006, doesn't it? Actually, interest is accruing from now until then, and you will end up with a pile of it if you don't pay the balance in full by New Year's Eve 2005. Because the finance company is waiting for its money, it also feels just fine about charging huge interest rates. The plans I looked into were all around 24-percent interest per year. Here's what this means: If you bought $3,000.00 worth of furniture and waited the promotional 18 months to begin paying on your purchase, your starting balance would be $4,166.40, with interest accruing at a very high rate every day the balance was not paid in full. Yikes!

Convenience Checks

Credit card companies often send out convenience checks, especially during periods of higher spending, such as the holidays. Some of the checks might look enticing because they offer low interest rates for a certain time period. Just as you might guess, your credit card company isn't really offering you a free ride because it likes you. If you look closely at the details (and please read them all), you'll notice that many of them offer terms that are much more favorable to the company than they are to you. If you use one of these checks to purchase something and use your credit card at the same time, the money you send in to pay your credit card will go to service the debt for the check (the low-interest portion) first. This means that the only thing the check did was get you to take on more debt. It's time to get out the shredder.

***CAUTION:* Always check the terms of convenience checks. Most often, your credit card company will specify that payments are applied first to the low-interest-rate credit, which means that the rest of your debt (presumably with a higher interest rate) doesn't get paid down at all. As a result, the credit card companies are making even more money on you because you're not paying down your high-interest-rate debt. What a great deal—for them.**

Home Equity Loans

Another possible hole to fall into is the home equity loan trap. The past couple of years I have seen ads for equity lines of credit of up to 125 percent of the equity in your home. Think about that. If you borrow all of the equity from your house and more and then, for some reason, need to sell it, not only will you not have anything to use for a down payment on another home, you will still owe on the one you previously had, plus realtor and closing fees. Borrowing more money than your home is worth is *always* a poor idea.

The key thing to remember here is that even if your home is appreciating like crazy, the other homes around you are appreciating as well, and you will always have to live somewhere. Another issue with home equity loans is the fact that you are putting your home at risk. If something awful happens and you can't make that payment, the bank will foreclose and you could lose your home and any equity left in it. Why take that chance, especially if what you're borrowing for is not necessary? Leave the equity in your home so if your finances take a downturn, you can downsize. If that happens, your equity will make your future house payment smaller and your life more manageable.

***TIP:* Protect your home at all costs. Very little is important enough to borrow against your home's value, and there are different ways to consolidate your debt without digging into your equity.**

GunkBuster's Notebook: How to Know If Your Debt Level Is Too High

It's easy to think that the level of debt that you are carrying is reasonable, even when you are spending bundles of money paying interest and late fees for your credit cards and other consumer loans, and you are taking on too much risk. Here are some tell-tale signs indicating that you need to reduce the amount of debt you are carrying:

√ You are unable to pay credit card balances. If you are unable to pay off the full balance on your credit cards every month, this may tell you that not only is your credit card debt too high, but you may have too much in secured debt as well. Having a couple of car payments and a high mortgage and then running up your credit cards with unbudgeted purchases is playing with financial fire.

- √ You have problems making minimum payments. If you are not paying your balances off every month and you are barely able to make the minimum payments for your credit cards, this is another red flag. Minimum payments are calculated by the credit card companies to maximize the money they can collect from you. If you are making only the minimum payments, it will take you years to pay off your credit cards, no matter what the balance. If you are in this situation now, you need to immediately stop using your credit cards and develop a plan to pay them off.
- √ You are tempted to trade home equity for credit card debt. If you have been tempted to take out a home equity loan to pay down your credit card debt, you should know that this is very risky and puts you in the position of losing your home if you become unable to make those payments. Adding to this risk is the fact that if you haven't addressed the overspending problem that got you in this position, chances are you will rack up more debt, which makes this vicious circle even meaner. You could, without too much trouble, lose your house.
- √ You are forced to make significant lifestyle changes. If you've had to significantly change your lifestyle to be able to afford the credit card bills you receive each month, this is a problem that needs to be addressed immediately. If you used to be able to take a vacation every couple of years and now that seems as impossible as a visit to the moon, the culprit could well be the size of your credit card debt. This often happens to people even when their incomes go up.
- √ You are a recent graduate with big debt. If you are a recent college graduate or you are starting out your professional career and find that your credit is so maxed out you can't qualify to purchase a house or take out a car loan, this is cause for alarm. Stop charging and get your credit cleaned up as soon as possible.

If you are wondering about your debt in relation to the rest of the U.S., consider that the average household consumer debt is $7,000, with the average interest rate running between 15 and 17 percent. If you are below this, it is still too much if you are paying any interest at all on unsecured debt. In a perfect world, the number would be zero. Some families carry much more than the average, and the stress that brings with it can be more harmful than the money it costs.

Get Serious About Paying Down Your Debt

Now that you're convinced not to build up more debt, it's time to get to work and get rid of the debt you are currently carrying around. You'll need to make some tough decisions as you progress, but remember the prize—a debt-free life, money in your savings account, a vacation at the end of the year, and extra funds to sock away in your retirement program.

This simple but very effective program involves a few easy steps:

- √ Gather all of the information on the debt you currently have. Include everything—car loans, credit cards, department store charge cards, and bank installment loans. You should have this information handy from your work in Chapter 3. It's very important to get a complete picture of your debt situation at this stage.
- √ Take a close look at the interest rates you are paying for the different credit card balances and consumer loans.
- √ Look to see if there are any loans that you can consolidate or move to another lower-interest card to start saving money on the interest that you are currently paying.
- √ Arrange your debt in the order of lowest balance to highest balance.
- √ Start paying off each debt, and as you pay one off, apply your additional money to the next one on your list.

I'll be giving you tips along the way so that you can speed up the process of paying down your debt. The important thing now is to make a simple plan for yourself and then stick to it. Once you begin the process, you'll be amazed at how quickly you pay off some of your debt and how the money you're paying will go to decrease your debt, as opposed to just paying interest.

As you move through the process of actually paying off your loans, I'll have you paying off your loans with the smaller balances first. I do want you to consider the interest rates that you are paying (as I will show you shortly), but that isn't the primary focus. It is hugely important to the success of this program to be able to develop a feeling of accomplishment as you pay off your loans. A little sense of "a job well done" can go a long way in encouraging you, and getting rid of your debt is just the encouragement you need to keep going.

GunkBuster's Notebook: Paying for the "Budget" Weekend Getaway

You've been working hard and you finally decide to take a weekend off and get the heck out of town. Your spouse is packing before the arrangements are even finished. You call around and you find the best hotel deal available ($85 per night) on a last-minute booking for two nights. You figure you're getting such a good deal on the hotel that you can afford the trip. You don't have the cash to pay for anything, though, so the whole weekend will be an addition to your credit card balance. Here's what the grand total could actually be:

Two nights at the hotel:	$170 (plus the taxes they don't quote, usually an additional 10%)
Two nights of dinners:	$155
Gas:	$50
Other meals:	$80
Entertainment:	$125 (What a great surprise that your favorite Elvis impersonator was in town!)
Gifts for the people watching the dog:	$45
Total:	*$642*

Your two- or three-hundred-dollar getaway has now officially at least doubled in price. If you're a fan of the MasterCard TV commercials, you might think that the much-needed trip away with your significant other was "priceless." If, however, you can't pay your credit card off immediately, facing the music of what has been added to your debt may leave you "All Shook Up."

The reality is that if the charges for your trip ($642) go on your 21-percent-interest credit card, they will continue to compound at an alarming rate, and if you pay only your minimums, you could still be paying for this lovely trip 10 or more years from now. Let's get even more "real life." The credit card fees you'll pay will be with after-tax dollars. Assuming that you are in the 30 percent tax bracket (for federal and state taxes combined), you'll need to earn 30 percent more for the original cost and 30 cents on the dollar for each buck of interest you pay on your "budget" weekend getaway. So, what do you think? Maybe get a pizza delivered, and rent *Blue Hawaii* instead? Total cost: About $25, and you don't have to miss the dog. Pay cash. Be romantic. Win-win.

Gather Up Your Debt Information

Now, let's get down to business. Gather all the paperwork of all the loans you want to pay off, including credit cards, other consumer debt, medical bills, loans from friends and family, and whatever other obligations you have hanging over your head. Make a list all of your debt balances, interest rates, and minimum payments. This is where you'll start to make some preliminary changes in order to decide what to pay first.

Review Interest Rates on Your Loans

Interest is like gravity. It's financial weight that we carry around. Every debt that you have is made of two components: principal and interest. With interest-bearing credit card debt, it's easy to get into a situation where the greater portion of the total amount you owe is made up of the interest and not principal. This can happen quickly when your credit card charges a high interest rate.

At this stage, take your list of debts and look for the loans that have the highest interest rates. If all of your loans have interest rates that are similar and reasonable, then you don't need to go any further with this analysis. You can skip this section and move on to start paying down your debt.

If you have some loans that stick out because of their high interest rate, take some steps to either consolidate those loans into lower-interest-bearing accounts, or find another credit card to transfer the balance to in order to save you bundles on the interest you will be paying.

Consolidate High-Interest Rate Loans

Consolidating your high-interest loans into a lower-interest loan is something you may be able to do if you have a decent credit rating. (I'll explain your credit scores and ratings in Chapter 10.) This can be especially effective now as many companies are offering very low (0 percent and up) rates and are marketing hard for your balance transfer.

Credit card companies often send out special offers to entice new (or existing) customers who want to consolidate their debt into a new account. You probably toss a few of these offers each week without even opening them. It is possible to get a balance transfer that charges you very little interest for an introductory period, or even until the balance transfer is paid off. Be very careful when signing up for these offers, however. A new twist that can be included in the low-interest offerings is charging a "transfer fee" on the transferred balance—sometimes as much as 3 percent. Know what you're getting into if you choose to consolidate.

***CAUTION:** If you sign up for a new credit card and consolidate some or all of your other credit card debt on the new account, don't ever use the new card to make purchases. Put the new card away and focus only on paying off the loan balance. If you must charge something, use a different card. This is very important as the low-interest deal the credit card company gave applies only to the amount you transfer and not to any additional charges you incur using the card.*

Assume that you have four credit cards and the unpaid total balance of these cards is $2,500. Because the interest rates on these cards are high, you decide to consolidate. You receive an offer in the mail that allows you to transfer your existing balances to the new card that will charge an interest rate of only 2.9 percent for the transferred loan balance until that balance is paid off. Doesn't this sound like a great deal? It is, in fact, a great deal *if* you can discipline yourself to use it wisely. Assume you take the offer and transfer over your balance of $2,500. Because of the lower interest rate, you are applying more money to your outstanding debt. After six months you might be able to pay down your loan balance to $1,300.

Compared to what it used to be, that balance looks so low that you decide to buy the dining room table you've put off, and you use the new card to pay for that purchase, costing you $800. The new amount you charged will be added on to your existing balance of $1,300, but unlike your previous balance, you may be charged a very high interest rate on the new $800 purchase, which will compound while you're paying off your transferred balance and continue while you pay off the now much larger new balance. Sneaky, right?

Debt consolidation by transferring loan balances can be a smart move, but you need to look at the offers available to you very closely. Credit card companies are in business to make money (your money), and they don't make offers that haven't been historically proven to do just that. It can still be a good move for your finances, however. Here are some general tips to help you consolidate wisely:

- √ Read the fine print very closely of any offer you are considering. Keep in mind that many offers are designed to benefit the credit card companies much more than you.
- √ Look for offers that do not charge you any type of transfer fee on the loan balance you are moving.
- √ Don't lose sight of the goal—the point of consolidating is to lower your interest rates and use any savings you can to pay down that balance even further.
- √ Take the money that you save from paying lower interest and plow it back into paying down your credit card balances. Don't fall into the trap of consolidating your debts to simply lower your monthly payment so that you have more money to spend on "stuff."
- √ Don't ever be late with a payment for a transferred balance. In some cases, you'll then be charged a very high interest rate until you pay off the balance of the loan. This is one of the items in the small print.
- √ Physically remove the credit card that carries the transferred loan balance from your wallet. If you consolidate all of your balances to one card, don't cancel all the other cards immediately, in case you have an actual emergency and need to use a credit card. You'll then have a choice and you won't have to use the card to which you transferred your balances.
- √ When searching for a lower interest rate to pay down a high-interest loan, the first place to look is your current credit cards. It's possible that you will get a solicitation to transfer balances to a card you already have, but keep in mind the principles set forth earlier in the chapter. Keep your balance transfers separate from other debt. Don't add them to an existing balance.

Once you are done reviewing the interest rates and consolidating where you can, you'll have an updated debt reduction list from which to work.

Start Paying Down Your Debt

Now that you have consolidated your debt to the lowest interest rates available to you, the next step in the degunking process is to look at your Monthly Expenditures sheet to see how much money you can allocate to debt repayment. The key here is to find as much money as possible in your budget over and above the minimum payments required by your creditors. Determine how you can free up more money than you might initially see, as paying off these debts and becoming debt-free is the goal. Then, fill out the Debt Reduction Form shown in Figure 6-1, listing your debts from the smallest balance to the largest. This form will serve as your debt reduction road map.

Debt Reduction Form

Debtor	Amount	Interest	Minimum Payment	Additional Money	____ Months	____ Months	____ Months	____ Months	____ Months

Figure 6-1
The Debt Reduction Form.

To help you get started, take a look at the sample shown in Figure 6-2. We'll be using this shortly as your plan comes together for paying down your debt. In this sample form filled out for a fictional client, notice that the loans are arranged in order of smallest balance to highest. The minimum payments are paid for all loans, but the extra $125 is all put toward the smallest loan until it is paid in full. All the money put toward that loan is then put toward the next smallest balance until that one is paid in full as well. Notice how the amount put toward the Visa loan is the full amount of what was put toward the Gateway loan, plus the minimum on the Visa loan? This process continues until all the loans are paid off.

REALITY CHECK: You didn't get into this shape with your credit overnight, and you're not going to get out of it overnight either. Start your plan, and stick to it, and you will quickly see the benefits of working to pay off your debt in this manner. Paying off all the debt will take time. Keep in mind, however, that the more you allocate to your debt repayment, the quicker it will be gone and the sooner you will be financially free of that weight you're dragging around. Sounds good, doesn't it?

Debtor	Amount	Interest	Minimum Payment	Plus Additional Money $125	5 Months	21 Months	35 Months	44 Months	Months
Gateway	$750	19%	$23	$148	Paid Off!				
Visa	$3,526	9.9%	$71		$219	Paid Off!			
Target	$4,259	13.9%	$87			$306	Paid Off!		
MasterCard	$7,000	0%	$100				$406	Paid Off!	

Figure 6-2
Debt Reduction form with sample data.

The procedure that you want to follow is this:

1. Start with the smallest debt and pay the minimum payment plus any extra that you have allocated for debt repayment until that debt is paid off.
2. Take all that you were paying toward that first debt and add it to the second debt (the minimum payment plus all the extra) until that one is paid off. Do you notice a compounding effect here? That money that's freed up is *not* more money in your pocket—it's more money to pay off debt.
3. Continue this procedure for each loan you have listed on your form. You will continue this process until you have paid off all of your loans.

The money that this person has allocated to debt repayment is $125, which is shown in the "Addt'l. Money" column at the top of the table. They start by taking these funds and making a minimum payment of $23 combined with another payment of $125. In five months, the first loan is paid off in full. The sixth month will begin the payoff of the Visa bill.

Following this system, this person can pay off $15,000 in debt in less than four years using an additional payment of only $125 per month. If they raised the additional money to $250, the debt would all be paid off in about 31 months. Your additional payments could be larger, or they could be smaller. The key here is to continue rolling over the payments from debts paid off to current debt.

CAUTION:* *Do not add to your debt while you are working through this repayment period. The process will never end if you continue to charge on the Visa or Target card or you take out a new loan.

The goal is to eliminate debt from your life and replace it with the smarter process of making purchases based on what you can pay for in cash. Because paying down your current debt will be a somewhat painful process, it is important to keep your eye on the goal—being debt free.

Can I Still Save?

Although it may seem impossible to both pay down your debt and save at the same time, it is simply a process of allocating funds. If you have an extra $200 per month over and above your monthly bills, use $150 to pay down debt, and put $50 in the bank as untouchable savings. It will take longer to pay down your debt, but it will also help keep you from having to use your credit cards while you're putting so much of your extra money toward debt repayment. After your debt is paid off, that money saved can be allocated to raise your emergency fund to the level it needs to be. Again, this isn't an overnight process, but by following the process to its conclusion, you will be in the position that you now crave—no consumer debt, the beginning of a savings account already growing, and well on your way to being fully financially degunked.

Paying Off Debt Is a Commitment

What I've shown you here is completely attainable. I have worked with untold numbers of clients who have used this process to get out of debt. Not only does this system work, it is designed to keep you motivated along the way. How satisfying is it to see debts paid off? There may be some people who can see the long-range benefits to paying everyone a small amount monthly until they are all finished, but the bulk of us like to see results, and a fine, measurable result is not getting a bill from Gateway or the furniture store in the mail ever again.

This could be you, and it could be you starting this month. If you follow this program, it will work. Depending on the level of your debt, it may take a longer or shorter period of time than the example, but it will work. And if it takes five years to pay off your debt, keep in mind that the five years was going to pass anyway. At the end of it, where do you want to be financially? Do you want to be out of debt or perpetually afraid of what bill is going to show up in the mailbox? The key is, as always, *do not add to your debt* along the way and stick with the plan until it's complete. This will take reorganizing your lifestyle to change the habits that got you into debt and lowering your monthly expenses as much as possible. So, get to it! Rework your Monthly Expenditures sheet to free up more money for debt repayment and savings, and be the first on your block to be debt-free.

GunkBuster's Notebook: Finding Money to Pay Off Your Debts

You've already seen that paying off your debts requires that you have a sound plan and that you stick to it. As the process moves along, it may be a challenge to find the money to pay down your debts. There are months when you'll feel it is impossible to scrape up even an extra dollar to apply to your debts. If you need some help, one book that I'd suggest you read is *Pay It Down!* by Jean Chatzky (Portfolio). This short book advocates that you look for ways to set aside $10 per day to apply to your debts. This might sound like a difficult thing to do each day, but once you start looking, you'll be amazed at what you can do without.

In addition to looking at your day-to-day activities for finding money, here are some tips to help you pay your debts off faster:

- √ If you get a windfall, such as a bonus at work or a check from the IRS for a tax overpayment (wouldn't that be great?), deposit the money and immediately write a check to the debtor you are currently paying down. Don't even consider using the unexpected money for a lifestyle enhancement or an unbudgeted expense. Slap it right on that debt, and smile when the next month's statement comes and your balance is so much lower.
- √ Look for things that you can downsize that won't really affect your lifestyle. For example, when was the last time you checked your home phone bill or your cell phone plan to look for features you don't really need? This could easily save you a little cash that could be applied to your loan payments each month.
- √ Get rid of items around the house you don't need. Most of us are swimming in clutter. We accumulate all kinds of things that we seldom use that could net us some easy cash without much trouble Have a garage sale, put up a sign at work to sell your almost new cappuccino maker, or get rid of unwanted items using online auctions like eBay. There will be much more about ways to find money around your house in Chapter 14. You might even have items worth a

great deal of money. Remember that the point of selling these items is to allocate all the funds you receive directly to your debt. No fair selling your old fur coat to buy a new one.

√ Don't put off making hard choices. If you have a lot of debt to pay off, it will take more time and cost you more money. The sooner you make some sacrifices, the sooner those debts will be paid off. Getting out of debt will lower your stress, increase your day-to-day enjoyment of life, and put you in a position to further your financial goals. Does a budgeted vacation sound good to you? Then get started, and keep yourself on the path.

Pay Your Loans Quickly and Stop Paying Late Fees

As you go through the process of paying down your debt, make sure that you always make your payments on time. Am I sounding a bit like a broken record? When you pay a bill late, you'll be charged late fees as well as finance charges. This can put a cramp on your ability to pay your debt down as quickly as you want to, and late payments can put a black mark on your credit report. Think about the wasted money when you make a late payment—a late fee of $15 to $35, extra finance charges on the late balance, and that much less money going toward paying off your principal. My guess is you worked hard for that money. Why waste it in that fashion?

One of the problems we are all facing is that credit card companies are giving us less and less time to review and pay our bills. You might open a recent bill and discover you only have a few days to pay your bill before you are charged late fees and additional financial charges. Why is this happening? Our bills are being sent later, giving us less time to get our payments in before being assessed with late fees and more interest. The law requires that there must be a minimum 14-day period between when a bill was printed and when it must be paid. Five years ago, the industry's average grace period between when a bill was sent and when it was due was 25 to 30 days. Today, this period is closer to 20 days, and even less in some cases. Credit card companies are getting smarter and demanding that they get their money faster, hoping you won't respond quickly enough. More money in their pocket is the usual result.

These changes mean that you need to be diligent about opening your bills as soon as you receive them. Note the date they are due and keep the bills sorted in the order that they need to be paid. Also, make sure that you pay your bills with enough lead time to arrive and get processed before the due date. With some bills, the clock is really ticking. To save you the problems of being late, you might want to look into setting up an online reminder and bill payment system for your credit card bills and loan payments. I'll be covering this in more detail in Chapter 15.

TIP: ***Because the window for paying bills is getting shorter, you might end up paying a bill a few days late. This can easily happen if you travel and you're not home to get and process the bill when it first arrives. If you end up paying a bill late and the credit card company charges you a late fee (you'll see it when you get your next statement), call the credit card company and complain. I've tried this before and it works. If you typically pay your bill on time, the credit card company will be able to remove the fee from your account. If the company still won't budge, say you are considering canceling the card. Keep in mind, credit card companies may reverse one or two late charges, but they won't do this on a regular basis. This will only work if you have a good payment history.***

CAUTION: ***Paying your credit cards late can hurt you over the long run. Not only will your credit rating be affected, but your credit card company may start charging you a higher interest rate on your existing cards. This means that the cost to pay down your existing debt will continue to go up. It is a waste of your valuable money and will make it harder to reach your goals. The only thing left to say about that is...yuck. Pay on time, and keep your money working for you.***

What to Do with Extra Money

I touched on this earlier, and this may be a tough one for some of you, especially if you have gunked-up finances, but it remains an important point. When you get a hunk of money in your hand, whether it's a tax return, a bonus, or a gift, it should get smacked right on the balance of the card or loan you are currently paying off. Imagine that. Instead of paying the $341 on the Sears card for the next three months till it's paid off, you can pay it off fully with the tax return, and you're getting a huge head start on paying off the Visa bill. How many steps closer will that get you to your goal? If you do it again next year, how many more debts can you retire? I know it is very tempting to take that money and get new carpeting or take a vacation, but those expenses are not in line with your long-term goal, let alone your Monthly Expenditures budget. If you absolutely have to have an immediate reward, take a small percentage of the money to do something inexpensive, like going to a movie or having the carpets professionally cleaned. Be reasonable, and keep your goals in mind.

Getting a bunch of money all at once is unusual. It's not how our finances usually work. As it is not the norm, you have to know ahead of time what you plan to do with the money or emotions and lack of foresight can take over. Don't let a windfall get away from you. Make the money work for you by dramatically lowering the balance (and not paying the interest you would have) on a debt that is hanging over your head. It will be immensely satisfying and a fine use of the big check burning a hole in your checking account.

Deal with Harassing Creditors

If you've gotten behind in your loan payments, you may be getting calls from creditors. This is yet another detriment to not paying bills on time. If the situation gets bad enough, the creditors may call you at work and at home and even have discussions with your superiors. At that point, it may be difficult to think straight and you'll likely feel that the best plan is to avoid these calls at all costs. There is, however, a much better way to deal with your creditors.

Over the past five years, creditors have become much more aggressive about trying to collect on past due loans. When the loans become significantly overdue, the creditors often turn the accounts over to collection agencies. Bill collectors from these agencies will start calling you as often as two to three times per week and won't give up until they get some money, even it it's not the full amount. Once the debt is in the hands of a collector, the only way they make any money is to collect it from you. If you ignore them, they will just try harder, leaving explicit messages everywhere. They will try to track you down at your job and through relatives. I've had clients who even had collection agencies calling their neighbors looking for them. Most of these tactics are designed to "shame" you into paying your debts or annoy you into paying them so that they just leave you alone.

This is your debt, and you do owe them this money. If you had the money, you probably would have paid them already. If you don't, you will have to find a way to scrape up something, but there are limits as to how far a creditor can go to collect money from you.

If you are in trouble with a creditor or a bill collector, here are some things that you can do:

√ Don't let a bill collector go beyond specified limits to get money from you. There are specific laws that they must follow. You don't have to listen to a collector be rude to you. A collection agency cannot call you before 8A.M. or after 9 P.M. They also are restricted from telling someone else about your debt and they can't threaten to garnish your wages. That can happen, but it would come through the courts as a judgment, not from the collection agency.

√ Contact the creditor of the debt or bill directly and try to work out a payment plan. If you agree to a payment plan and follow up on making the payments, the calls will stop. The creditor just wants to get paid and if you make the agreed-upon payments, they will leave you alone.

If you are getting rude calls from a collection agency or if you think that an agency is crossing the line and harassing you beyond the legal limits, send them what is called a "cease and desist" letter. A federal law called the Fair Debt Collection Practices Act has been passed that forbids collectors from contacting you if you tell them to stop. You letter should instruct them to stop contacting you in connection with the debt that's owed. This does not remove your responsibility from paying the debt, but it does stop the collection agency from harassing you about it. Not having the daily harassment of debt collectors can be a huge relief, but keep in mind, if you use this reprieve as an excuse to forget about the debt, that doesn't make it go away. Having a defaulted debt will stain your credit report and will lower your credit rating, keeping you from receiving good interest rates and opportunities in the future. It is still your debt, and you should be finding a way to pay it, whether or not you are being called by a collection agency. Get in touch with your creditors, decide on a payment plan you can manage, and pay off the debt as you would any other.

GunkBuster's Notebook: Advice for Credit Abusers

Most people in credit trouble had good intentions on how to use credit cards and pay them off as soon as possible. Things may have gotten out of control at some point, and after that, the debt seemed impossible to manage. If this has happened to you, don't despair. Get yourself back on track. You can change this, and it can start now.

If you find that you've made a debt reduction plan for yourself in the past and haven't followed through, here are some obstacles you might have encountered with some tips to help you get by them:

√ Are you a victim of too much credit switching? It's easy to convince yourself that switching your credit balances around to save money is a good way to save on interest, but if your spending isn't under control, all you might be doing is getting further into debt. If you are having trouble paying your credit call bills, stop switching and focus on paying your existing bills one at a time in the process outlined in this chapter.

√ Are you a shopaholic? You won't be able to pay off your loans if you can't control your spending. If you find that you can't stop shopping, there are organizations you can look to for help.

√ Did you lose your motivation for paying off your debt because your balances changed so little over the course of a year? Using debt consolidation companies can be a good thing, but since they pay a small amount to each creditor per month, your balances don't seem to change much over the course of time. It can be discouraging after a couple of years to see that your total amount owed hasn't seemed to decrease. Part of the plan outlined here is to keep you motivated by paying each debt off in full from the smallest balance to the largest, keeping you on track and encouraged.

√ Did you lose your job without having a safety net? It's easy to overuse your credit cards if you don't have an income and have bills to pay. When you lose a job unexpectedly, cut back on your expenses as quickly as possible and avoid using your credit cards to replace your lost income. Perhaps you have savings you can tap into or a family member or close friend can help you stay on your feet. Once you get a job, face your credit situation immediately (including paying back that generous family member and replacing your savings) and do everything you can to get back to paying your loans down.

√ Did you go in debt to start and fund a failing business? Staring a small business is difficult and risky. When you are in the midst of trying to run a business, you may feel tempted to use your credit cards to pay expenses and keep your business afloat. If your business fails, you've now accumulated a pile of debt with no way to pay it off. It is a huge risk to fund a business with your personal credit, and needing to pay business expenses in this manner is a good clue that your business is headed south.

A Word (Okay, Several) About Bankruptcy

You've probably known someone who's declared bankruptcy. Maybe you've declared bankruptcy at some point in your financial life. We all know of companies that have gone belly-up. This has become a disturbing trend in this country, and it seems that more people are seeking bankruptcy as a way out of their financial problems. The number of personal bankruptcies rose 7.4 percent from 2002 to 2003 to over 1.6 million, and in 2004 1.6 million people or families declared bankruptcy. Here are some statistics on business- and non-business-related bankruptcies during 2000–2004.

Business and Non-business Filings (Years Ended September 30, 2000–2004)			
Year	**Total**	**Non-Business**	**Business**
2004	1,618,987	1,584,170	34,817
2003	1,661,996	1,625,813	36,183
2002	1,547,669	1,508,578	39,091
2001	1,437,354	1,398,864	38,490
2000	**1,262,102**	**1,226,037**	**36,065**

Source: Administrative Office of the U.S. Courts, Office of Public Affairs, Washington D.C.

The Ethics of Bankruptcy

There are a couple of large issues to think about when considering bankruptcy. First of all, it's not fair. You accumulated these debts. You told the credit card companies, or the car dealer, or Nordstrom's, that you would pay them what you owe them. You picked out the clothing, you put it on your credit card, and when you signed, you were agreeing to pay them what you charged. Getting in too deep is no good reason to stiff the people who gave you credit. The people you owe money to deserve what you promised.

Another issue with bankruptcy is that when you declare bankruptcy, somebody is still going to pay for your debts. The credit card company will make up for your bankruptcy by charging more interest or higher fees. The department store will raise its prices and the rates on their cards. Mortgage lenders will raise their fees, making it harder for others to secure mortgages. Even though you may think your bankruptcy doesn't account for much, your action contributes to the cost of credit.

Imagine yourself in your creditor's place. Say that someone bought your lawnmower and told you they'd bring you the money in a week. A week came and went, then a month, then the rest of the summer, and then you got a letter from an attorney saying not only would you not be getting your money, but the people were keeping the lawnmower. Doesn't seem right, does it? Ultimately, you will have to make the ethical decision about whether declaring bankruptcy is right for you,but I believe that the larger lesson about degunking your personal finances is for you to take personal responsibility for your own financial destiny. Owning up to past mistakes is part of that degunking process.

For most people in credit trouble, bankruptcy is not a necessity—it's an easy way out. It often takes something difficult and satisfying, like pulling yourself out of debt, to learn and understand how not to get back in the same situation. Work the process instead, save your credit, and be responsible about your debt.

Alternatives to Bankruptcy

If you feel you are so deep in financial gunk that you're drowning, there are a lot of steps you can take before you declare bankruptcy. There are consumer-based groups that will, for a fee, work with your creditors to lower your interest rates and put you on a debt-consolidation and repayment program. If you seek this type of credit counseling, it will show up as a hit on your credit report, but not as big a hit as bankruptcy.

CAUTION:* *Be very careful when choosing a consolidation program as some require a large up-front fee (not good) or have programs that are very detrimental to your credit standing. I heard of one program lately whose philosophy was to not pay anything to any creditors for a year and then bully your creditors into taking a much smaller settlement. When asked, they said it would, indeed, trash your credit, but you'd pay less on each card. They didn't mention how you would ever get credit again, however.

Consumer Credit Counseling Services is a nationwide consumer-based, not-for-profit group that may be a good place to start. The programs may change by city or office, so I am not wholesale recommending them, but my experiences with this organization thus far have been good. Check several different programs before making a decision about signing up for this type of service. Before signing anything, however, try to work things out yourself. It's very possible you can get your own interest rates lowered and get on a plan that will net you better results than an organization can get. You need motivation and you need determination. Avoiding bankruptcy and the residue that comes with it should be very good motivation, and the satisfaction you'll feel as you get your credit back in good shape will fuel your determination.

Bankruptcy and Your Credit Rating

Filing bankruptcy will also have a hugely detrimental effect on your credit score. Strangely enough, though, it will not keep you from getting credit cards. In fact, credit card applications will probably flood your mailbox after you declare bankruptcy. Credit card companies are not dumb, after all. First of all, they know you probably got into trouble with credit cards, and by filing bankruptcy, they know you haven't fixed the problem. They also know you can't file bankruptcy again for seven years. It is common for credit card interest to be in the 30 percent range for those who have declared bankruptcy. If they can get you to max out your card again and charge you 30-percent interest, even if you file bankruptcy again, they will have made more than enough to cover their expenses and soak you good. They are in it, as always, for the money.

Any credit you receive after filing bankruptcy will be substantially higher than if you managed the situation yourself. Anyone that will give you credit will make you pay through the nose, and for as long as possible. If a process is not followed to get out of debt, all bankruptcy will do is clean the slate to fill it up again, at much higher interest rates, and with no end in sight to this vicious cycle.

Summing Up

You are not helpless when it comes to paying off your debt. Contained in this chapter is a concise, manageable plan to pay off the debt you currently have and keep you motivated to incur no further debt as you get closer to being debt-free. As difficult as this sounds to you now, the gratification you will feel as you watch your debts diminish and disappear will be real. This process can begin as soon as you commit to the process of degunking your consumer debt. Like any work, it won't always be fun, but it will always be beneficial and very rewarding. The sooner you start, the sooner you will be finished. As you continue working through this book, you'll learn more and different ways to cut expenses and free up yet more money to pay off the anchor of debt that's dragging you down.

I'm proud of you already.

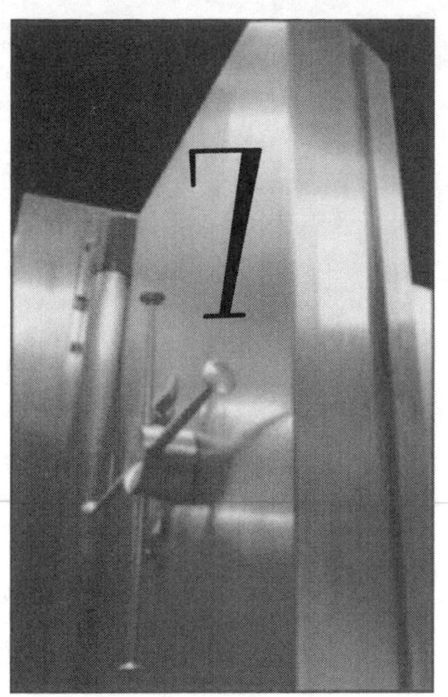

Degunking Your Home and Mortgage

Degunking Checklist:

- √ Determine if your house is right for you.
- √ Assess whether you have the right mortgage or if it's right to refinance your home.
- √ Avoid costly refinancing traps.
- √ If you are a first-time home buyer, follow a smart strategy to purchase your first home.

Now that you've learned how to get your consumer debt under control (and paid off as soon as possible), it's time to turn your attention to your home. Degunking your home will involve two phases. In this chapter we'll look at ways that you can select the home or apartment that is best for you and ways that you can improve your home mortgage, if you have one. If you don't currently own, I'll help you develop a strategy for purchasing your first home. In Chapter 8, we'll open the door to your house and take a look at your actual living expense. You'll be pleasantly surprised by the simple things you can do to reduce your living expenses but still enjoy a comfortable lifestyle for you and your family.

Your home is most likely your largest financial asset but also your biggest expense. If you select the home that best fits your needs, it's a good start to reducing or eliminating a lot of your financial gunk. It's possible to make decisions on where to live or what type of home loan to use and then end up paying for a less-than-perfect choice for many years. Fortunately, there are some things you can do immediately concerning your home to save you money and improve your finances.

Choose the Right Home

In this section, the word *house* or *home* means wherever you live. It includes apartments, town homes, condominiums, rental houses, purchased houses, or that cute studio above the Chinese restaurant that you rent from your aunt.

The largest single payment that most people make is their rent or mortgage. When choosing where they live, people usually choose the largest, most expensive place they think they can afford. This is true whether a single person is looking for their first apartment or a family is upgrading to a larger home. When nearly anyone tells you the story of how they ended up where they live, there is usually a line in it that goes something like, "It was a little more than we wanted to spend, but we knew we could make up the difference somehow."

***CAUTION:** Lenders help this thinking along, often giving mortgage approval for much more than the consumer can afford. The mortgage business has become so competitive that lenders are often willing to approve people with less-than-stellar credit, and they're also handing out big mortgages to individuals who can obviously barely afford the payments. Don't get suckered into this situation – it will become a living nightmare for you and your family. Once you're in a place that is more expensive than you planned, the stress builds as you constantly try to figure out how you'll pay for it. The feeling of being trapped (especially if you've bought the place) is locked in and becomes something you can never escape from.*

Here's the good news. You're not as stuck as you think you are.

Degunking your house payment will include opening yourself up to the possibility of change. Now, don't get nervous. I'm not saying you have to sell your house or move out of your perfect apartment. I'm just saying that it's something that should be considered in your overall degunking plan. So, in the following paragraphs, talking of the *possibility* of selling or moving is just that—a possibility, not a decision. Okay? This is an option to play around with and consider. Now, wipe the sweat off your forehead and we can continue.

Don't Be "House Poor"

It's common in large and expensive cities like New York and San Francisco for everyone to be "house poor." In these places, there is such fierce competition for decent housing that people will pay nearly anything—and put up with a host of inconveniences as a result—to live in desirable and safe neighborhoods. I know of people in those cities who pay over half their monthly take-home pay just to live in tiny one-room apartments that are close to transportation or in "cool" neighborhoods. Luckily, most areas of the U.S. aren't as expensive as these cities, but wherever you live, you will have to make choices concerning what you think is important in your housing and get a firm grip on what you can really afford. What are your priorities? You will probably have to make some tough choices. It would be a rare situation to get absolutely everything you want. What is most important?

- √ Would you pay higher rent in order to have a desirable location?
- √ Would you pay lower rent but have more space?
- √ Would you live in a neighborhood with only so-so public schools?
- √ Would you get a larger space that doubles your commuting time and travel expenses?
- √ Would you get a cheaper space that's far away from your friends and interests?

Before making a housing decision, think carefully about what you're prepared to spend, and why. It's tiring and expensive to move yourself and your family out of a bad housing situation, so make the best housing decision that you can from the beginning. Make sure that what you choose is affordable and reasonably convenient for your needs. With some preparation and thought, you can avoid making a housing choice that will leave you house poor and miserable.

GunkBuster's Notebook: How Can You Tell When You Are House Poor?

Many people become house poor without even immediately realizing it. One day, they realize they can't afford to pay their housing expenses along with their credit card bills and other loan payments. Their only way out may be to either refinance their house or sell it. To keep this from happening to you, here are some signs to watch for:

- √ Your home mortgage is greater than 25 percent of your income.
- √ What you pay monthly for your mortgage payments, homeowner's insurance, utility bills (don't forget to include your cable TV and Internet access), any homeowner's dues, and maintenance costs is greater than 38 percent of your monthly take-home pay. (Add what you pay yearly for each of these items and divide the total by 12 to determine the actual monthly outlay required to stay in your home).
- √ You can't get by without both you and your spouse working to pay your mortgage and other household operating expenses, and you have no money left for savings and an emergency fund. What if one of you loses your job?
- √ In the past few years you have needed to refinance your home mortgage to lower your monthly payment in order be able to afford to live there.
- √ Your housing costs have stretched your budget so thin that you cannot afford to spend any money on entertainment or take a vacation.
- √ You can't afford basic maintenance on your house, such as replacing a leaky roof, repainting, or yard work.
- √ There is no near-future hope of your situation changing, and the condition of your home is suffering from lack of upkeep, lowering its value.

If any of these items sounds familiar to you, you are probably house poor. This is an unhealthy situation and can make your life and finances seriously uncomfortable, as well as lowering the value of your home. If you are house poor, you should think now about when and how to change your housing situation.

The Problem with Upgrading

It is common in our culture to move to larger living spaces as our household income grows. But is it necessary to live in the largest home you can afford? It's possible (notice I said "possible") that you now live in more house than you need. A way to save a chunk on your living expenses is to downsize where you live and lower (sometimes by a large amount) what you pay to have a roof over your head. I have worked with dozens of people and families that took one step too many in upgrading their homes and were then perpetually strapped for money as a result. You can become house poor quickly by overstepping your financial boundaries in order to live in a bigger, better, or trendier place. In my experience, living in a too-expensive house becomes an albatross around the neck of the wage earners in the home, who then have to work harder and longer to support the new dwelling; often, the ones paying the bills get to spend even less time in the home as a result.

It is, after all, just a house. It doesn't represent your worth or how you are judged by those who love you. It won't make you happier, and it won't fulfill your dreams. It's a place to live, and the level of importance you place on it is up to you. There is nothing at all wrong with liking your house or wanting a better house than you now have. The issue at hand now is the cost. Can you afford where you live now? Would it profit your financial degunking plan to lower your housing expenses by moving to somewhere less expensive?

Is It Too Big?

Think about your house. Have you noticed how easy it is to fill up all the space available? It's probable that however many places you've lived in, you have easily adapted to more space, and now can't imagine how it was to not have that third bedroom or the second half-bath. It would be hard to fit back into a smaller area, wouldn't it? I know it seems like a strange idea to leave your present home and downsize, but the truth is, you would live through it. In the course of moving, you would probably get rid of a ton of things that are gunking up your basement, attic, garage, or storage space, and in a short time, you would accustom yourself to less space.

In our culture, a home can be a status symbol, and it is very difficult for some to people let go of that when their finances require it. In working with people, I ask them what their "lines in the sand" are concerning their situation. Is it vitally important for them to stay in their home, even when the numbers say otherwise? Is staying in the same school district what is important? What are they willing to give up to keep their oversized and overpriced house?

It's common for people to hang on to their house as long as they can, often to their financial detriment. I worked with a couple who thought they would be willing to give up everything to stay in their house. It was their first home, lovingly chosen and decorated, and their kids were happily ensconced in the schools and neighborhood. They cut down their lifestyle to the bare minimum and kept to a strict budget. The problem was that they had taken on too much to begin with, and as time passed, and even working as hard as possible (taking on part-time jobs and side work), they found (to my great joy) that the house had become a hungry monster, eating their money, time with their family, and most of their energy. They sold the house, found something smaller and more manageable in a neighborhood close by, quit their part-time work, and went to a movie for the first time in a year.

I couldn't talk them into selling their house, and I didn't try. They had to find out what living there was truly costing them in terms of money, time, and energy. I'm not trying to talk you into selling your home, either, but the questions presented in this section are very good questions to ask yourself. What is living in this house really costing you?

The first thing to look at is whether you are living in more house than you need. If you bought the house when the kids were growing up and now they've moved out, it could be a good time to downsize your space and your monthly housing payment. Even in the growing-up years, a family with children can usually live with fewer bedrooms or bathrooms than they originally think they can. A single person can sometimes do without the extra bedrooms they think they need, such as an office or a guest room. You can always give up your room for an honored guest and bunk on the couch. It all depends on what you're willing to do to reach your financial goals.

Is It Too Expensive?

The second way your home can be too big is simply by costing too much. No matter what the size, if it's more than you can afford, it's too much. Thinking back to the entitlement section in Chapter 1, remember that you are not deserving of a three-bedroom, two-bath town house just because your friends have one. How much you are spending on your mortgage or rent payment? Is there money being spent in housing that could go a long way to paying off your debt? Look also at the rest of the Monthly Expenditures sheet that you filled out in Chapter 4. Have you cut costs everywhere else and still can't reach your goal without lowering your housing expense? Are there things you don't want to give up that mean less to you than your current address? Is it possible that being able to visit your dad in Arizona is more important than living where you do? Perhaps being able to give the kids more opportunities (playing a musical instrument, the eighth grade class trip, or a better dance program) means more than that fourth bedroom. So, decide. You're in charge. Make a bold choice based on all of the information you have, and be happy about it. It doesn't mean you will never again have a second bathroom. But it does mean that you're being responsible now with managing whatever gunk you're stuck in, and when it's degunked, your opportunity for housing choices will be better than it is now. Won't that be fun? And, just think—you will have earned it.

Degunk Your Mortgage

In Chapter 6, you learned how to degunk your unsecured consumer credit. Since we are focusing on how to degunk your housing and living expenses, it's now time to take a close look at your home mortgage, the main component of your long-term debt. I'll show you how to degunk your existing mortgage or the best way to go about deciding how to purchase a house if you aren't currently a homeowner.

Having a home mortgage is "good debt," as this loan is used to acquire an asset—your home—which should appreciate in value. You can also take tax deductions for any interest you pay on your home mortgage. Even though your home mortgage is a better type of debt, it doesn't mean you should go wild and purchase a house you can't afford or settle for a financing plan that doesn't fit your needs.

When it comes to degunking your existing home mortgage, here are some of the important considerations:

- √ Reviewing the current terms of your home mortgage.
- √ Refinancing if you are paying an interest rate that is significantly higher than the current rates available. If you are considering refinancing, make sure that you closely examine all of the costs involved.
- √ Reducing the length of your mortgage.
- √ Making extra payments each year to pay your loan off faster. Making even one extra payment per year can reduce the life of a 30-year loan by several years.
- √ Avoiding loans that promise to save you money in the short run but cost you more in the long run.

This chapter will show you how to work through these issues and also provide some degunking help for first-time home buyers.

CAUTION:* *Because interest rates have declined so drastically over the past few years, many people have rushed to refinance their existing mortgages. This in turn has created quite a demand for new types of loans. When evaluating these financing options, you need to be very careful. You should always be cautious about getting into any situation that allows you to significantly reduce your payments for the short term, as you'll likely pay much more, or be forced to refinance again, in the long run.

The Temptation to Refinance

In the section "Choose the Right Home" earlier in this chapter, I asked you to think about whether you have too much house, whether you're house poor, or whether you've upgraded beyond your means. You should have a good sense of what the answers are to these questions. Let's say that you've decided you're living in an appropriately sized house, and it's generally within your budget. You're doing fine financially and making your payments on time without a struggle. Then, on late night TV when you should already be in bed anyway, there are commercials that entice you with the following offers:

- √ Refinance and get a 3% mortgage!
- √ Pull equity out of your home to pay off bills and consumer debt!
- √ Get a second mortgage and pay off debt!
- √ Borrow up to 125% of your home's value!

You should be suspicious of all these claims—they simply don't make financial sense once you've analyzed them.

What the following sections will outline is how you should think about changing your mortgage if you believe it's creating gunk in your financial life. Be careful and get informed: a mortgage is a serious, important piece of your financial picture and should not be toyed with lightly. (Good books have been written about how to apply for a mortgage or refinance your current mortgage. Check those out if you need more in-depth information on mortgages.) On the assumption that you have a mortgage and already know something about the process, here are some important degunking points.

Look at Your Current Mortgage

When it comes to degunking your home mortgage, you first need to examine the characteristics of the mortgage you already have. In reviewing the terms of your current home mortgage, look at the length of your loan (30 or 15 years), the interest rate that you are currently paying, and the balance due.

Current Terms

Depending on when you took out your mortgage and your credit history, you may have an amazingly good deal or a 10-ton weight around your neck. If you are within a percentage point of current rates for your type of mortgage, you're doing pretty well and should probably not refinance and take on the accompanying charges. If, however, you are seeing interest rates that are consistently more than 1 percent lower than what you are paying, you might consider refinancing.

When I say, "your type of mortgage," I mean mortgages that have the same terms as your current one. If you are carrying around a 30-year fixed mortgage at 8.25 percent, for example, you should probably look at refinancing because standard rates are currently much lower. At that point, you may even be able to shorten the term of your loan because the money you'll now be paying for interest will be so much less than you've historically paid.

Accelerate Payments

Instead of refinancing, some people choose to accelerate their mortgage payments. There are a couple of advantages to doing this:

√ Additional monthly payments (over and above your payment amount) are applied to the principal of the loan. If you make one extra mortgage payment per year, for example, you can make a significant dent in your principal and shave *years* off an average 30-year mortgage. This works even if you take one mortgage payment per year and split it up over your year's worth of payments. For instance, if your mortgage payment is $1200 and you send $1300 every month, the life of your loan will be substantially lowered. Another choice is to increase your mortgage payment as much as you are able, which will be applied on a monthly basis and reduce your principal that much faster. Even an extra $25 to $50 per month will make a difference, since the extra amount goes directly to paying on the principal of the loan. To make certain this happens as you wish, note on your payment slip and check, "extra $50 to principal." That way, the mortgage company cannot mistake your intentions.

√ If you don't want to refinance, accelerating payments is a good way of voluntarily paying off your mortgage early. Most mortgages don't have a prepayment penalty, but be sure yours is specified that way. If you refinance, you're locked into the new payment schedule. If you don't refinance, you can pay whatever additional amount you can afford. Another important point to add to this is that you will probably need to budget the extra money you're allocating to your mortgage. It's rare that you'll have the extra money just sitting around.

TIP: Because mortgages usually have a fairly low interest rate (at least compared to most credit cards and installment loans), any extra money that you have should go to the following bills first:

1. Credit card debt, especially high-interest rate cards
2. Other consumer debt and installment loans
3. Home equity loans or lines of credit
4. Student loans
5. Automobile loans (when the interest rate is higher than your mortgage)

In looking at other places to put your money, prepaying your mortgage is one of several options to raise your net worth. There are other options listed later, but the key on where to save is determined by the interest rate you're receiving as opposed to the interest rate you're paying. If your mortgage is at 6 percent and you're paying with taxable dollars (which raises what you pay by your tax rate) and your 401(k) is making less than that, then by all means put the money into your home. It won't be liquid until you sell, unless you take out a second mortgage or refinance, but prepaying into an appreciating asset can, in the long run, be hugely beneficial. Imagine the freedom of owning your home free and clear! As far off as this may seem, it is very possible and will become even more possible once your consumer debt is paid off and you are able to accelerate your payments even more. It is important, however, to remember that your net worth should not all be tied up in one asset. Don't neglect your other long-term investment opportunities, and keep up your budgeted additions to your varied investments. There will be much more about investments in Chapter 9.

Should I Refinance?

If you're in financial trouble, you may be considering whether you should refinance your home. The first question to ask is why. What is the point of refinancing? As I mentioned previously, refinancing to pay off your consumer debt is risky and can often lead to more debt, especially if you haven't mastered the problem of overspending. Taking money from your equity is not recommended unless there is an emergency situation of some kind, and that would certainly not include the need for a backyard pool.

If you're considering refinancing because there are lower interest rates around and the lower payment would give you cash during the month to pay off your consumer debt faster, invest more, or pay off your home in 15 years instead of 30, then it may well be a good idea.

Here are some guidelines to consider before refinancing:

√ Can I easily qualify for a refinance?

√ Will the benefits outweigh the costs?

√ Will I be able to reduce my monthly outlay?

√ Will the interest rate be an improvement over what I have now?

√ Will the overall cost of the loan be less than what I have now?

√ Can I afford the fees associated with this refinancing?

You may need to do some digging to get the answer to these questions. It may take calls to several mortgage companies and some number crunching with someone who knows the ins and outs of mortgages and refinancing. If you find it would be to your benefit, and you have the right reasons, then by all means, consider refinancing.

REALITY CHECK: There is a refinancing frenzy going on these days. Anyone who owns a home is likely to be inundated with offers in the mail for home equity lines and refinance options. All these lenders make it sound easy, cheap, and fast. What is the truth behind all this easy money? Lenders make huge profit on their mortgages and lines of credit. Your financial gunk is not their concern, nor are the difficulties that the loan you request may create for your family's budget. They certainly don't care about the long-term implications on your net worth. After all, the money they're lending you is secured with *real* property—yours. They're happy to sell you the loan, and they'd like you to pay on it as long as possible. Don't forget: the longer you're indebted to them, the more money they make.

Fixed or Variable Rate?

With all the low interest rate offers around today, you would think most people would go for that 4.5-percent mortgage, right? As good as that looks on the outside, much more study would need to be done to know if this is the right loan for any particular person or family. As with other types of credit, there are different ways to get a mortgage and different ways to get stuck with something that doesn't fit your needs. I'll briefly compare two types of mortgages—fixed rate and adjustable rate—but you should do further investigation on your own to decide which type of mortgage is a good way to help degunk your finances. These mortgages will work the same whether you are refinancing or getting a mortgage for the first time.

Fixed Rate Mortgages

Fixed rate mortgages are just that—the interest rate of the mortgage stays fixed for the life of the loan regardless of whether it's for 15, 20, or 30 years. The only increase you will see in your mortgage payments will be the result of increased property taxes or other withholdings, such as insurance premiums (if you pay them into your escrow account). With a fixed mortgage rate, you will probably see an increase of your monthly payment equal to the percentage your real estate tax has gone up. You can count on this amount going up every year, so you need to plan for an increase with each new year's budget.

Variable Rate Mortgages

Variable rate mortgages (also called ARMs, or adjustable rate mortgages) offer one major benefit over fixed rate mortgages: ARMs often have a lower initial interest rate than fixed rate mortgages, although after a "lock-in" period (which can range from six months to five years), your interest rate will "float" (or vary) according to the fluctuation of the federal reserve interest rate or some other index, often giving you a much higher rate at that point than the current fixed rate mortgages. While this results in a lower interest rate to start and consequently, a lower monthly mortgage payment for the lock-in period, I generally wouldn't recommend an adjustable rate mortgage, especially if you are trying to closely control your budget. Most adjustable rate mortgages are designed to be short term and usually necessitate getting a different mortgage in a specified amount of time. Adjustable rates are just that—adjustable—and being tied to the prime rate or some other measurement can easily get you more gunked up if you are unable to get a different loan when your lock-in period is over. There are instances when this is a good idea, however. This may work well if you know you're moving in two years or if you are investing in property you know you aren't going to keep. It's always a possibility, though, that your plans will change. Perhaps the move fell through and, to make matters worse, you have trouble getting a new mortgage. You'll be stuck paying the inflated rates for the meager benefit of lower interest for a couple of years.

I have had many clients hurt with ARMs over the years. One couple took an ARM fully meaning to get a conventional mortgage after the initial low-interest period. When that time came, however, the economy had taken a downturn, the man had been laid off, and they couldn't get a new mortgage. Now they had only one income and their mortgage payment had almost doubled. Yuck.

CAUTION: If interest rates go up in the next few years, people with ARMs could see their mortgage payments rise dramatically. Even if interest rates stay the same, most ARMs are structured to be a certain number of points over prime, and your payment will certainly go up. If this situation makes you uncomfortable, or you don't think you can accommodate a higher mortgage payment, an ARM is probably not the mortgage instrument for you.

If you plan on moving or refinancing your home before the lock-in period has expired, an ARM might be a good loan for you. If you are uncomfortable with interest-rate uncertainty, or if you're unsure of whether you'll qualify for refinancing after the lock-in period has expired, avoid this type of loan. For further reading, look at **www.eloan.com** or your local mortgage lender's site, which should offer extensive information on these and other types of loans.

Other Types of Mortgages

There are numerous other styles of mortgages out there, as you'll discover when you start investigating your financing options. Some loans that have received a lot of press are balloon loans, interest-only loans, and reverse mortgages. Here are my thoughts on these mortgage products:

√ Balloon mortgages. Balloon loans are short-term mortgages that have some features of a fixed rate mortgage. The loans provide a level payment during the term of the loan, but as opposed to the 30-year fixed rate mortgage, balloon loans do not fully stay the same over the time it would take to pay off your home. Balloon loans can have many types of maturities, but most first mortgage balloon loans have a term of five to seven years. At the end of the loan term, there is still a remaining principal loan balance and the mortgage company generally requires that the loan be paid in full, which can be accomplished by getting a new mortgage. This is not a good mortgage option if you are having financial problems. Although it provides a predictable payment to start with, it requires refinancing at the end of balloon period.

√ Interest-only loans. If you're planning on living in your house for only a year, this type of loan is an option. If you're planning a longer stay, do not take out an interest-only loan. These loans are exactly that—interest only—and so build no equity or net worth. Since the principal never gets paid, you will pay the same huge interest payment for the life of the loan, unlike a fixed rate mortgage where the longer you pay on your loan, the more of your payment goes toward your principal. I can picture a happy lender clapping his hands in glee at the thought that you are going to pay him interest that never ends and that at the end of it you will own nothing. What a great deal for him. I'm breaking out in hives just thinking about it.

- √ Reverse mortgages. This is a special federally insured program for people over the age of 62 who own their homes. It basically converts the equity in their homes into monthly income, which is seen in the form of a monthly check for as long as they live in the home. For more information on this option, see **www.reverse.org** or **www.aarp.org/revers**.

Don't Use Home Equity to Pay Bills

There are several options that are frequently advertised on TV and radio for creative ways of using equity lines of credit. They all promise that you'll be debt free if you just refinance or set up a home equity line of credit. I've stated this before, but it bears repeating. Never use home equity to pay bills. Here are my thoughts on these offers:

- √ *Pull equity out of your home to pay off bills.* This offer is to refinance your home and "cash out" a portion of the equity to pay off consumer debt. One of the things you're doing here is converting short-term debt (such as a credit card balance) into a long-term mortgage. This will result in a higher mortgage payment for you, as well as loss of the equity value in your home. You will also be paying off this debt over the life of the mortgage. For example, by doing this you've converting a $3,000 credit card balance (for example) into a 30-year loan. That's a terrible idea and can't possibly be a part of your long-term goals. Don't do it.
- √ *Get a second mortgage to pay off debt.* What you're doing with this option is paying off unsecured debt (credit cards) with a secured debt (which is guaranteed by the deed to your home). Think about this one. If you default on your credit cards, you get a black mark on your credit report. If you default on your second mortgage, you're out on the street. Again, bad idea.
- √ *Borrow up to 125% of your home's value.* This option combines the worst pieces of the first two scams…I mean options. Now you have a secured and an unsecured loan on your house. What happened to that equity that you've been building up? Gone. You own nothing and you are upside down on your mortgage, which means you owe more to the mortgage company than the home is worth. Forget this one, and tell everybody else how bad it is. My main (and loud!) advice here is, just say no. *Do not use the equity in your home to pay off debts.*

TIP:* *Don't turn an unsecured debt into a secured one! By borrowing on your home's value to pay off unsecured debt, you put your home in jeopardy if your finances happen to worsen. Don't jeopardize your home's equity and get sucked into the home-equity scam.

These types of loans are designed to be cheaper in the short run but really cost you more (and make more for the mortgage company) in the long run.

Adopt a First-Time Home Buying Plan

For most of us, buying a home will turn out to be our biggest investment. Instead of throwing away money on rent and other expenses, with home ownership you can build equity and raise your net worth. It also gives you a feeling of permanence that may be more difficult to attain if you rent and have to move often. Buying your first home can be a challenge, however, especially if your finances have been gunked up in the past. Fortunately, most people with a good plan can achieve their goal of purchasing a home.

Although purchasing your first home might seem a little scary, there are six important steps you can follow to help you work through the financial clutter and confusion:

1. Make sure that your current consumer debt is under control and that you've done everything you can to improve your credit score.
2. Assess the true impact that purchasing and operating a home will have on your budget.
3. Have your emergency fund in place so that buying your new home will not totally deplete your savings.
4. Try to prequalify for a mortgage so that you'll know what you can spend.
5. Search for and purchase a home that fits your real needs and budget.
6. Make sure that the mortgage you obtain fits your long-term goals.

Get Your Consumer Debt under Control and Improve Your Credit Score

Many clients come to me with the goal of wanting to purchase their first house. They hear about low interest rates and are anxious to get into their own house before interest rates rise again. I understand that completely. Buying my first house was one of the best financial and personal moves I ever made. If you're feeling ready to buy and all your spare time is spent on the Internet and going to open houses, you need to stop the train for a few minutes and take a close look at your debt situation. From what you learned in Chapter 6, you are now probably in the process of controlling and paying off your consumer debt. If you're struggling to make those payments, then now is probably not the time to take on more debt. This can be disastrous to your goals. Once you purchase a home, it's not only your mortgage payment that will add to your expenses.

There will be costs associated with owning a home that you've never thought of, and chances are you're thinking about getting some new furniture, a few rooms of window coverings, and a lawn mower. Then, much to your surprise, the fridge dies. This actually happened to me after buying my first house, and it was a sorry day indeed when I went out and charged that appliance because buying the house had tapped us out of cash. Some of this advice is hard won, and painful to remember. Don't buy until you have your financial ducks in a row.

The other important item you need to look at is your credit score. I'll be showing you how to work with your credit report and improve your credit score in Chapter 10. What you need to know now is that your credit score will impact the type of loan you'll be able to get, how much interest you'll be paying, and the fees you may pay for closing costs. Having a higher score can save you a bundle in immediate and long-term costs, so it is well worth the time and effort to try to improve your credit score before you start house hunting. If your real estate agent calls in during this process and tells you she has just located the perfect house for you, bite your lip and tell her you have other priorities at the moment but you'll call her as soon as you're ready to look.

Determine Your True Costs and Plan Out a Budget

The easy part of buying a house is determining how much you can afford to pay each month for your mortgage. The hard part is factoring in all of the other costs. Most people learn the hard way by plunging in and then realizing later that their mortgage payment is only a part of the actual costs. If you are currently renting a house, you already know you need to budget for expenses such as utilities, phone, cable TV, and renter's insurance. But with your own home, you'll have other expenses as well, including repair and maintenance costs, insurance, homeowner's association dues, and property taxes. As part of your planning and budgeting, it's imperative for you to consider all of these expenses. If you are working with a real estate agent to target certain houses and neighborhoods for a possible purchase, you should ask for as many financial details as you can, so there's no need to guess. You should be able to get good estimates for all of these costs. For costs such as insurance, you'll need to do some of your own homework and make a few calls.

Build a Needed Savings Cushion

It's common for people I've worked with to think that once they've saved up a little money for a down payment, they are ready to purchase their first house. Coming up with a down payment is an important savings step, but you shouldn't stop there. In addition to the down payment, you'll need money to handle your closing costs, moving expenses, deposits for utility companies, initial insurance payments and a little extra for expenses that might sneak up on you. In Chapter 9, you will be encouraged to build up a savings account of three to six months of your living expenses. This is even more important as you purchase your first home.

Two questions that I hear quite a bit are, "How much money do I need for a down payment?" and "How in the world can I save that much?" The answer to the first question has a lot to do with how much risk you feel comfortable taking on and how low you want your monthly payment to be. Today, it's possible to qualify for a loan that allows you to purchase a home with very little money down. These types of loans were unheard of years ago. As more and more people are taking on greater amounts of debt, banks and other lending institutions have changed the standards of what they require for mortgages, allowing much higher ratios of debt to income than in years past. This doesn't mean taking on as much debt as possible is a good idea. It's your money and your good credit that is at stake.

The best case scenario is to save up at least 20 percent of your home's purchase price. If you put down any less, you will be required to purchase private mortgage insurance that will be added on to every payment you make until your equity reaches 20 percent. If you don't think that will be possible in this lifetime, check with several mortgage companies and find out what the differences will be to your payment and fees with a selection of down payment options. Choose the option that best fits your needs, keeping in mind that the sooner you get to 20-percent equity, the sooner you can stop funneling unearned money to the lender. Keep in mind that your down payment is merely a portion of what you'll need to actually get possession and set up the kitchen table handed down from your grandmother. You'll also need to save money for your closing costs. To get a good estimate of what those costs will be, ask your mortgage person for a written estimate. New charges can always crop up at the last minute, but this will give you someplace to start. On average, plan on spending at least $2,000. Moving costs can add up as well. If you're planning on your 10 best friends, a rented truck, and pizza afterward, you're looking at about $500, depending on the size of the truck. If you are looking forward to professional movers who will pack it all up and put it where it goes in the new house, you can multiply the first number by 10. When you total up just the extra charges, the cost of getting into your new home will still be at least $2,500, and it will probably be substantially more. Add on your down payment and that's a lot of bananas you need to put away. Fortunately, in the next chapter I'll show you how you can degunk your basic household living expenses to come up with extra money that you can set aside for a new home purchase. In Chapter 9, I'll also show you how to get a good savings program in place.

For now, here are some quick instructions to help get the money put away that you'll need to buy that cute, perfect place. Pick something in your price range. Figure out what it would cost to live there, including all of the things you don't have to pay for now (all these things were mentioned in this chapter). Figure your budget to include those expenses. Take the extra money you would be spending every month (higher mortgage payment, real estate tax, association fees) and put it in a savings account specifically earmarked for your home purchase. This way, you'll be getting practice on what living in a place like that will actually cost you, and you'll be building savings for the down payment and expenses. Wow! Yet another win-win situation.

Prequalify for Your Mortgage

Prequalifying for a mortgage means you have a company willing to lend you a certain amount of money toward the purchase of a home. Then, as you're house shopping, you know exactly what you can and cannot afford. It helps when the place with the toolshed the size of the rest of the house is making your husband salivate but it's over your preapproved budget. Sorry, honey.

Getting prequalified for a mortgage is much easier than it used to be. With some mortgage companies, you can get information back in as little as an hour. The mortgage company will pull your credit report, ask you specific questions about your income and debt, and have you fill out forms. Depending on what the information tells them, you can prequalify for different types of loans. Conforming loans (conventional fixed and standard ARMs) are reserved for those with a credit score of 600 and higher. FHA loans (conventional loans with a smaller down payment underwritten by the government) are available to those with a 575 score or higher. Subprime loans can be approved for people with a score of 500 to 600. These loans are the most expensive and the least attractive, like the two-year ARMs charging high interest. If you have a credit score less than 500, it will be very difficult to get a home mortgage.

It is an important point to a seller when the proposed buyer is prequalified. It means there won't be time wasted waiting to see if the buyer can get a mortgage and taking the home off the market, but not knowing if the mortgage will come through. Closing can be scheduled quickly, and the transaction can be smooth and fast, to the benefit of both buyer and seller.

Be aware that just because the mortgage company says you can afford a home worth $250,000 doesn't mean you can. Get preapproved, but know that only you are aware of everything financial that goes on in your home, and you know what you can manage and what you can't. The big toolshed house can still be more than you can afford, even if the mortgage company prequalifies you for that amount.

Match Your New Home to Your Real Needs (and Look for Deals)

Earlier in this chapter we looked at how important it is to match up the home you choose with your real needs and actual budget. It's possible, however, that when you begin looking for your first home, you may find that market conditions get factored in and you can't always find exactly what you want for what you can spend. Most first-time home buyers end up being shocked by how little they can purchase for what they can afford. At that point, it's common to get discouraged and end up spending considerably more than what was originally planed.

As you progress through the home buying process, use your budget and your common sense as your guiding force. Here are some simple tips you can follow to help you make the best purchase decision:

√ Keep in mind that this is your first house. You'll probably live in the house for a few years, make some improvements to it, and move on. It is rare for a person or family to stay in one house forever. If you can't find the perfect house for your budget, be patient. Your dream house may be more affordable the next time around, after you've built up some equity and aren't paying that nasty private mortgage insurance.

√ Make sure that the house you select is worthy of the debt you are taking on for it. Be realistic about what condition the house is in, and make certain you understand what the house will cost you. Get professional opinions. You will be taking on a big debt (and a lot of operating overhead) in an area in which you have little experience. Borrowing this much money is something that shouldn't be taken lightly.

√ As you travel around, look in the paper for homes that are for sale by owner. Bypassing the real estate agents can save you at least 6 percent of the purchase price. On a $200,000 home, that would equal $12,000 that you don't have to pay. Most people selling their own home have already figured that savings into the price, but do some comparisons to other recently sold properties in the area to be sure. Don't be concerned about the paperwork—you'll need a real estate attorney at the closing anyway, and they won't charge you much more to officiate over the original contract. It certainly won't cost you $12,000.

GunkBuster's Notebook: Do Your Own Marketing Work and Save

When I finally convinced my mother to move back to our area from Florida, we wanted to find her a nice place to live and treat it as investment property. We scoured our town because we wanted her close by and found what we thought would be the perfect area for her. It was a coach home, all on one floor, with the right amount of bedrooms and bathrooms and an indoor accessible garage. This was at a time when properties of this type were much in demand (how's that for luck?), and listings that came on at 9 A.M. were selling by noon for the full purchase price. This annoyed me. Using an idea I got from my dentist, I sent postcards to every unit matching our criteria in the complex and waited for a couple of days. The postcards stated what our need was and asked anyone that was considering selling to contact us before signing with a Realtor. We got four calls from people ready to sell. We saw all four units, ruled out two for space reasons, flew my mother in for the day to pick the one she liked (after seeing tons of pictures online), and signed a contract the next day. We saved $7500, got just what we wanted, and had people fighting for our business.

- √ If you are working with a real estate agent, don't let them talk you into buying more house than you can afford. No matter how friendly you become with your agent, don't forget that they are in the business to sell you as much house as they can. They get paid on commission, and you'll be left to make payments you can't afford long after they get their check.
- √ Look for neighborhoods that are improving. If you're budget is tight, you probably won't be able to afford a neighborhood that is fully established and nicely manicured. On the other hand, make sure it is a neighborhood that is moving upward and not down. "Falling apart at the seams" isn't a good neighborhood description when it's time to sell. Focus instead on an area that is getting better. If you drive around a neighborhood and see a lot of dumpsters in driveways filled with old kitchen cabinets, that's a good thing. It means that the folks who live in the neighborhood are fixing up their houses. These are typically the places where you can find good deals and be with people who care about their homes.

√ Look for neighborhoods where there are more homeowners living there than renters. Neighborhoods that have a higher percentage of renters tend to decline faster. If you are unsure about this, ask your real estate agent for help.

√ Look for houses that have poor landscaping in good neighborhoods. Someone else's hatred for yard work can be your bonanza. When the weeds pile up, the house looks like an unattractive buy. Don't discount such a house—it can be a beautiful home waiting to happen. You might find a great deal for the price of a weed whacker.

√ Buy the smallest house on a street in a good neighborhood instead of the biggest house. You've probably heard this before but it bears repeating. The smallest house in a good neighborhood is usually the easiest one to sell, which means that you'll be able to get your money out of it when you are ready to move on.

√ If you have kids (or you are expecting to have them), look for the neighborhoods with the best schools. Homes located in neighborhoods with good schools tend to appreciate faster than homes in neighborhoods with lower-quality schools. Check more than the test scores that the schools provide. Ask questions and find out if the schools are really good. Talk to other parents, and visit the schools during the day while school is in session. You'll have to speak to the school first, for security, but it will be worth your time to avoid making a mistake. Sometimes, even good schools aren't worth what you might have to pay to live there. In one California neighborhood (according to National Public Radio), the homes increased in value over 35 percent in one year because that particular neighborhood contained schools that had the highest test scores. Parents were flocking to the neighborhood because they wanted their children to be at the "best" school and hugely overpaying for houses in the process.

√ If you are comparing neighborhoods, do a little research and determine which neighborhood on average has homes that appreciate the most in value. Not all neighborhoods are created equal, and homes in some turn out to be wiser investments than others. Do your homework first and you might spot some interesting trends.

GunkBuster's Notebook: Be Careful of the Fixer-Upper Money Pit

If you are looking at homes in a neighborhood that is too expensive for your budget, you might feel tempted to purchase a house that is priced below market value because it needs some repairs. This might seem like a good idea in the beginning, but get a grip before making that purchase.

You need to take a very close look at the situation and ask yourself the following questions:

- √ Do I have the time to take on a project like this?
- √ Do I have the experience for this work, or will I have to depend on someone to help me?
- √ Do I really know how much it will cost to make the repairs and do all of the necessary work?
- √ Am I willing to give up most of my free time over the next year or two (or more)?
- √ Am I willing to live in a house that will be under construction for the foreseeable future? Is my spouse willing to live in that situation?
- √ Do I have a backup plan if I end up taking on more than I can handle?

Most home improvement projects don't turn out exactly as planned. They take much longer and they cost much more than projected. I tell my clients to estimate the costs and schedule and then double everything—both time and costs.

Get the Best Mortgage

After reading about the different types of mortgages in this chapter, you probably have a good idea which would work best for you. Now is your chance to show your deal-getting colors. Start shopping the different mortgage companies in your area to find the very best deal on the mortgage you have chosen. This will take some phone time and a legal pad on which to make notes, but the money you save can be substantial and will last the life of your loan. The housing market isn't what it was a few years ago, and mortgage companies are back to needing your business. Make a deal. Tell them what you're getting at other mortgage companies. Get them to sweat a little. See what you can get in the way of lower interest rates or lower fees. It won't hurt to ask. Compare all the offers, and choose the one that benefits you most.

Summing Up

The most important thing you've learned in this chapter is how to manage your rent or mortgage. Determining if this piece of your budget is too large is critical, and deciding what would be appropriate for your needs is an exercise that may stretch your imagination but will help you make good future decisions about your housing. Also discussed was how to decide if refinancing is a good idea for you, and how to choose your best fit from the several mortgage options available. If you're looking to purchase a home for the first time, you've come to the right place. You now may have more information than you even wanted, including the message that it may not be the right time for you to buy. The point here is to keep your eyes on the long-term goal—and the best way to get there. If it is the right time to buy, remember what to look for in a neighborhood, how to get a better deal on your financing, and not to ever roll the cost of a hot tub into your mortgage, which I hadn't mentioned but will tuck in now.

Stay tuned! The degunking continues.

Degunking Your Housing and Living Expenses

Degunking Checklist:

√ Get your utility bills in order.

√ Find the best deals on telephone services.

√ Follow some tips to save money on your basic expenses, such as utilities, cable, groceries, and packaged goods.

√ Eliminate waste from other household expenses.

By now, you've organized your finances. You've faced the truth about your personal debt, you've taken a close look at your home mortgage, and you have a new, realistic budget in place. You've developed a debt-repayment plan and are working toward becoming debt-free. With these steps, you've taken enormous strides in getting your financial life gunk-free. Congratulations! But, if you're not yet completely satisfied with your new fiscal belt-tightening system, I have yet more suggestions on where you can save (and find) yet more money in your budget.

This chapter will help you further hone your household budget to free up more money to put toward debt repayment, savings, or other living expenses. In many cases, you have a lot more money than you think you do—it's just tied up in expenses that you haven't thought you could control, like utilities or food. Close management of these areas can net you a good portion of extra money each month, and by taking a really good look at what you're spending in other areas as well, you can often find money that could be better spent. This "found" money can have a huge effect on your bottom line. Imagine finding another two or three hundred dollars per month to put toward debt repayment or savings! That money could go a long way toward getting you to your goal, and it might be already in your checkbook—you just don't know it. Let's explore some ideas here—read on!

Put Your Utilities on a Budget Plan

Most people don't question their utility bills. They come in the mail and we pay them without giving them much thought. Even when we get a nasty surprise in the middle of December, like a $450 heating bill, we just pay it, loudly complaining, of course, but without a plan in place to avoid that same situation in the future. A couple of years ago, the price of natural gas went ballistic, and in the Midwest, people were getting socked with bills that were triple what they were used to a week or two before Christmas. It wasn't an especially jolly time.

The people that weathered that storm best were those who were on the "budget plan" for their gas, a system where you pay the same amount all year round. In summer, when you use gas only to cook (and we in the Midwest barbeque in the summer), the money in your account builds up. In our frigid Chicago winters (and in yours), you use the money you saved over the summer and add to it with the budgeted amount you pay every month, leveling out what you owe with what you have saved up. For example, by paying $121 all year toward my heating, I now have over $500 credit (over and above paying all my gas bills through the year) toward the bone-chilling, breath-stopping, nose-freezing weather that's coming. It's a good feeling, even though I still hate the cold.

***TIP:* Most gas and electric companies have a budget plan available. Unless you don't have a good payment record with the company, utility companies are usually happy to sign you up for their budget plan because it means they will probably get their money from you in a timely manner. Most companies will pay interest on the credit amount, although the rate is quite low. The point of these plans is to create a forced savings account for your utilities to help you even out your monthly expenses—and save you the pain of the huge gas or electric bill in the middle of the very cold or very hot season. It makes it easier to budget your utilities if you know how much you're going to pay every month, so in mid-winter, or mid-summer, you're not dreading the arrival of the bill. My gas company looks over the budget plans every four months. If they feel the gas prices are going to go up or my usage has increased, they will adjust the bill accordingly. If the winter has been unseasonably warm or you have decided to use the wood burning stove instead of gas heat this year, they will lower the bill. However they alter it, feel free to call them if you are confused or don't agree with the changes. It's their job to answer your questions, and you are the customer, after all.**

The point of a budget plan is to make it easier for you to plan your personal expenses. It can be hard to save up for the whomping big electric bill you know is coming in August, and you usually don't have a space on your Christmas list for the gas company. If you pay the same utility amounts all year round, you won't be afraid to go the mailbox, no matter what the weather.

***TIP:* Another way to save money on your electric bill is to try to do activities that require more electricity, such as the laundry, during off-peak hours. Most utility companies charge a higher rate for their services during the day than they do during off-peak hours—usually after 9 P.M. on weekdays and all day on weekends.**

Shop for Telephone Services

Phone companies—until they have you under contract, anyway—are bitterly competitive. Every one of them desperately wants your money, and they will tell you almost anything to get it. Some of what they say is true, and some is open to interpretation. For instance, saying you can call anywhere, anytime for $49.99 per month may make you think that's what you'll be paying. What may not be mentioned is the applicable taxes at 10 percent to 20 percent, or the fees they have to add by law that aren't in the original price. And, if you don't have an unlimited plan, there are per-minute charges that can stack up if you use more minutes than your plan provides. Some of the hidden charges have names you can't even decipher, like "Federal Universal Service Fee," or the "State Infrastructure Maintenance Fee." I don't know who gets this money, but it's on every phone bill I receive. The bill can get up to about $70, even though you are still on the "plan" you originally requested at only $49.99. A big target area to degunk in your personal finances is in the telephone and telecommunications services you receive. As with utilities, these bills are seldom examined once you start getting these services. Beware: Hidden and unexpected charges are lurking everywhere, and lucky for you, better deals are out there—you just have to be a dedicated degunker!

Land Lines

The key to getting the best deal on a land line is to be an informed consumer. Land line accounts (the phone that plugs into your wall) work differently than cell phone accounts. Land lines are rarely on a contract (as opposed to cell phones, which almost always are), but they do have a variety of service options available.

Service Plans

When you're shopping for a land line, start by asking your friends what deals they are getting. It's very possible the company you are with now has a better deal than the one you're currently receiving. Many land line companies run similar, if not identical, promotions, and staying with your current company can be less frustrating and less expensive than changing, so give them a call and see if they have a better plan for you. Tell them you're looking for cost savings, and that if you don't get them you'll go somewhere else. They will be motivated to find something you will be pleased with. Your phone company spends a good deal of money on marketing to attract new customers, so if they lose you, they would have to spend quite a bit of money to either get you back or replace you.

To begin this process, look at your phone bill. Are you using less or more minutes than you are being allowed for local or long-distance service? If you're using more, it is usually beneficial to up your allowance because $5 can usually buy you a ton more time and using more than your allotment can add up to more bill quickly. If you don't make a lot of long-distance calls, ask if you can get a better rate for local calling only. Again, look at your own usage patterns and see if your provider can give you a better deal. Saving even $10 a month will make a difference in your degunking plan.

TIP: If your home phone bill is high because of the long-distance calls you make, there is another choice. Instead of using your phone company for long-distance service, shop around for the best deal on calling cards. Some cards offer rates as low as three cents per minute. They also offer very low rates for international calls. If you find a card that offers you a better deal than your phone company, buy one and cancel your long distance. You can use these cards from any phone because they use an 800 number to access your call. You can even put the calling card access numbers onto the speed dial program on your home phone to automate the process. Not only will you save money making your calls, but you'll avoid having to pay the annoying taxes that you get charged for your long-distance phone service.

Extra Services

Another part of your land line bill that can cost you is the list of services for which you're paying. Voice mail, three-way calling, call forwarding, and call waiting are usually individually charged and can be expensive. Even if a company tells you it's a "Five Accessory Package," you will find it broken out individually on your bill. What can you do without? How often do you actually need to forward calls? If you don't need it, get rid of it. Using the company's voice mail service at $4 per month is much more expensive than buying an answering machine. I paid $30 for my machine several years ago and have saved several hundred dollars of unneeded expense as a result.

CAUTION: Be on the look out for a "linebacker" charge on your phone bill. What is this? It's an insurance charge that some phone companies add to your bill to cover the cost if a repairman needs to come and fix a problem with the phone line inside your house. This rarely happens. If you are being charged this fee, call your phone company and have them remove this option.

Information Calls

Another money waster is information calls. Your phone company will probably provide you with any phone books you need or want. (I get at least three delivered every year that I recycle immediately.) If you are looking for a business number, it is almost always available on the Internet. If you don't have a personal phone book for numbers you use consistently, go to the Dollar Store and get one. There is no such thing as a $.35 information call anymore. Information charges start at $.95 and are sometimes as much as $1.95 each. International information can cost up to $10.00 a pop. Look up the number in the phone book, already. If you have to use this service, okay, but don't waste $20.00 per month on information calls because you can't be bothered to dig out the book.

Cell Phones

Cell phones are a different animal entirely. As their service is almost always contractual, you need to be very careful when you sign up. A two-year package that doesn't fit your needs can be counterproductive and expensive, and if you change packages in the middle of the contract period, it usually extends your contract from the date of the change. Make sure you read the entire contract carefully because the small print probably mentions that opting out early lands you a stiff penalty, often in the neighborhood of $200 per line.

Luxury or Necessity?

Before signing a cell phone contract, look at what you can afford. A cell phone is a luxury, not an absolute necessity, no matter what our culture says. Go back to your monthly expenditures sheet and see what is allocated for cell phone usage. Get a plan that gives you the most minutes for what you can spend, and use self-discipline to keep within those boundaries.

***CAUTION:** If you have children or teenagers who want a cell phone, think twice about providing one. As with your cell phone plan, there will be usage charges, minute allowances, and long-distance and roaming charges that will creep into their bills. Are you paying their cell phone bills? This can be a budget buster for you, and I've had clients whose cell phone bills ran a few hundred dollars per month for multiple phones. Can you afford this?*

There are more than financial issues concerning teenagers and cell phones. A cell phone is a ticket to a very private life for your teen. Most teenagers with cell phones do all of their communicating through their own number and rarely use the house phone. They can call, text-message, and use the walkie-talkie feature, and as a parent, you lose the opportunity to know who is calling your teen. There is no reason for a teen to use a cell phone while in the house. If you want to provide one for when the teen is not at home (or have the teen pay for their own usage) to make it easier for you to contact them or for them to request a ride home, fine, but when they get home, the cell phone becomes family property, in the custody of the parent.

Some people are doing without a land line entirely and using the cell phone as their only phone. Do some research, look at your own calling habits, and make an informed decision before doing this. Be aware, as well, that there is growing concern about possible health issues concerning constant cell phone usage.

Consider a "Pay As You Go" Plan

If you have had financial issues concerning your cell phone in the past and know you won't keep to your allotted minutes, consider getting a prepaid cell phone. You buy the phone, and then buy the minutes separately. It's akin to a phone card, and when your minutes are used up, you go buy more. This promotes self-discipline and keeps you from receiving a surprise $350 cell phone bill. Many a budget has been gunked up by managing a cell phone poorly, and an unpaid bill gone to collections will put a black mark on your credit. You don't want that kind of gunk on your credit report.

The moral of this story is that if you choose to have a cell phone, think it through from the beginning. This is an easy place to gather financial gunk, and if you have a mess to clean up from the last cell phone, get to sweeping. Pay off the last bill before getting another number, and get a prepaid phone to train yourself to do better.

Waste Not. Pay Not

There is great potential to remove financial gunk from your life if you look at the way you manage your household. Toilet paper can be $1 roll at your convenience store or $.20 a roll at a big retail store. Coffee can be $4 a cup at your local international café or $.25 a cup if you make it at home. Dog food is cheaper when you buy big bags whenever you get it. Taking a good look at how you manage your household can result in significant savings and thereby help degunk your budget. From the edicts of our mothers ("Turn off the lights when you're not in the room!") to finding a store that sells what you most need for less, money can be saved from the get-go by simply not wasting it. There's nothing wrong with spending what you can afford for utilities, food, and repairs, but why spend more that you have to if there's an option to spend less?

Utilities

Utilities seem like a necessary expense, but in actuality, you have a lot of control over how big your utility bills are. Although my husband and I consistently meet at the thermostat (me turning it up, and him turning it down), we still keep our bills as low as possible by turning the heat down at night and doing our best, by using storm windows and plugging drafts, to keep the heat in the house instead of around the house. Here are a few ideas for saving on your utilities:

√ Programmable thermostat. I highly recommend a programmable thermostat, which costs less than $50 at your local home improvement store. These nifty devices allow you to preset your house's temperature so you don't have to fiddle with it. If your house is empty during the day, you can turn the heat way down and set it to warm up again an hour before everyone arrives home. The same is true of your air conditioning. This device will save you *hundreds* of dollars over the course of a year.

- √ Low-water landscaping. You can reduce your water bills by switching to low-water landscaping. Do you really need a full acre of lawn around your house, or can you do alternative landscaping with low-water plants? This, too, can save you hundreds per year. It can also save you part of your Saturdays when you don't have to mow that golf course of a backyard!
- √ Low-flow toilets. While we're on the topic of saving precious water, you can easily convert your existing toilets to operate more efficiently by purchasing a low-flow conversion kit from your favorite hardware stores. These kits cost about $15, and if you're handy, you can make the conversion in about one hour.
- √ Water heater. Turn your water heater down when you are away. Most water heaters provide a "vacation" setting that will save you money on your utility bill—gas or electric depending on how your water heater operates. If you plan to be away from your house for a period of three or more days, you should put your hot water heater on the vacation setting.

Utilities do make our lives more comfortable, but wasting these resources by misuse costs us money. Pay attention to the little inserts you receive in your bill with suggestions on how to lower costs (you know, the things you throw away without reading), and take to heart the thought that many of our natural resources are not naturally regenerating substances. Saving money and the environment is a double bonus, and by becoming simply more aware of your usage, you can lower your bills and live a little "greener" as well.

Cable

Cable is a line item for most people, but it can be unnecessarily high for someone whose finances are gunked up. When asked, most people will say they need cable for improved reception, which can certainly be true. When you call a cable company and ask for the rates for its least-expensive package, you will usually be given a rate of around $40.00 per month. That is not entirely true. That may be the lowest rate for a package that includes some premium channels, but every company is required to provide what is, in essence, local service. This gives great reception to all the major stations and a bunch more besides. I pay $8.52 per month for cable, and that includes all the local stations, Pax, the Animal Channel, the Travel Channel, lots of stations I can't remember, and all-day car racing, which is so darned exciting I can hardly stand it. Cable is a luxury no matter how you look at it, and if you're looking for something to cut, cable, or at least more than the local basic package, is an obvious choice. Cutting your service down to the basic will also give you the benefit of reducing some of what you may not want coming into your home anyway, so saving $30.00 to $80.00 per month can be extra beneficial.

Groceries and Packaged Goods

Food is a necessity, but here you have complete control over how much and where you purchase. There are two major points here:

1. Find the least-expensive stores in which to shop.
2. Don't pay full price for anything.

Finding stores in your area can be an adventure. The larger chain stores will be high for most items, unless they are having a special. You will probably end up with two favorite stores: one for fresh food (fruits, veggies, dairy, deli, and meat) and one for packaged items (Cheerios, crackers, and the like). Your fresh food place will probably be a free-standing, privately owned store. In the Chicago area, these stores are getting more and more popular, and the prices on the fresh items go at about one-half the cost of similar items at the larger chain stores. The one exception here is milk, but even then, at $2.29 per gallon, the cost is substantially less than the $3.89 they're asking at the local big chain grocery store. Check your area. My guess is you'll find a treasure you may not have known was there.

For packaged goods, a "no-frills" store with lower prices is probably best. Do a comparison shop and see how much you save by shopping less fancy, and while you're at it, try generic brands on things like crackers, cereal, and frozen vegetables. Often, these items are packaged in the same plant with different labels on them. Wouldn't you be proud to pay one-third less for something that was the same product in different packaging? Experiment a little, and find what you like. It may not always be completely successful. For instance, I would not recommend Cub Foods private label of Grape-Nuts cereal. It was so bad I put it out for the birds, and they even let it sit out for a couple of days before eating it.

Chain Stores and Big Box Retailers

The big chain stores can be useful for you. They will run several specials every week, called "loss-leaders," that you can take advantage of, but commit to buying only what is dramatically on sale and nothing else. It can be a trial to pass up all those end caps of tempting items placed so your cart practically runs into them, but put on your blinders and go directly to the $1.69 per pound chicken breasts, or the $1.99 Cheerios, and then get the heck out of there. If there is a good sale, buy a few of what you need (staying within your budget, of course) so that you are not in the position of "needing" something that's full price next week. Chicken freezes well, and I always have a few boxes of Cheerios on hand.

A membership to Costco or Sam's can be beneficial to you if you go in as an informed consumer. Not everything there is cheaper—sometimes it is just bigger. They do have incredible deals on some items, though, and the trick is to find out what you use consistently and check the prices there against what you would pay at your local store when that same item is on sale. You have to weigh the price of the membership against what you can save. If you find you can do well, then go for it. I have had clients, however, who say they overspend there because of the selection of'"stuff" that they may not be budgeted for, or need (like that nice 2-carat diamond ring next to the generators). Shop at these stores with the same discipline you use at the mall. Don't buy things you don't need just because they're there and may be cheaper than they are at the department stores.

Sales and Coupons

There are two other ways to save money on household items: sales and coupons. The first I heartily recommend as part of your new degunking lifestyle. The second is optional and can save you money if you have the patience and discipline to use coupons well.

Never Pay Full Price

It's essential that as part of your degunking plan you commit to saving on food by not purchasing anything at full price. If it's not on sale, don't buy it. This isn't as hard as it sounds. Look around your grocery store on your next visit. Will inexpensive rice cakes taste the same as expensive ones, which is to say, will they both be as equally tasteless? Will porterhouse on sale taste the same as it did at full price yesterday? Is milk on sale any different than at full price? Everything goes on sale at the grocery store, so get in the habit of taking a look at the ad before you go and searching for the sale tags when you're there.

***TIP:** Most major grocery stores have affinity programs in which "members" get discounts off of commonly purchased items. If you shop at these stores for the sales, those programs will save you a few bucks on every visit, and all you have to do is sign up to become a member.*

Searching for sales is more doable with packaged foods than with fresh produce, but making it an objective when shopping can save you a bundle. The key here is to not "need" anything. For example, buying a big jar of Miracle Whip at full price can run you $3.49, but on sale it will run you $1.99. If you use this product regularly, buy two. Now you're not in a position to need it for a long while, and you're getting two for nearly the price of one. Having to run and get one when you're out and the tuna is already in the bowl will cost you the full $3.49, not to mention creating irritation by having to drop everything and go to the store. When pork chops are on sale, buy a bunch and freeze them for future use.

Even with fresh foods, choices of menu can be made with a mind for what is cheaper this week. Fruits and vegetables come into season at different times, and craving peaches in July is much less expensive (and tastier) than craving them in February. You are not a slave to your taste buds, after all, and reasonable decisions can be made about what to eat and when. Try to eat what is in season and you'll find you're spending less at the grocery store.

Coupons

Some people love couponing, and some people hate it. Personally, I don't have the inclination to search the Sunday newspaper supplements for coupons—but I know lots of people who do. If you use coupons for what you regularly buy, you can save real money, and if you organize well, it doesn't have to be a bunch of little pieces of newspaper flying around at the checkout. It's certainly another way to degunk your shopping budget, and if you get your children involved, it can be a way to teach them about shopping for food when they're still young.

Eat at Home

I probably don't have to tell you that eating out constantly, even if it's just for lunch, can represent an expenditure of *thousands* of dollars per year. Unless you're on an expense account—and it can be wasteful no matter who is paying for it—that's cash that's coming straight out of your budget.

If you're serious about degunking your budget, then one of the fastest improvements you can make is to start taking your lunch to work and eat at home more often. Restaurant meals and takeout food, while more convenient for busy people who have already put in a 10- or 12-hour day, are expensive and not usually as healthy as what you can make at home. If you can enlist the members of your household to help cook dinner a couple nights more a week and to brown-bag their lunches, your household will see at least two benefits:

- √ More spendable cash in the budget at the end of the week
- √ A healthier diet

There. Bon appétit, and do it cheap.

Summing Up

In this chapter, we examined your housing and living expenses with the goal of finding additional savings on these costs. You can save an awful lot of money by just looking around at what you spend to feed, house, and heat your family and tweaking this piece of your budget. Even though most people don't think about saving money in their utility budgets, it is possible, and now you know how. In addition, there are easy savings to be had with telephone, cable, and grocery expenses. This is such basic, practical stuff that it can become second nature to consider it as you move forward in the degunking process. If you don't forget your financial goals and you make good choices concerning your food, your home, and your utilities, you will end up exactly where you want to be in the future. You will be amazed not only at what you can do without, but how painless it will be in the long run. I have had clients without number who have trouble remembering how they managed to spend so much on food when now they manage quite well with half that amount. Household expenses are still choices that we make, and the best decisions pay such great dividends that once you get started, you'll get quickly in the swing. Oh, and when you're done reading, don't forget to turn out the light.

Degunking Your Savings and Investments

Degunking Checklist:

- √ Create a savings plan and learn how to pay yourself first.
- √ Discipline yourself to set aside a portion of everything you earn.
- √ Recognize the true monetary cost of your dreams.
- √ Review and fine-tune your current savings strategy so that you balance your priorities.
- √ Learn how to save in the correct order.
- √ Learn about risk and know where your money is going.
- √ Develop a plan that will maximize the money you have to save for your retirement.
- √ Learn about the power of investing.

Saving and investing is not just for wealthy people. Nearly everyone can, and should, save for the various things in life that they know are coming and can prepare for. If you know you want to own a home, saving for it is necessary. Saving for emergencies is imperative. Your car won't last forever. Eventually, it will break down, and if you don't have funds stashed away to fix it, you'll be back in the leaky boat of running up your charge cards in order to be able to get to work. Sending your kids to college is an expensive proposition, and getting them married can be as modest or as pricey as your finances and constitution can stand. Retirement is another can of worms altogether.

It is rare that you are handed money to pay for life's major events. The key is preparation and being able to put aside some current gratification to pay for a future financial benefit. No matter how you look at it, saving and investing is a good idea. The questions are how to do it, how much to set aside, where to put the money you're saving so it does you the most good, and how much time you'll need to reach a goal. Through all this, you will need to learn how to monitor and fine-tune your investments over time.

The answers to the previous questions will be based largely on you personally. How old are you? What do you need to save for, and how quickly? How much risk are you willing to take? How much time do you have to monitor your investments? There are, thankfully, some rules of thumb to help you decide and many professionals to help fill in the gaps where you are lacking in knowledge or understanding.

In this chapter you'll learn to degunk your finances even further by getting on the road to building a savings plan. If you've already started to save, I'll help you take your plans one step further and fine-tune your investments. You'll learn how saving and investing are two complementary actions necessary to help you reach your goals. First, you'll degunk your savings strategies in order to have money set aside, and then I'll show you how to put those savings to work for your future benefit.

Create a Savings Plan

As with any endeavor, you need some goals. What do you want the outcome of your saving or investing to be? Here are some possible savings goals (depending on your living situation):

- √ Retirement
- √ Emergency situations
- √ Home purchase

- √ Wedding—yours or a child's
- √ Raising or adopting a child
- √ Infertility treatments
- √ Your children's college education
- √ New or used car
- √ Family vacation
- √ Major home renovation
- √ Second home

If you have never saved before, now is your chance to start. As with almost anything that will benefit you, it may be a difficult habit to ingrain into your budgeting practices, but if all it takes is minimizing your lifestyle some to keep from eating nothing but Ramen noodles when you're in your 80s, it seems quite worth it to bear down a bit now.

In the 10 years I've been working with people and their money, the clients that make me the saddest are those elderly couples who did not save for their future and who are now both old and ill. Their years of earning potential are long gone, and the best they can hope for is that Social Security will hold out and their children might be able to help now and then. It is a bleak picture, and I wish it on no one. I can't imagine you want your "golden years" to consist of endlessly scraping for money for bills and prescriptions. I worked with one couple who each worked a few hours a week doing jobs no 70-year-olds should have to do. When they got paid, they had to choose which medicines to buy (they couldn't afford them all) and how to make do with the little food they could get with the rest of their wages. What made this situation so very sad was that they got in this position by making poor choices for most of their marriage, taking all the equity out of their home for lifestyle enhancements, and spending all they had as they earned it. Aside from helping them manage the little they had, there wasn't much I could do for them aside from suggesting they get some help from their children. Get to work on this, and keep this from being your future.

REALITY CHECK: Look around at your life. What are you spending money on that is temporary (clothing, meals out, vacations) and is making it hard for you to save? Will that steak you ate last week seem like money well spent if you have to borrow to send the kids to college or have nothing saved for retirement? Hindsight is 20/20, but when looking at a possible purchase, ask yourself if this is something that will likely end up in the donation pile. Stop and think about your future wants and needs.

Would this money be much better put to work in a savings or investment account? Don't discount small additions over the long haul. Interest doesn't just compound against you. When it's money sitting in your account, it compounds for you.

GunkBuster's Notebook: The Cost of Funding Your Dreams

If you're not convinced that you need a savings plan in place, you probably haven't thought about what you want the future to look like and what things really cost. Most long-term financial goals come with hefty price tags. Here are some estimated costs to consider:

- √ The initial cost of purchasing a house (aside from your monthly mortgage) will be $20,000 to $30,000 once you factor in the down payment, closing costs, and moving expenses. This figure could be higher if you are planning to purchase a house in a more expensive area or one that requires renovation.
- √ Home renovation costs could be anywhere upwards of $10,000 to $20,000 for an average kitchen and $5,000 to $8,000 for an average bathroom. A basement renovation could be $20,000 to $30,000, depending on what you decide you want. A new roof could be $5,000 to $10,000. Cheaper renovations, such as carpet and paint, also bring value to a home but still require substantial costs.
- √ A dream vacation for two weeks in a tropical location or a trip to Europe could cost you $6,000 to $10,000 for a family of 4 ($2,500 for airfare, $2,000 for hotels for 10 nights, and a minimum of $1,500 for meals and other expenses). More modest vacations can be had for much less, but it is important to know what to expect and plan for it. A cottage in Wisconsin can cost $1,000 for the week if you count in cheese and beer.
- √ Purchasing a new car could cost $25,000 to $40,000 or more. If you have your heart set on a luxury model with all of the latest safety features and other gadgets, your total will be quite a bit heftier. A later model used car in good shape will be less, but still in the $10,000 range.

√ Raising children is an expensive proposition. Statistics show it costs as much as $250,000, but those numbers are found by a complicated method that never made much sense to me. To keep it simple, think of it this way. You will provide every need for these hungry little mouths until they can provide for themselves. Clothing, food (my daughter could eat her weight every day in steak, if she was able), sports uniforms, entertainment, school costs, medical expenses, drivers-ed fees (a harrowing time for all parents), college—there is a never-ending line of expenses and endless hands held out to be paid. They're worth it, don't get me wrong, but it does get expensive almost immediately, and if you are not prepared, it can be forever a frustrating scramble to keep up.

√ Sending a son or daughter to college could cost you as little (!!!) as $40,000 for a state funded four-year degree and as much as $160,000 for a private college. In recent years, college tuition has been rising faster than inflation. If this trend continues, you could need much more than you think to fund your child's education.

√ A retirement nest egg could require you to sock away as much as $1,000,000. With life expectancies rising and Social Security at risk, you'll need to take more control over your retirement. Thank goodness compound interest is working *for* you in these circumstances. (We'll go into this in much more detail later in the chapter.)

Fortunately, you won't need to fund all of these activities today. Unfortunately, you will need to factor in inflation as you start to design and fund your savings plans. Even with the inflation rate as low as 3 percent, you'll need twice as much money in 25 years to match the buying power you have today.

Set Aside a Portion of All You Earn

This is a concept called "Pay Yourself First." Say for a moment that you are getting your first full-time job. Out of your check, you put aside money in savings, the company 401(k) plan, and possibly other investments. With what's left, you figure out what your lifestyle will look like. You don't get the bigger apartment before knowing how much you need to put away for the future, and saving becomes as second nature to you as paying off your credit cards in full every month. If you have children, you need to start immediately saving for their college education. When you are finally an empty-nester and looking at retirement, you can sleep well and soundly, knowing you will be financially solvent in your later years, beholden to no one. Just think how good you'll feel being able to jump on a plane to Bermuda at a moment's notice for the really exciting Bingo games when the mood strikes.

Even if you didn't start saving with your first job, it's not too late now. Although it may include some lifestyle changes on your part, and some degunking initially if you are gunked up, saving isn't out of line for anyone, and paying yourself first is the best way to make sure it happens. Imagine the likelihood of saving if you pay all your bills, go grocery shopping, get your hair cut, pick up that suit you've been looking at for a month, and then save what's left. From month to month, and year to year, there will be situations that crop up in your life that will make saving the money you intended very difficult. So, make it easier. Do it first.

REALITY CHECK: Once you get into the habit of paying yourself first, you'll be thrilled at how easy it is. Most of the things we do with our money are based on the habits we pick up over the years. If you get in the habit of saving like this, there will be no question of doing it any other way.

Hide What You Save

It's a good idea to never see the money you're going to save. It can be deposited directly to a savings account and the 401(k) plan and never be part of your net paycheck. Then, it doesn't feel like money you could have spent—it was never in your hand to begin with. If your check is deposited directly into your checking account, you can designate a portion to go to a savings account with very little trouble. That way, it's not sitting in your checking account—it is building up in savings instantly. Good deal. You'll appreciate getting those statements with growing balances a lot more than yet another long cruise in the Caribbean with fruity drinks speared with pineapple and an umbrella. Well, okay, maybe not right away, but hopefully you can see far enough ahead to know that some things will have to be eliminated so that you can meet your long-term goals, and part of that may be trading this year's tan for enough money to pay for medication in later years.

Make Your Savings Automatic

A great reason to use a direct deposit feature is that your savings will be automatic and occur on a regular basis. The less you have to think about it, the less you'll be tempted to spend the money another way. This way, you also won't second-guess yourself and try to rationalize that the money should really be used to update the stereo system in your car. Most people who save a lot of money do it a little at a time. You might think you need to win the lottery or receive an inheritance to have a stash of cash to invest, but in reality, most people do it by bits and pieces—consistently and modestly. The more you automate the process, the less hassle it will be for you. If you set up an automatic system, you can always review it once a quarter and make adjustments as needed.

Make Your Savings Tax Deferred

The importance of tax-deferred savings cannot be overstated. (See more on this topic under "Building Your Retirement Savings" later in this chapter.) Tax deferred means to put money aside (1) before it is taxed or (2) into plans that don't tax you on the investment earnings. If you've been part of your company's 401(k) plan, you know that a pretax contribution (in other words, your contributions to the plan are not taxed as ordinary income) is a great bang for your buck. With these types of tax-deferred savings plans, you will also often get your company's matching contribution, up to a certain percentage—which translates into *free money*. The money will be taxed when you take it out of the plan, but your tax rate will probably be lower at that point in your life and the money will have earned substantial interest over the life of the investment.

TIP:* *If your company has a 401(k) plan, be sure to contribute the maximum amount to take advantage of the company's matching program, if at all possible. For example, if your company will match 50¢ for every dollar you contribute to the 401(k) plan up to 6 percent of your salary, your goal should be to contribute 6 percent of your salary into this plan. If you can only afford 3 percent of your salary to start, that's great as well, but set your goal so that you can reach the maximum to fully take advantage of the match. In this example, the "company match" essentially guarantees you a minimum 50-percent return on your investment! The result is that although you're contributing 6 percent of your salary into this plan, the amount invested for you is in fact 9 percent of your salary. If your plan allows you to invest this money into mutual funds that get an annual return of 8 to 10 percent, that's an even better deal. Where else can you get this kind of investment return? Nowhere! And best of all, it's tax free until you remove the money from the investment vehicle.

Review Your Current Savings

If you are already saving, you're ahead of the game. You'll probably be surprised to learn that in the U.S., the average household only saves about 1 percent of its income. By comparison, Germans save about 10 percent and the French save nearly 16 percent of their income. (Source: Organization for Economic

Cooperation and Development, October 2002.) If you're not sure what to do about your current savings, read on. You should now take a little time to review your savings history. The goal is to see if you are on track for what you are hoping to accomplish. If you have fairly typical goals such as saving for a new child, house, college for your kids, a wedding, and retirement, your saving chart might well look like the one shown in Figure 9-1.

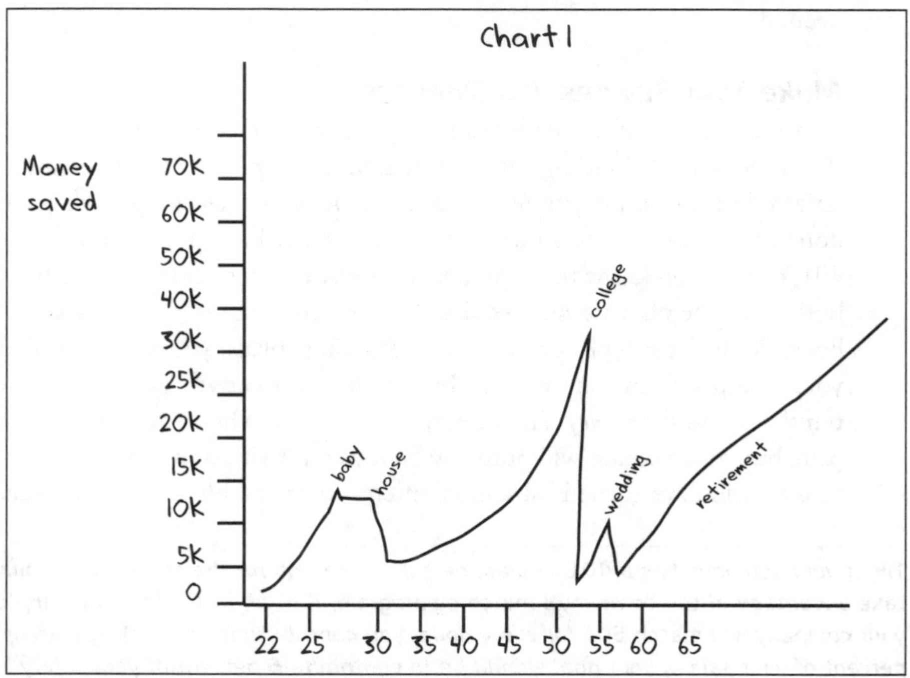

Figure 9-1
The process of saving for different activities as you age.

Notice that the chart shows how a couple has saved for the things they knew would happen and had some money available to meet their goals. After each goal was met, savings were then accumulated to meet the next goal. Although this chart seems to cover the bases, there is a problem lurking. The issue with this otherwise very pretty chart is that retirement is not addressed until all the other goals are met. Then, when the weddings are finished, attention is paid to retirement, which can be less than 10 years away. It will be difficult in that short span (investment wise) to save enough to set up comfortably for retirement, and the magic of compounding interest will not have the time it needs to do its work. The lesson here is that a successful savings plan needs to factor in the element of time.

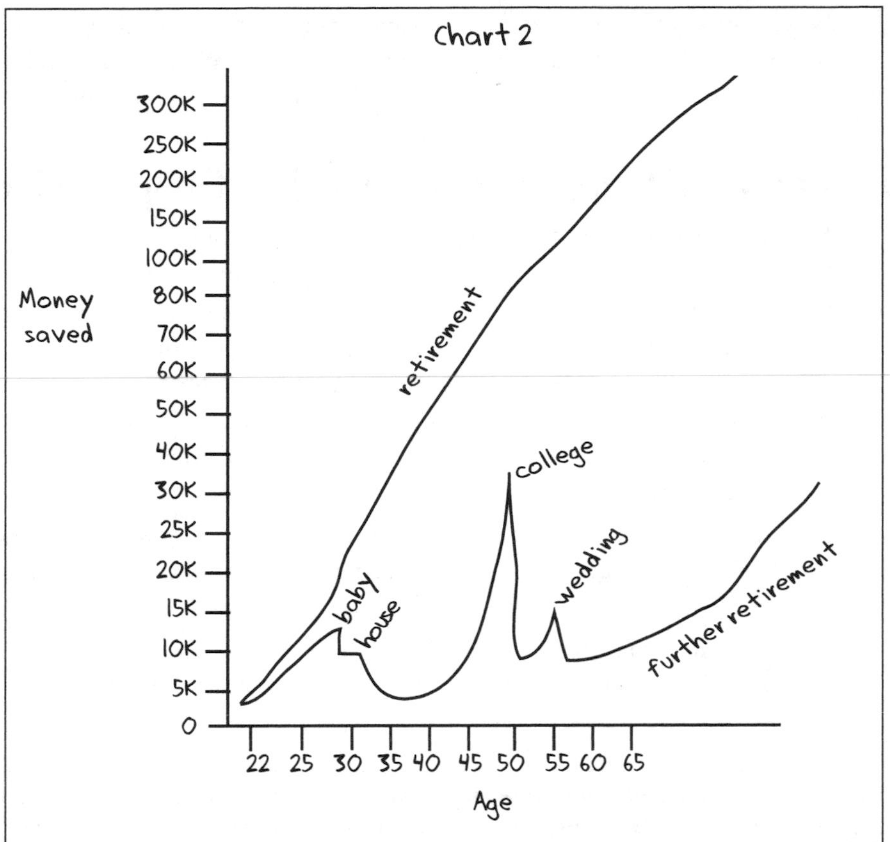

Figure 9-2

Using a concurrent savings strategy will help you balance your savings priorities.

Figure 9-2 shows a much better approach. Notice now how our example couple starts saving for retirement immediately. In fact, retirement is given the top priority early on because more savings will be needed to fund retirement than any other activity, and the earlier you begin putting that money away, the longer it has to compound. Retirement savings are being addressed concurrently with all of the other savings. Look at the differences. The final amount available at retirement is based on how long the money has time to grow. Taking the concurrent savings approach allows you to better balance your priorities with the amount of time you have to save.

There is a tremendous difference, which can make you happy if you're 22 and unhappy if you're 45. You can't make up the earnings you missed, but you can go at it harder now. By saving a larger amount per month now, you can substantially increase the amount you will have to live on at retirement.

Now you know the differences of how your money can accumulate over a period of time. The next question may well be how much to save and how to go about saving for different categories. Stay tuned. It's all coming.

Develop a Plan to Save in the Proper Order

You now should know that saving for retirement should start with your very first job. Determining how to manage the rest of your savings mix might be a bit more confusing. Should you focus on creating an emergency fund, or is it more important to set up that college fund for your children? How much do you need to allocate for other activities, such as saving for a new car or a much needed vacation? Although it's still true that everyone is different, some basic principles will apply to most people. Your savings, in order of necessity, can be looked at this way:

- √ Plan on saving 10 percent or more of all earnings for retirement funding. The first 10 percent is a minimum and can be increased immediately if you are able or as your income increases.
- √ Other than the emergency fund, this 10 percent should stay constant throughout your working life for later life, and other saving is on top of this, not out of this.

TIP: As you are considering how to allocate your retirement savings, here's a simple first strategy you can take. The initial portion of your retirement savings should go into your 401(k) (or equivalent) plan at work to maximize the amount the company is matching. If the company matches 3 percent, you put in 3 percent. You are now doubling your money, right out of the box. Don't pass that one up.

Building Your Retirement Savings

Once you start saving consistently for retirement, you may have questions about the best way to go about choosing your investments. Should you take on a lot of risk and invest in stocks because you're worried about not having enough money when you retire? Or should you play it safe (after all, this is the money you'll need to live on someday) and invest only in cash and bonds? I'll be showing you how to approach investing later in this chapter and how to degunk your current investment strategy (if you have one), but for now we'll focus on some important techniques to help you maximize your retirement funds. As you'll learn, you should develop an investment strategy than you understand, that you can manage, and that matches your tolerance for risk.

Understand Your Tolerance for Risk

A good place to begin is to discover your risk tolerance for long-term investments. There is a test you can take at **www.rce.rutgers.edu/money/riskquiz** that will give you some insight into how chancy you want to get with your money. Keep in mind: just because you have the capacity to be risky doesn't always mean you should be. Balance is a nice thing, but knowing your tolerance for risk is helpful when planning your retirement strategy.

TIP: One way of looking at the risk decision and to help you decide how to invest, no matter your risk-taking ability, is to use your age as the portion of investments in fixed income and 100 minus your age as the portion of investments in stocks. For example, if you are 37, you would place 37 percent of your investments in fixed income vehicles, and 63 percent of your investments in stocks. If you're 65, then 65 percent will be fixed income vehicles and 35 percent will be stocks. The thought here is that stocks will make more money in the long run but are riskier. The closer to retirement you are, the less risk you'll want to take with the money you already have and will soon need.

Create a Retirement Savings Goal That Fits Your Needs

You need a goal when it comes to retirement. Does that phrase sound familiar? To create a realistic goal and plan, you need to try to think about how you live today and then fast-forward to your retirement. Here are some of the questions you'll need to ask yourself:

- √ Do you still expect to have the same lifestyle when you retire? Will your spending patterns be the same or different?
- √ What activities will you want to focus on in your retirement years?
- √ What are you willing to give up if your income declines when you retire?
- √ Are you willing to move to a less expensive house or geographic area?
- √ Are you willing to work part-time when you retire?
- √ Are you willing to delay your retirement to save up extra money and to keep from draining your retirement savings?

Ever present in money matters of all kinds is the need for goals and a point to work toward. Retirement is certainly no exception. One common goal for retirement might be to be able to live in the style you are living now when you retire. That probably means that from all your retirement income sources, including Social Security (we hope), your employer retirement package, traditional IRA or Roth IRA funds, personal savings, and income from other investments, you can replace the cash flow you are now producing to support your lifestyle. It's important to note that you will probably not need to save any further money during retirement, and can hopefully live off of what you have spent all these years accumulating, so the part of your current budgeted funds going to savings can go to living expenses. The Social Security Administration estimates that most people will need five sources of income to draw on when they reach retirement age:

- √ Earned income from employment during retirement years: 36 percent
- √ Income from investments: 23 percent
- √ Income from a company pension: 20 percent
- √ Social Security: 19 percent
- √ Other: 2 percent

Let's apply this to real numbers to see what retirement might look like. Assume that you'll need to have a yearly cash flow of $50,000 in today's dollar. This means that you would need to earn approximately $18,000 from some type of part-time job, your investments would need to provide you with $11,500 of yearly income, and you would need to draw $10,000 from both Social Security and a company pension. If one of these income sources were missing, such as a company pension, you'd need to make up this portion by working more or taking more from your investments.

REALITY CHECK: What this says is twofold: Many people will still need to work during their retirement years to make up some of their lost income, and Social Security will only cover about 20 percent of their income needs. If you build up a savings cushion, you'll be able to skip having to work in your retirement years and also be able to ensure that your total retirement income better matches your current lifestyle expectations.

Know Where Your Money Is Going

It's essential that you consciously decide and know where your money is going. If you invest a dollar, what happens to it? For many of us, this dollar just seems to disappear into investment heaven, and what happens to it after that is for the more investment-minded to know and for us to try to discern from the incomprehensible investment statements we receive and put into a shoe box without opening. Starting now, make sure you can read your investment statement when it comes. You also want to be able to track the deposits and withdrawals as they happen. If the statement seems to be written in hieroglyphics, get someone from the investment company to explain it to you. If they can't or won't, ask their boss to explain it to you. If the investment is so confusing you can't understand it after making some inquiries, you should find one that you feel more comfortable with and can fully understand.

Fine-Tune the Retirement Plans You Have

Retirement accounts come in all types of flavors: 401(k) plans, SIMPLE (small business IRAs, traditional IRAs, Roth IRAs, and SEP-IRAs if you have a business, Keogh plans, company-sponsored pension plans, not-for-profit sponsored annuity plans, and deferred composition plans. To take control of your retirement planning and savings, you need to take the time to understand what you currently have and how the plans are set up. (If you need help understanding the jargon and basic retirement plans, see the GunkBuster's Notebook in this section.) There are two major steps you need to take to get a grasp on what you have:

1. Look at your company-sponsored plans.
2. List and evaluate any personal retirement accounts.

Employer-Sponsored Plans

The first thing to investigate is any employer-sponsored pension that you might have. You'll want to determine if your pension is part of a defined benefit plan or a defined contribution plan:

√ A defined benefit plan is one where you work at an organization for a certain number of years, your employer (and possibly you) put money into the plan for the time you work there, and when you reach retirement age, you receive a pension. The amount of the pension is usually dependent on how much you made in the last four years you worked for the company. You cannot change how the money is invested or what funds to invest in—it is up to the administrators of the plan to make enough money to pay the retired employees what they are due. This type of plan, although still available in some large company, government, and municipal settings, is becoming less common.

√ Much more common is the defined contribution plan. 401(k) and 403(b) plans are examples of defined contribution plans. Here, your employer may match a portion of what you put in to the plan, and you can decide for yourself how much more to invest, up to a certain amount. These plans are based on investing in mutual funds, and a plan may have as few as 5 or as many as 50 funds from which the employee chooses. This is a good place to put your risk-taking information to use.

If you find that you don't have much money saved in a pension plan, you'll want to direct your savings to a company-sponsored plan as soon as possible. The first benefit is that you will get an immediate tax break for the money that you contribute to the plan. The second benefit is that you may receive "free" money toward your investment if your company has a matching program, and you become vested.

EXAMPLE: Assume you make $50,000 per year and that the company you work for has a matching program where they will contribute fifty cents for every dollar you contribute, up to a prescribed amount. If you contributed $8,000 one year, the income that you would pay taxes on would be $42,000. Your company would contribute $4000 to your retirement account, making the yearly contribution $12,000, which would begin compounding interest immediately. Not only would you now have $12,000 in your retirement account making tax deferred money, but you would save $1,600 to $2,400 in taxes. Is this a smart financial move or what?

Your Personal Retirement Plans

After you put what you can into your employee-sponsored plan, your next investment dollars should go to either a Roth IRA or a traditional IRA account. The Roth IRA is similar to a traditional IRA, but the money placed in it is after-tax income. Here is the good part about the Roth IRA: as long as the money has been in the account for five years and you are 59½ years old when you withdraw it, there is no tax on any of the money in the account. Within those boundaries, the money and all the earnings are tax exempt. Way cool. There are limits as to how much per year you can put in a Roth account, and you must earn less than $95,000 as a single person and $150,000 as a couple to be eligible to open one, but if you can, this is a good place to grow money.

Traditional IRAs

A traditional IRA works for those in the higher tax brackets, but this account is tax deferred, not tax exempt. The money that fills an IRA is pretax earnings (subject to limitations), so you don't pay tax on it when it goes in, but you do pay tax on the contributions and the earnings when you withdraw them at retirement, again, at whatever tax rate you are in at that time. As mentioned, there are harsh penalties if you withdraw the money early (with a few oddball exceptions), but it is a nice deduction on the front end and can help your money grow more quickly without being taxed initially.

The current limits on tax-deductible IRA contributions are as follows:

YEAR	AGE 49 & BELOW	AGE 50 & ABOVE
2002–2004	$3,000	$3,500
2005	$4,000	$4,500
2006–2007	$4,000	$5,000
2008	$5,000	$6,000

Investment Vehicles for Retirement

When you hear the fancy term "investment vehicle," what's being referred to is where your money is being invested. *Where* you invest your money is as important as *how much* you invest. As you probably know, there are oodles of mutual funds, stocks, and bonds to buy. I suggest keeping them all within your grasp and not in far-flung places—here a CD, there a stock, everywhere a bond, bond.

***TIP:* It is your responsibility—because it's your money, after all—to educate yourself about investment options. Even though you may not be good with these concepts, it's time to learn. There are many good investment books out there that can help novice investors further understand all types of investments. Check with a friend or your investment person on which book to buy and get educated on what is happening to your money.**

Although it doesn't release you from the responsibility of understanding your investments, an investment advisor house can handle all of your investments for you. Make certain that it is insured by the Securities Insurance Protection Corporation (SIPC) and that it handles the types of funds in which you want to invest. SIPC doesn't protect you against making bad investment choices, but it does protect you against someone making off with your money. Another plus to this strategy is you will have someone at the other end of the phone or e-mail that can answer your questions about all of your investments. The larger companies (Vanguard is one example) are a good place to start checking. Keep in mind that if someone will be helping you handle your account, it will cost you something. Thoroughly check out all of the charges, commissions, and service fees before getting involved with any investment firm.

***TIP:* In the investment world, high-risk equals stock investment, and low-risk equals fixed income vehicles, including CDs, bonds, and money market funds. There is usually no commission involved in working within these funds, so you can make changes without incurring charges, and there is someone in the company you can speak to if you need more information on a particular fund. When you retire, you get the money you put in and the earnings, taxed at whatever rate you are being charged when you remove the money from the fund.**

GunkBuster's Notebook: Dealing with All of the Retirement Plan Jargon

Keeping track of all the retirement plan jargon and rules can make you want to go do something more fun, like wash windows. It seems that every year something new comes along that we need to understand. Here is just some of the terminology you'll see frequently:

- √ Traditional IRA: An individual retirement arrangement, contributions to which may or may not be deductible depending on the taxpayer's modified adjusted gross income and whether they are covered under an employer-sponsored retirement plan. Earnings within a traditional IRA grow tax deferred. Distributions from a traditional IRA are taxable, except to the extent they represent nondeductible contributions.
- √ Roth IRA: Contributions to Roth IRAs, which were introduced in 1998, are not deductible. Earnings grow tax free and qualified withdrawals are also tax free.
- √ SEP-IRA: An arrangement whereby an employer makes contributions to an employee's individual retirement account (IRA) or a self-employed person contributes to his own plan.
- √ Rollover IRA: The conversion of an employer distribution—such as an employee's 401(k) plan—or an existing IRA to another IRA without taxable consequences. This action must take place within 60 days of receiving the distribution.

Source: H&R Block.

Create an Emergency Fund

Everyone, as you know from previous chapters, needs an emergency fund. After putting the matched money amount into your 401(k), the next step in building your savings should be creating a fund that would cover from three to six months of your monthly expenditures. Hopefully, you have some of this already in place from instruction in previous chapters. Then, if someone in your household gets hurt and can't work, if you get caught up in a restructuring that erases you off the org chart, or if a tree falls through the roof, you are covered for some stretch of time without the wolves howling at your door. If you take money out of the emergency fund at any point, you must put the money back before other saving or investing can be done. That means, if you're saving for a house and you suddenly need to take $1,000 out of your emergency fund, the money in your emergency fund needs to be replaced before adding more money to your down payment fund. When your emergency fund is complete, the rest of your first 10 percent in savings can go directly to investing in your retirement.

Home and Children

Next in the pecking order would be saving for a home or a child, if you choose to have either one. If you are saving for a home, the time it takes to get a down payment together will directly relate to the percentage at which you're saving. If you make $50,000 per year and need $10,000 to put down on a home, at a possible 6-percent savings per year, it will take you 3.33 years to save enough to go house shopping. If you increase your house savings to 7 percent (out of your monthly expenditures, not by reducing your retirement savings), it will take 34.2 months—less than 3 years. The house down payment will cause a large withdrawal of the accrued savings, and then it's time to start over.

Saving for children is a different kettle of Legos. You can save for what you know will be needed, but these bundles of love are literal money eaters until sometime in their 20s, and it can't all be planned. As I have two big bundles myself (ages 17 and 22), I know this is a continuous stream of outgoing money and not an amount you can save before they're born. There will be an immediate need to change your monthly expenditures sheet to account for diapers, food, babysitting (only if you want to stay sane), and soccer equipment, so the ongoing expenses may be more of an issue than the cost of the crib and doctor. It is imperative to plan for these higher costs and for the time needed for a parent to be off work. The good news here is you still have your emergency fund and retirement is still building up in the background.

Another child-related expense is adoption, which currently runs anywhere from $5,000-25,000 in the U.S., depending on which agency you use. Luckily, many employers offer benefits to individuals who adopt children, often called Flexible Spending Accounts (FSAs), which allow you to put aside pre-tax dollars to pay for such expenses.

Higher Education

Once you're in your home and have your children, it's time to begin saving for college. Keep in mind that college is a personal and family decision and some families are not able to pay for a college education for their children. There are grants, scholarships, and loan opportunities that can help a child get to college if the family is unable or unwilling to help.

As with most savings plans, starting early is a big help. With the cost of college rising much faster than the cost of inflation, the sky can be the limit when trying to educate a child. Decisions when the time comes on where to attend need to be made as any other financial decisions are made—what is the actual need, how much money is available, and what are the options? For those with less to spend, community college can get your first two years of required courses out of the way for a fraction of what a state school would cost, and finishing part-time so as not to accumulate debt is a great option for those without resources set aside. A community college can be about a third the cost of a state school, but they usually offer only a two-year degree.

To find out what you may need for a four-year degree, a good first step is to contact one of your state schools and get some numbers from them on the costs of tuition, room and board, and books. Virtually all colleges and universities have Web sites with this information readily available. If you decide on a private school, you can at least double this number, and the more illustrious the school, the more times you can double it. For undergraduate work, Harvard's rate for one year of education in the 2004–05 school year was $39,880. Books are extra.

TIP: 529 Plans. If a parent chooses to help pay for a child's education, the government is an actual help here. There is an investment vehicle called the 529 Plan, which is run by individual states as a section of the Internal Revenue code and is designed for the sole purpose of encouraging saving for higher education. After-tax dollars (money you have already paid tax on) are invested in the plan, which is somewhat similar to a Roth IRA account, and when the money is taken out to pay for higher education, the money and its earnings are not taxed. This is a good deal. Some states offer a tax incentive for investing in their state plans. As well, if the child for whom the account is opened decides instead to go into professional snowboarding, the money can be transferred to another child, back to the parents, or to the child's children, as long as it is used for higher education of some type and the new beneficiary is related to the previous one. If the money is taken out for any other purpose, tax rules and penalties similar to those involved in prematurely removing money from an IRA would apply.

If your child gets a scholarship and doesn't need the money you have saved, you have a couple of options. You can take out of the account an amount of money that is equal to the scholarship, and the earnings on that portion of money will be taxed at your regular income rate, which works out the same as it would if the money was in a savings or money market account. The money can be left in the account in case there is more schooling on the horizon for this child, or it can be transferred to a relative of the child. You can empty the account, but that will put you in the line of fire for the penalties and taxes on the entire amount.

You can and should prepare for your child's education. Putting money away when they're in diapers is a good way to start, and making use of the government's attempt to help the process is a good way to continue. If your child isn't in diapers anymore, you can still make inroads in saving for college.

It won't happen overnight, but it will help when the time comes to pack them off to college with tears and a semester's supply of Easy Mac.

Take Advantage of the Power of Investing

Now that you've learned how to degunk your savings, it's time to focus on the investment side of things. The two activities are separated in this chapter because it is important to first focus on setting priorities for the different areas that necessitate savings: retirement, emergency fund, and education. This approach helps you plan for your goals instead of focusing only on how to invest your money. Many people I've worked with have gunked up investment programs because they spend their time changing their investments around and worrying daily about minute changes. They forget that their long-term goals are to keep looking for ways to add to their savings, both long and short-term.

TIP:* *Your savings are the fuel that drives your investment program, but they make up only half of the equation. The other important ingredient is time. The more time you have, the more opportunity your investments will have to make money. Don't procrastinate when it comes to starting your investments.

Any successful investment program requires you to set goals, set aside assets (usually making some type of sacrifice), assess your level of risk-taking, and select investment vehicles that are right for you. The advice that I'll be providing to degunk your current situation involves the following six-point plan:

1. Determine what your savings goals are.
2. Estimate how much money you'll need to reach your goals.
3. Determine how much time you have.
4. Determine your tolerance for risk.
5. Build a investment portfolio that meets your needs.
6. Review your investments every six months and rebalance your portfolio when necessary.

This may seem like a lot of work, but we've discussed some of these steps already. Earlier in this chapter you learned how to create goals for your savings and estimate how much money you'll need to reach them. We can now focus on using time wisely, building an investment portfolio (or degunking the one you currently have), and reviewing and fine-tuning your portfolio as necessary.

GunkBuster's Notebook: The Three Investing Fundamentals You Never Want to Forget!

While many people think that investing is too complicated or that the stock market is only for sophisticated Wall Street types, I'm here to tell you that it's not beyond your grasp! There are three fundamental ideas that, if you understand them, will work to your advantage:

- √ Time is on your side. Time can indeed heal most investment mistakes.
- √ Don't underestimate the power of compounding. Investment earnings, if left alone, make more and more money over time.
- √ Slow and steady wins the race.

These three ideas are powerful components to your investment life and should help you to start and stay on your investing plan.

Let Time Be Your Number One Asset

There's an old saying about investing: It's time, not timing. This means that even though most people would love to have a crystal ball to tell them which stock to pick to make them an instant millionaire, the millionaire next door is actually the guy who's been saving consistently for 40 years.

I know of a man who did a very good job on his retirement savings. From the day he started his first full-time job, he put aside the maximum amount he could toward his company's 401(k) plan. The company only matched to certain percentage but allowed employees to add additional funds up to a ceiling amount per year. As this friend continued his working career, he based his lifestyle around what was left from his check after savings and investing, not by what he made. As he reaches retirement, he looks back and sees that the investment strategy he was taught from his father, which was to save early and live moderately, kept him in good stead. He lived comfortably, put his children through college, took some vacations, and will have enough in retirement to continue to live in the manner to which he and his wife are accustomed. It wasn't that this man made millions in his working years—the key is that he lived according to the principles he set forth early in his working career and stuck by them.

What a legacy from this man's father! What can we, as parents, hand down to our children in financial matters? What do we want them to know? My friend has given this treasure of information to his children as his father did for him.

Whether they choose to follow it is their choice, but I believe part of our responsibility to our children is to help them manage the world of finances in a way that will benefit them long term and model for them moderation and saving as part of that equation. If we don't do this, where will that information come from for our kids? The media? Movies? Their friends? Just like other areas of principle, this one needs to come from us, the parents. Teach them well. They, like my friend, will be grateful later.

The earlier you put yourself on a savings plan, the better off you'll be. If you use the advice given here—put it away and wait—you will be assured to have money set aside for your future goals and retirement.

The Power of Compounding

You've probably heard this before, but the importance of compound interest is an enormously powerful concept. Inflation can erode the buying power of your earnings. With banks offering 2 percent or less on most savings accounts and inflation running at 3 percent per year, you won't make any money leaving your savings in your local bank.

> **EXAMPLE:** Let's say you have $5,000 in your bank account and decide to put it into an investment with an 8-percent annual return. During the first year, you will earn $400 on your investment, giving you a total of $5,400. The second year would deliver another $432, or 8 percent on both the original $5,000 and the $400 gain. Your two-year total is now $5,832. By comparison, if you had put that money into a bank savings account drawing 2 percent a year, you'd only have $5,202. The longer you leave your money in the account without making withdrawals, the faster it will grow. By year 10, your money would be worth around $10,800. If you added $1,000 to that account every year, starting with year 2, the total would be over $24,000 in that same 10-year period! All you have to do is (1) contribute regularly and (2) leave it there.

Slow and Steady

If your finances are gunked up, it's probably hard to conceive of having hundreds of thousands of dollars in savings and investments. There is a lesson here: don't look at the top of the mountain—focus on taking one step up at a time. Remember once again that slow and steady wins the race. Put yourself on a plan. Commit to your goals. Don't let impulse spending, lack of planning, or unforeseen expenses destroy your dreams. Plan for your future. Take your financial life seriously. With a good attitude, and a reasonable plan, your nest egg will hatch chicks that will lay more eggs. That's either an example of compound interest or an example of how to make an omelet. Either way, you win.

Building Your Investment Portfolio

As you begin to build your investment portfolio or degunk the one you currently have, let these be your guiding principles:

- √ Invest only in things that you understand.
- √ Take a long-term view with anything that involves a significant amount of risk.
- √ Focus on some proven asset classes (stocks, bonds, income producing real estate, and cash) and avoid trendy or unproven investments.
- √ Diversify (choose an asset allocation strategy) to reduce risk while you maximize your return.

Don't invest in something just because you hear about it on the news, and don't rush into that hot new mutual fund you read about in the doctor's office waiting room. Do your own research and look for investments that have been around and have proven themselves over time. You worked much too hard to earn your money, degunk your finances, and put savings aside to throw it all away in a risky investment you don't know much about.

Select an Asset Allocation Strategy

Before plunging into any type of investment (stocks, mutual funds, bonds, money market account), you should take the time to think about how you want to allocate your money. This allocation will have a lot to do with how much time you have to invest and how much risk you feel comfortable taking. If you have a lot of time, you can take on more risk. You'll be using the following types of investments to build your allocation mix:

- √ Stocks or mutual funds. These investments provide the highest return over a long term period (historically), but they also involve the greatest amount of risk. Equity mutual funds are less risky than individual stocks because they typically invest in many different types of stocks.
- √ Bonds, CDs, or bond mutual funds—These investments provide moderate returns and moderate risk as compared to stocks.
- √ Cash. Your lowest returning option but the least risky as well.

When it comes to selecting an allocation, there is no one-size-fits-all solution. As a starting point, use the chart shown in Figure 9-3 to select a strategy that matches with your needs. The examples shown on the left are considered conservative and designed for short-term investments. Slide all the way over to the right and you'll find an allocation that is for someone who has a lot of time to invest and can afford to take on a lot of risk. By taking on more risk, your return could be much higher, but you need to make sure that you can invest for a longer period of time.

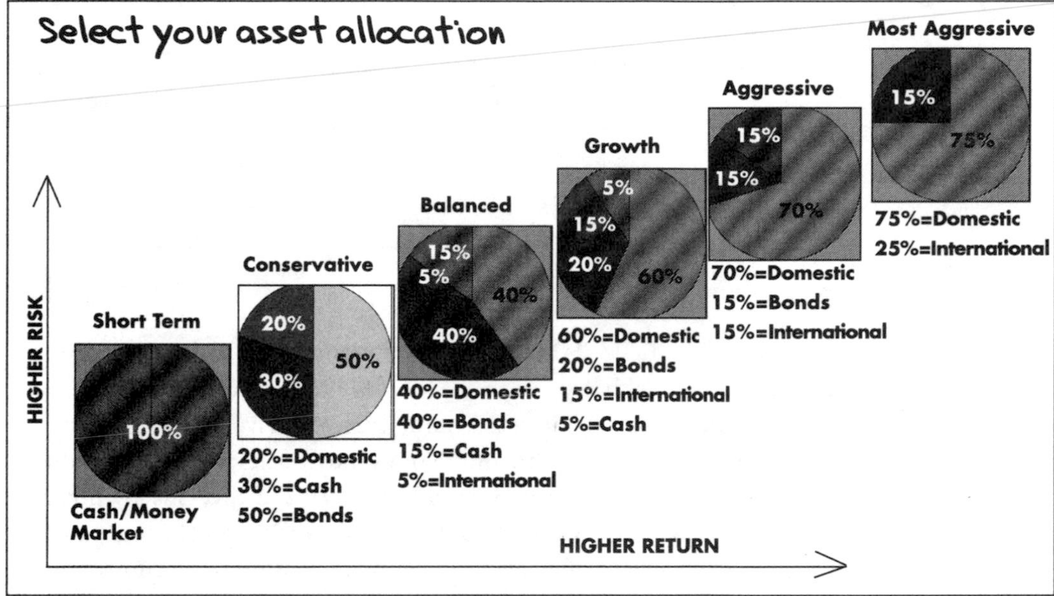

Figure 9-3
Sample portfolios to help you determine an allocation mix for your investments.

If you already have some investments in place, I suggest that you review your investments and determine how your assets are currently allocated. This is an important step, especially if you are planning to invest new money. It's very easy for our investments to get gunked up and out of balance over time.

The Importance of Diversification

You've already learned about the first way to diversify your investments: select an allocation that includes stocks, bonds, and cash. Taking this a little further, you can diversify a little more by selecting investments for each asset class. Table 9-1 lists some of the assets that you can choose from to help you diversify further.

Table 9-1 Assets classes and options available for diversification.

Asset Class	Options	Risk Level
Cash	Money Market	Low
	Bank account	
	Short-term CDs	
	Long-term CDs	
Stocks/Mutual Funds	Individual U.S. stock (large company)	Medium to high
	Individual U.S. stock (small company)	High
	Large U.S. stocks mutual fund	Medium to high
	Small U.S. stocks mutual fund	High
	International stocks mutual fund	Medium to high
Bonds	Municipal bonds	Low
	Corporate bonds	Low to medium
	U.S. Government bonds	Low

The options listed in Table 9-1 aren't exhaustive. There are many more to choose from. The idea is that you should look for investments that help you spread out your risk. For example, let's assume that you have $10,000 to invest and you decide to put 60 percent of your savings into stocks and equity mutual funds. This gives you $6,000 that you would then want to diversify by investing in vehicles such as mutual funds holding stocks of large U.S. companies, mutual funds holding stocks of small U.S. companies, and mutual funds holding stocks of international companies. Your allocation might look something like this:

- √ Investment: $6,000
- √ 50 percent ($3,000): Large company mutual fund
- √ 25 percent ($1,500): Small company mutual fund
- √ 25 percent ($1,500): International mutual fund

Although this full amount is invested in stocks, you would have some diversification because your investment would be in different types and sizes of companies.

Diversifying in this fashion is important because diversified portfolios tend to provide less volatile returns over the long term. This is a fancy way of saving that you can make more money and lower your risk all at the same time. That would be the goal, would it not?

***TIP:** If all this talk of diversification makes your head spin and you are worried about having to track all of your investments, you might want to investigate some of the "all-in-one" mutual funds that are provided by successful money management companies such as Vanguard, Fidelity, and Charles Schwab. These all-in-one funds do the diversification work for you and have low fees, which means more of your investment dollars will end up in your pocket and not theirs.*

Make Investing Automatic and Don't Time the Market

One of the best ways to keep your investments from getting gunked up is to set up an automatic investing plan. You can do this on a monthly or quarterly basis. Instead of trying to time the market, put in money on a regular basis. This approach works best if you set up an automatic investing plan, forget all about it, and then review your statements when they come in for the correct deposit information. This technique of putting in money on a regular basis is called *dollar-cost averaging.* Studies have shown that investing this way produces the best results for investors over the long run.

It is important when learning about investing to understand that a little knowledge can be a dangerous thing. Learning about your investments may well give you the idea that you can do it much better yourself and save the fees and commissions that you're paying an investment company.

STORY: Talking to another budget counselor recently netted the very sad story of a man who, upon retirement, did what he had always wanted to do—took out all his investment money from the vehicles where it had sat for 40 years making money for him and began managing it himself. Within one short year, he had cut his money in half, and in trying to make it back quickly, lost the rest. This man and his wife, both in their 60s , had to go back to work just to be able to make their mortgage payment, and they recently had to sell their home and downsize considerably. What heartbreak this decision caused!

This doesn't mean no one should handle their own investments, but it does mean that good counsel and help from people who do this for a living is essential if you aren't experienced. Most importantly, if you want to learn to play in this sandbox, don't risk your financial security to do it. Set a small amount aside, and work it for a few years to see how you do.

Monitoring and Fine-Tuning Your Portfolio

I wish I could tell you that all of your work will be done once you figure out how you should allocate your investments and send your checks off. Investing is a dynamic activity because you are investing in companies that are constantly changing. For proof, turn on the financial news. One week your favorite company announces record profits and the next week the board of directors has fired the CEO because he's spending too much time exploring the country in the company jet. Not only does the market change, but your needs and goals are constantly changing also.

To keep your plan healthy, you should review it at least once every six months (or when you have a life-changing event). When you review your plan, you should check the following:

- √ How are your investments performing overall? (If you are having a down period, don't be too fast on the trigger and make a change. Just take a note. Compare your investment results to the overall market.)
- √ Is your allocation getting out of balance because some of your investments have significantly outperformed others?
- √ Do you have an investment that has become too risky to hold?
- √ Do you need to add more money to your investments than you were planning because you overestimated how your investments would perform?

GunkBuster's Notebook: Consolidating Your Assets

After you have been investing for a while, it's easy to get gunked up by overdiversifying and opening up too many accounts. You might have money invested in IRAs, SEP-IRAs, and after-tax invested mutual funds. Each quarter finds you swimming in investment statements. Having so many different funds and accounts can make it difficult to track what is really going on. If you have statements coming at you from all directions, you should consider consolidating your investments. To consolidate, you can open an "all-in-one" account at one of the larger financial management companies such as Vanguard, Fidelity, or Charles Schwab. These accounts are easy to set up and allow you to move all of your investments over, often with little or no cost. This way you'll get one statement that will typically show you at a glance the asset mix you have chosen with all of your funds. Having a single road map can help you stay organized and keep your level of understanding where it should be.

Summing Up

In this chapter, you learned how to create a savings plan with the principle of "pay yourself first." You learned how to discipline yourself to set aside a portion of everything you earn and how to review and fine-tune your current savings strategy so that you know how to balance your priorities. I showed you how to save in the correct order. You also learned how to evaluate investment risk and how to develop a plan that will maximize the money you have to save for your retirement.

This is a good start, but by no means is it an exhaustive explanation of how savings and investments work. It's up to you to further your education about investment options. Just as you wouldn't buy a used car without thoroughly investigating its history, neither should you blindly assume that investments will take care of themselves.

The hugely important point is to *save*—and to start as soon as possible. Depending on your level of financial gunk, it may take some time before you are in shape to invest more than your minimum level. Keep handy the thought that the money you save today will fix the furnace when it spews water all over the basement, buy a stroller for your new baby, send that same baby to college, and feed you when you're old. This is reason enough to change your habits today to make that happen. Learn enough to understand where your money is going and what it does when it gets there. It doesn't have to be complicated, and it doesn't have to be horrible. It just has to happen, and the sooner you start, the more you can plan your future instead of letting your future simply happen to you.

Summing Up

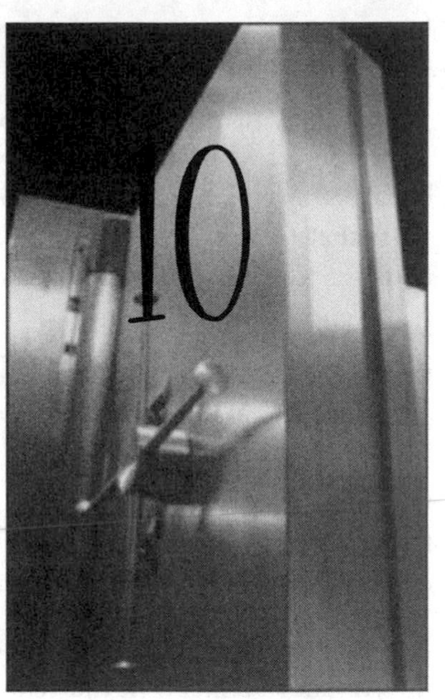

Degunking Your Credit Report

Degunking Checklist:

√ Learn about credit reports.

√ Understand what is on your credit report.

√ Obtain copies of your credit report.

√ Learn how to read and interpret your credit report.

√ Report errors on your credit report promptly and in writing.

√ Discover the five most important pieces of information that affect your FICO score.

√ Find out about the four easiest ways to improve your credit score.

√ Discover how negotiating with a lender can improve your score.

√ Learn how your spouse, ex-spouse, and children can affect your rating.

Perhaps you have a recollection of a teacher standing over you, shaking a finger in your face and spewing out that dreaded threat, "If you don't behave, this will go on your *permanent record!*" Even if you didn't know exactly what that meant, it was ominous, wasn't it? A permanent record! Something that lasts forever and comes back to haunt you in later life, even if you've been really good for a long time.

For adults, the closest thing we have to compare with this fear is when we look at our first credit report. We discover that this report has recorded every financial move we've made since our first credit transaction. It haunts us with the reminder of when we misbehaved with our credit lines, and it never seems to forget anything. Your credit report can have items on it that go back 20 years, even though the accounts listed have been closed for almost that long.

For many people, their credit report is exciting reading—right up there with investment statements in the "Gosh, I can't wait to read that!" category. Unlike your investment statements, however, this little puppy can either help or hurt you in getting a mortgage, can raise or lower your interest rate on a car purchase, can be a wealth of information about credit accounts that you haven't used for years, and can be a good indicator of identity theft. So, even though you probably don't relish the thought of poring through every line of your credit report, it's important that you do so. If you're serious about finding the gunk in your finances, your credit report is an important indicator of where that gunk exists. Remember that if there's gunk in your credit report, that particular gunk is out there in the open, available for any potential creditor to see.

Like it or not, your credit report is on file to be used by anyone who is considering lending you money, and what it says can make the difference between a happy call from the mortgage company or bitter disappointment in the form of higher interest rates, higher fees, or denial of a loan altogether. If you want your credit report to be squeaky clean, you're going to have to do some reading. But don't worry—everything you need to know about credit reports will be explained here. At the end of this chapter, you'll know how to degunk your credit report so that your financial records are reflected in the best possible light. Another important benefit of this chapter is that you'll learn how to go through your credit report and take action to improve your credit score.

What Is a Credit Report?

A credit report is a standardized financial summary that is designed to help lenders decide if you are likely to pay them back on time if they loan you money. Credit reporting agencies have developed some standard measures of credit worthiness. Some of these standard indicators are payment history (whether you pay bills on time), default history (if you've ever defaulted on a loan), number of credit accounts you have open, percentage of available credit that you use, and the types of credit that you are currently using. Compiled all together, this data constitutes your credit report. Banks and other lending institutions see your credit history as the best indicator of whether you are creditworthy. Like it or not, this report is a snapshot of your credit risk at any particular time.

When you go in to buy or lease a new car, for example, and the salesman asks if he can pull your credit report, he is asking if his company can access all available data about your financial history. If you agree, that dealership will access your credit report and look at your creditworthiness. If you don't agree, you will either need to pay cash for your car or get a loan elsewhere (pay cash, pay cash!). If the salesman comes back in a few minutes with a smile on his face, that's a good indication that you probably have a high credit score and are a good credit risk. You can bet that he'll be flexible on his credit terms to get you into that new car. If, on the other hand, he comes back with a serious, worried look on his face, that may mean bad news for you: a higher interest rate on your car loan or possibly being denied a loan altogether. The point here is that a good credit score will determine what you pay for credit and whether you're eligible for credit at all.

CAUTION:* *Your credit report is not only used by those to whom you give permission. More and more, your credit report is being accessed by others, including potential employers, landlords, utility companies, insurance companies, and even government agencies. Your credit report is not private information, and many companies are now using credit reports to weed out potential employees or customers. Your car insurance company, for example, may look at your credit report along with your Motor Vehicle Report and determine that you are a high-risk customer because you have a low credit score. Your insurance rates would be higher than someone having the same driving record, but better credit. People in the military may even find that their security clearance is affected by their credit report.

What a Credit Score Does

Credit reporting agencies sum up all the financial data on your credit report and come up with a credit score for you—your "grade," at it were. Credit scoring is beneficial to lenders and borrowers alike. It can give a fast, objective measurement of the risk the lender is taking in giving you credit. Imagine trying to decide whether or not to lend someone money just based on their appearances or their promise to pay back the loan. The process would certainly be inconsistent and unfairly biased. The point of a credit score is to provide a level playing field, so regardless of whether you're wearing old jeans or Armani (hopefully bought at T.J. Maxx), if you have a high credit score, that car salesman is going to adore you.

A credit score is designed to be objective and does not take into account race, religion, marital status, or gender. By looking at an applicant's credit score, lenders can focus only on the facts of the borrower's financial health and do not have to count on their "feelings" or "intuition" about a particular individual. Because of this objectivity, loans can be approved much more quickly than in the past, and it is now common for mortgages to be approved in hours instead of weeks. Online availability of credit scores also makes it easier for retail stores and car dealers to make near-instant decisions about credit worthiness. The problem that this produces for you, the consumer, is that you can now leave that dealership within hours with a car that you didn't intend to purchase and perhaps can't afford—along with a newly gunked-up financial situation. Just because your credit score might allow you to borrow doesn't mean you necessarily should. (Check back to Chapter 1 if you need a refresher course on how your finances can get gunked up.)

Your Credit History

Even if you've had past financial problems, your credit report will still be somewhat forgiving. Good recent payment habits will go a long way to clean up a soiled credit report. For example, if you defaulted on a loan last year but cleaned up your act and have made timely payments for at least 12 months, any new potential lender will look favorably on your good (recent) payment history. It won't get you the same good rate as someone with a great history, but it will help. Similarly, if you had a history of good credit two or three years ago but you've recently been making late payments, that will count against you. Remember that credit scores weigh credit problems with positive information, both past and present.

From a lender's perspective, more may go into their decision to extend you credit than your credit history. Most lenders will also ask about earnings and debt ratio before making a decision. Depending on your credit score, your lender will have various programs from which to choose to make credit available to you. Keep in mind, however, that if you have a lower credit score, the programs you are offered will have high interest rates; the better your score, the lower the interest rates and the more willing the lender will be to help you obtain credit. Forgiving your past mistakes isn't the same as forgetting; there are still consequences for past errors, even if credit is now available. That reason alone makes it very important to keep a close eye on your credit score and see to it that it stays as high as possible.

Identity Theft

Identity theft is becoming a huge problem in this country. There is big business in illegally obtaining a person's credit information and then using that information to purchase goods and services. If you're the victim of identity theft, your credit report could be in ruins for years. Therefore, getting your credit report is imperative if you are even slightly suspicions that you have been the victim of this crime. As you'll see later in the chapter (see the section "What Your Credit Report Reports"), your credit report will list all credit that has been reported in your name and accompanying social security number. After reviewing this list, it should be immediately obvious to you if the recent loan for that new Wave Runner was not your doing.

In speaking to my local detectives about identity theft, I learned that the major lasting problem seems to be getting the charges off your credit report. You are, in most cases, not liable for the money borrowed on a loan or charges made on your credit cards, but that doesn't immediately erase the marks on your credit. If the law was broken locally (someone got a loan in your town using your name), the police will investigate. In many cases, however, the problems happen across state lines or even in another country. In that case, the local police there would have to make the arrest (if they found the perpetrator), and the victim (you) would have to go to that location for the court proceedings in order to testify. Since the victim is rarely able or willing to travel at their own expense to do this, identity theft crimes don't rank terribly high on the priority list for police, who probably have criminals to catch who are easier to apprehend and prosecute.

Benefits of a High Credit Score

The most important benefit of high credit scoring is that credit becomes less expensive to the borrowing consumer. If lenders make better choices as to who their borrowers are, there will be fewer defaulted loans, which means less money the lenders have to recoup on the future loans they make. As a very practical result, for instance, mortgage lending rates are lower in the United States than Europe because of the credit reporting information available here, and that affects positively the amount of money available from lenders. Fewer defaulted loans means more money is available to be borrowed at lower interest rates.

If you have a high credit score, what this indicates is that you pay your bills on time and you use your credit in a reasonable manner. I've seen lots of clients, as well, with high credit scores who were in serious debt, but because they kept making timely payments, the credit reporting agencies still considered them a good credit risk. The bad news for these clients—and they *knew* it—was that their good credit score didn't reflect the impending crisis that their credit gunk was creating for them. Sooner or later, if you keep making minimum payments and increasing your credit lines, your financial situation will come crashing down around you. (See more about this in the section in Chapter 6 called "Stop Adding to Your Debt.") If you have a good credit score, work to keep it.

What Your Credit Report Reports

Your credit report is a detailed credit history, but only as it has been reported by your lenders. It's possible that some details of your history aren't even on your report or that old information or incorrect information is clouding your credit picture. What should appear on your credit report is what kind of credit you have, the length of time various accounts have been opened, and (most important to a lender) if your bills have been paid on time. Your report also details the amount of credit you've used over the years and whether you are now looking for new sources of credit. All of these factors give your banker a much more complete view of your credit habits.

***CAUTION:** Keep in mind that every time you let a car salesman "pull your credit report," it will show up as an "inquiry" on your report. If you end up applying for a mortgage and the lender sees that you've had six or seven car dealerships inquire about your credit in the last month, they may ask for an explanation or, worse, scrutinize your credit even more closely. The lesson here is to **be very cautious about who you allow to review your credit report** as you may have to explain these inquiries when it comes time to apply for an important loan. Don't let anyone pull your credit report until you are sure that whatever loan you are considering is, in your mind, a done deal. As you will see later in the chapter, you can get your own credit report at no charge, so there is no need to have someone pull it in order for you to see it. By the time you are ready to make a purchase, you should be reasonably sure your credit is good enough and that you can well afford what you are trying to buy.*

Get Three Credit Reports

There are three major credit reporting agencies: Equifax, Experian, and TransUnion. It is a good idea to get a report from all three of them once a year. Due to a recent law, you are entitled to one free report per year from each reporting agency. This is a huge new bonus for consumers, who can now easily check their report for mistakes. The free reports don't provide you with a credit score, only the information listed on your credit report. This is incredibly helpful. Left unchecked, a plethora of errors on a credit report can destroy your chances of getting a loan for a car, a home, or other major purchase. I recommend that you get all three reports at least six months before making a large purchase for which you will need credit.

***TIP:** The time to find out there's something wrong with your credit report is not when you are trying madly to get financing for the all-time perfect house and you're in a competitive bidding situation with another buyer who is preapproved for a mortgage. If you need to degunk your credit report, it's best to find out ahead of time. You'll need to give yourself time to clean up the errors and then apply for a loan so when the lender pulls your credit report, it's spic-and-span and raises no red flags.*

All three reporting agencies offer a 3-in-1 report that lists all information from the three agencies. This isn't a free service, however. The agencies can, for a price, provide you with either the one credit score from their company or, for more money, all three scores along with the combined information. I recommend this last option. You will certainly save money, instead of paying for three separate credit scores, and it's nice to have all the information on one document.

***TIP:** By September, everyone in the U.S. will be able to go to **www.annualcreditreport.com** for a credit report (western states are available now). You're entitled to one free report from each of the three major credit bureaus every 12 months.*

Clean Up Your Credit Report

If you find mistakes on your credit report, such as accounts labeled past due that have been paid or defaulted accounts that you paid off long ago, you will need to notify the reporting agency immediately. They must investigate the issue and get back to you within 30 days.

The best way to clean up your credit report, when you've found errors, is to do the following:

1. Make sure that you fully understand each listing in the credit report, and be certain that you understand what's an error and what's not. Each credit report will come with fairly complete explanations of what each entry means.
2. Create a list of the errors in your credit report.
3. Notify each credit reporting agency of all the errors in writing. You should list each error and what the situation really is. Keep your explanations brief and simple—a sentence or two, if possible.

4. Notify the lender that has reported the erroneous information and ask them to correct their entry on your credit report. Again, keep your explanation and request simple and straightforward. (See Figure 10-1 for a sample letter.)
5. Keep a copy of your correspondence. Instructions on where to send correspondence to the various agencies is included in your credit report.

46 East Glen Avenue
Ann Arbor, MI 48108

January 4, 1970

American Bank
Visa Card
P.O. Box 83132
Studio City, CA 98108

RE: Account 3344-XXXX-YYYY-9999

To Whom It May Concern:

I notice that on my Experian credit report, the above named Visa card account is still listed as open. I closed this account in August 2002. If you have not already done so, please close this account immediately and report this information to all credit reporting agencies, labeled as "closed at consumer's request."

Thank you for your immediate attention to this matter.

Sincerely,

Joseph H. Schmoe

Joseph H. Schmoe

Figure 10-1
Sample letter to lender requesting a correction to credit report.

If you are in the process of getting a loan, make sure your lender knows you are trying to correct the mistake on your credit report. Be aware also that the lender hears this particular line all the time, most often from people not nearly as honest as you are. Don't expect them to proceed with your loan on your word that the defaulted loan on your report was indeed paid in full. They may have been born at night, but they probably weren't born last night. To avoid discovering errors in your credit report when you're in the middle of applying for an important loan, it's essential that you know what your credit report looks like before sitting down with a lender.

In the next sections, I'll show you how to read your credit report and translate some of the jargon so you'll know what it's really saying about you.

Read and Translate Your Credit Report

There is a lot of information in a credit report, so it might seem intimidating at first glance. The thing to know, though, is that all the entries will have the same type of information, so once you learn how each entry is set up, you can cruise through each listing and quickly see what's correct and what's not. If you are going to degunk your credit report, it's very important that you look at every piece of information on the report and correct any and all errors. I know that this process may be time consuming, but errors in this document can threaten your overall credit picture. The time you spend correcting mistakes now could save you money in the future. Let's begin at the beginning.

Personal Information

At the top of most 3-in-1 credit reports will be the name or names of the people applying for the report—you alone or you and a spouse. Your Social Security numbers will be listed alongside your names. Immediately check for correct spellings of names and for correct Social Security numbers. Your address and date of birth will then be listed. Under your address will be the listing of the applicants' names and dates the information was reported.

TIP: Check carefully that all personal information, names, dates, and numbers are correct. If they are not, notify the credit reporting agency immediately.

What Your Credit Score Means

If you are receiving credit scores from each agency, these will be listed next. There will be a score for each applicant, not each couple. Because there are three major credit reporting agencies, each one will have made its own assessment of your creditworthiness, and it's possible that you'll have three different credit scores. Also, because these three agencies don't talk with each other, you will find that some items are listed on the Experian list, for example, and won't appear on the ones for TransUnion and Equifax. Don't fret about this, though, as it's likely that your credit scores for all three agencies are pretty close.

If the report is for a couple, you may each have information stored in the credit agencies that predates a marriage and this is worked into your score. Looking at these numbers for each individual on the application, check for significant differences. The numbers will not be the same, even if they have the same information, but you might get suspicious if there is a gap of more than 50 points in credit scores from the three agencies. This could mean either that one agency is reporting something negative that the other two are not or that one agency is reporting something positive and the other two have not been informed of it. In either case, it warrants further investigation on your part. This is one good reason why it's important for you to go through each listing for each credit reporting agency. If you can fix your credit score, it will benefit you greatly to do so.

Credit scores range from 300 to 850. The higher the score, the better for you. For instance, someone with a score of more than 720 can expect an interest rate on a home mortgage to be substantially lower than the rate for someone with a score of 560. The difference can be as much as 3.5 percent, which can translate to hundreds of dollars per month, depending on the size of your loan. Those with scores above 760 get the best rates, while those with scores below 600 pay substantially more for their credit. Later in the chapter, I'll discuss how your score is computed in "Understanding Your FICO Score."

GunkBuster's Notebook: Is There Such a Thing as a Perfect Score?

For those of you high achievers out there, you might be wondering how you can obtain a perfect score—assuming that this sort of thing is possible. Before we get to that, let's look at where different groups of Americans rank:

- √ The average American's credit score is in the 670s.
- √ Only 11 percent of the population have a credit score of 800 or better. (If you make it to this level, you deserve a big pat on the back.)
- √ Only 1 percent have a credit score of 850.

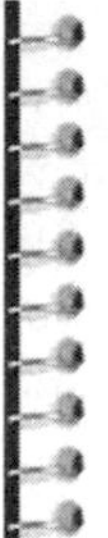

If you hit 850, you're lucky, smart, careful with your money, and especially good at degunking your finances. To achieve a score as high as this is not easy, however. One of the requirements is that you must have paid all of your bills on time during the past seven years. You also must have a minimum of 30 years of credit use and you need to have between four and six revolving credit accounts.

Account History

Next on your credit report will be the credit accounts you have had open in the past and closed; accounts you still have open but are inactive; and current, active accounts. For each account, it will list when the account was opened, when it was last active, the credit limit on the account, and the highest balance. It will say what type of account it is: revolving credit card, mortgage, secured loan, auto loan, or line of credit. Then it will list, by date, payments that were 30, 60, or 90 days late on that particular account. As credit reports are done in real time, the listings of past due, payment, and balance pertain to what was happening on the day the report was generated. This is another good reason to make sure that all your bill payments are current before a report is requested by a lender. Near the bottom of each account, it will state if the account is closed (either by the consumer or the lender) and, if it is a credit card account, if the card was lost or stolen.

After your accounts are listed, there will be contact information for each of the creditors listed, making it much easier to call them if anything is gunked up on your report or if you just want to thank them for all the interest you have paid to them over the years. (Okay, probably not.)

TIP: The contact information listed in your credit report may come in handy, especially if you've discovered errors in your report. Even though you may have long ago thrown out all those department store credit card receipts and records, at least this report will list the name and address of that lender. You can search for the phone number (if not provided) on the Internet, contact the store, and ask them where to send correspondence requesting a correction on your credit report.

Inquiry Information

The next section on the report is inquiry information. A "hard" inquiry is when that car salesman was given authorization (by you) to pull your credit report. Many people don't know that allowing someone to just *ask* for your credit information will result in a listing on your credit report. You don't have to apply for the loan, fill out an application, provide a signature, or do any paperwork. The mere act of allowing an inquiry gets a notation on your permanent record. The inquiry section will include all requests for your credit information. If you're trying to obtain a lot of new credit, this can be a red flag for a lender. If you have several recent inquiries for new credit cards on your report, a lender will certainly wonder why you need all this new credit and where the money will come to pay for it.

Some inquiries don't count against you, and these are called "soft" inquiries. Getting a credit report for yourself does not count, nor do multiple inquiries from credit card companies checking to "preapprove" you for a card. It would become an official inquiry once you filled out the paperwork and actually requested the credit card. If you are shopping for good rates on a loan or a car and multiple lenders check your credit in a 14-day period, it counts as only one inquiry (thank goodness, or you'd have no points left). Additionally, your score ignores all requests made in the 30 days before your current score was computed. Then, if you find a loan within 30 days, the inquiries won't affect your score during your rate-shopping blitz.

Other Data on Your Credit Report

There is a lot of miscellaneous data on your credit report, and some people are surprised to find the following types of information on themselves.

Public Records

In the public records section will be listed any negative statements concerning your credit history, such as a bankruptcy, a tax lien against your home, the fact that there is child support you may not have paid, or any continuing or dismissed suit against you. If anything shows up in this section that shouldn't be there, it is certainly cause for alarm and needs immediate action if you are trying to get credit, or if you are trying to get a good night's sleep.

Social Security Number

The next section will list when your Social Security number was issued and under what names it has been used. It should list, for all applicants, their current and former addresses. It will also list if you have been reported as deceased to the Social Security Administration. If that is the case, it's another reason to lose sleep—and you will obviously need to correct this misinformation immediately.

Other Names

Listed near the bottom of the report are any other names you have gone by, such as maiden names or your name before you went into the witness protection program (not really—my apologies to the government). At the very bottom it will state where the information for the report originated—usually the credit reporting agencies discussed earlier.

Understanding Your FICO Score

Since kindergarten, it seems that the world has been grade-obsessed. Someone always wants to know who the smartest kid in the class is and where they rank in comparison. Our credit score is something else we can use to grade ourselves—and either help or hurt our self-esteem. Let's not go there. Let me say right now that the good news about your credit score (also known as your FICO score) is that you can change it. First, though, you have to understand it. That's what will be covered in these sections.

There is actually rhyme and reason to how your FICO score is computed. Though different recording agencies count individual entries to your credit report in slightly different ways, the path by which they come up with your overall score is basically the same. There are five areas of your credit reporting that make up your FICO score, and although they are considered in varying percentages of importance, they all help determine if and at what cost you will get credit:

- √ Your payment history (35 percent of your score)
- √ The amount of your indebtedness (30 percent of your score)
- √ How long you've had credit (15 percent of your score)
- √ How much recent new credit you have (10 percent of your score)
- √ The types of credit you have (10 percent of your score)

We'll go through each of these items in more detail in the following sections.

Payment History

The most important area of your credit reporting is your payment history. Thirty-five percent of your score counts on whether you have paid past credit on time, have been delinquent on loans or have missed payments, or have any public records (bankruptcy or foreclosures) concerning past loans. Although late payments certainly gunk up your credit report, an overall good report can stand the hit of a missed grace period once in a while. If you make a habit of paying your bills late, however, this can take quite a few points off your score.

Amount of Indebtedness

Thirty percent of your score is based on how much you owe to the various creditors listed on your report. Owing a lot of money on several different accounts may indicate you are overextended and are more likely to pay late, or not at all. In addition to the total amount you owe, the score takes into account how much you owe on what types of accounts, such as mortgages and credit cards. Your score does not mark you down for having debt. Often, having a small balance and making regular payments can look better on your report than having no balances at all. A creditor wants to see that you are handling debt responsibly. Paying off an account every month looks great as well and can help a younger person establish credit without paying monster interest charges. Your score will also take into account how close you are to the limits on the accounts you are using. From the creditor's standpoint, someone close to maxing out their credit cards may have a more difficult time keeping up payments than someone who has small balances on a couple of accounts. Paying down installment loans (a car loan, for example) looks good to creditors, and the higher the percentage that's paid off when applying for more credit, the better.

How Long You've Had Your Credit

Your credit score is also based on how long your credit has been established. Fifteen percent of your score is decided by your length of credit history. The amount of time all of your accounts have been open will be averaged, and this information will affect your score. In general, a longer credit history will reap a higher score, but even someone with a shorter history can have a very reputable score if their credit has been used wisely from the beginning. The key here is if you are trying to establish credit, don't open several accounts in a short time. Rapid account buildup can look very risky to a potential creditor.

Recent New Credit

Ten percent of your credit score is determined by how much new credit you have recently taken on and how many inquiries into your credit have been made in the last two years. Again, opening new accounts is a sign of taking on more credit and lowers your score. Inquiries are counted carefully, as mentioned previously, and the FICO Wizard is very smart when it comes to knowing which inquiries were initiated by you, which are for the same type of loan (shopping for a mortgage), and which will actually impact your credit score.

Types of Credit You Have Established

The fifth area of concern when computing your credit score is the type of credit you use. Ten percent of your score is based on this category. This part of your score will take into account the mix of different types of credit you are utilizing, such as whether there is a mix of, perhaps, a mortgage, a couple of credit cards, an installment loan, and a retail account. If the entire debt load is in unsecured credit cards, that is a warning sign to a creditor. It is, of course, not necessary to have a loan in all the various flavors of credit available (in case anyone was using this as an excuse to run out and get that plasma screen TV to round out their credit usage), and it is also not advisable to open accounts that you don't intend to use. Although the types of credit you use is not a key factor in determining your FICO score, this information will be used more heavily if your credit report doesn't have other information (the other items mentioned earlier) on which to base your score.

Improve Your FICO Score

Now you understand how the FICO Wizard computes your FICO score and, in real terms, the different areas from which your score is taken. You now have somewhere to start if you want to change your score and get the best available interest rates I mentioned earlier. To that end, the following sections will explain—in very real terms—what you need to do now to improve your FICO score. As with all money management, it's not magic, it's consistency. If you follow this advice, there will be a definitive, measurable improvement in the next six months.

Pay Bills on Time

I know this sounds simplistic, but the easiest and fastest way to improve your credit score is to pay your bills on time. As you now know, over a third (35 percent) of your credit score is determined by whether you pay your bills in a timely manner. If you have missed payments, for any reason, it's important to get current and stay current. The longer you stay current, the better your score will be and the faster it will improve. Keep in mind that "late payment" usually means 30+ days after the payment due date, so there's no need to wring your hands just because you sent in the mortgage payment a day or two late. Still, don't tempt fate—pay all bills by their stated due dates.

***TIP:** If you have accounts that have gone to collection or you have previously missed a loan payment, what should you do? Paying off the loan will certainly help your credit score, but it will not erase the incident off your report. Furthermore, paying off the loan is probably not realistic if it's about to go (or has already gone) to collection. The practical thing is to try to negotiate with the lender and start making regular payments. Three positive things will happen as a result:*

1. *Your credit score will improve.*

2. *You'll whittle down the debt.*

3. *You'll be under less stress because you have a manageable payment plan in place.*

Your credit score will still take this negative information into account because it is still your history, but your new score will also reflect your positive actions if you start to make regular payments. After six months of making regular payments on this loan, your score will improve.

If you are going through the Perfect Storm in your finances and are having trouble making your payments, contact your creditors before it's time for them to report your difficulties to the credit agencies. The truth is, all they want is their money. Often, contact initiated by you, resulting in a payment plan that you can stick to, is all it takes to keep your creditors happy and prevent them from making a negative notation on your credit report. A proactive approach on your part will solve the problem before it has a chance to lower your score.

Keep Credit Card Balances Low

Again, I know this sounds simple, but keep your balances on revolving credit (credit cards) low—which means below 30 percent of your credit limit on *each* account. High balances on several cards will lower your score. If you have high balances now, follow the steps in Chapter 6 to pay your cards off, and don't run them up again. It doesn't help your score to move the money around from account to account, though you may get lower interest rates that way. Closing unused accounts has no positive effect on your score, either. (See more on this topic later in the section'"Other Tips for Improving Your Credit Score.")

Plan to Shop for Credit

When you are taking on new credit, do your rate shopping within a focused period of time so your FICO score will see all the connected inquiries as one. Note that checking your own FICO score and credit report will not count as an inquiry if you get the report directly from one of the reporting agencies or another entity authorized to provide that service to consumers.

You should also plan major purchases for which you will use credit. For example, if you're shopping for a vehicle or new appliances for your home, have all the credit inquiries happen within a 30-day period. Your credit report will reflect that you were applying for similar types of credit within a given period and it's clear that you were shopping for a specific item.

However, if you're applying for a mortgage and the lender sees that there is a different credit inquiry from you every month over the past 12 months, that creditor is going to wonder about your creditworthiness and your spending habits. The lesson here is to plan your major purchases, especially if they're going to involve credit.

Have Manageable Credit Limits

A low FICO score is a result of your previous actions, but the financial realities are that companies want to give you more credit. If you have had poor credit in the past, and you have learned from your mistakes, opening a new account and using it responsibly can raise your score in the long run. If you have not yet learned, stay away from getting more credit until you have developed and maintained a balanced budget for at least six months. Then, get one card with a very small limit, and pay off what you charge every month.

Other Tips for Improving Your Credit Score

Aside from the more blatant ways to improve your score, there are a few things that may not be obvious from the start that can be helpful. As with any other system, it's important to know the rules of the game before you decide to play.

Don't Cancel Credit Cards

One of the first temptations most people have when they have a lot of credit card debt is to start canceling credit cards that are unused. What this does to your credit score is to lower the overall credit you have available, raising the percentage of credit that is used. Therefore, the ratio of the amount of credit available to amount of credit used is higher, making your overall credit picture look worse. If you are going to make a major purchase, keep the cards to acknowledge your credit limit, but don't run up your debt by using them.

EXAMPLE: You have $20,000 of unsecured credit on four credit cards. You owe $10,000 total on these cards, which is 50 percent of your available credit. If you cancel two of the cards, lowering your total unsecured credit to $12,000, you now owe 83 percent of your available credit. This looks much worse to a credit reporting agency, and your FICO score will drop precipitously.

TIP: Once you pay off your debt, feel free to close some accounts. If you have little used credit on your cards, which is your long-term goal, the ratio will be very low and there will be no reason to keep all of those other accounts open. If you are entirely too tempted by having the cards available to you, it still may to best to close the accounts, no matter what the effect on your credit rating. Don't tempt yourself with available credit if you know you won't be responsible. If you run up all the cards again, it will have a negative effect on your credit anyway. You know yourself—if you can keep the cards without using them, fine. If not, get rid of them permanently.

Don't Consolidate Debt on One Credit Card

For convenience, many people in serious debt might be tempted to do their own debt consolidation and put all their credit card debt on one card. As I mentioned earlier, if you can, it's important to keep balances on any one card below 30 percent of your limit. It's actually better, from a FICO score perspective, to have your debt spread over several accounts. This is only good advice, however, if you have a decent interest rate on all of your cards. As mentioned in Chapter 6, you have to balance what you're paying in interest with the effect on your credit score. Getting your debt paid off will be even more beneficial to your credit score, so don't spend thousands more in interest to keep your levels below 30 percent.

Negotiate with Lenders

Lenders are much more willing to negotiate than you may think. To help degunk your financial situation a bit more, here are a few items that you should consider negotiating with your lenders:

√ Percentage rates. If you're not in serious financial straits yet but you've noticed the rates on your variable rate credit cards inching up—indicating that your FICO score is declining—call your credit card company and ask them to lower your rates. Again, the argument for this is that your other cards have much lower rates. This won't actually improve your FICO score, but it will lower the amount of interest you're paying, thus helping you to pay off your principal faster. Better yet, transfer your balance to a lower-interest non–variable rate card.

√ Payment plans. If you're having serious financial problems and simply can't afford to make your monthly payments, call your lender and discuss the situation. Remember, all the lender wants is its money. You may have to make several calls and talk to an array of supervisors, but if you show a willingness to pay off your debt, most lenders will work with you. They may drop penalties and some interest charges, or perhaps lower your interest rate for a specified length of time. And, if you ask, it is possible that they won't even ding your credit report. Again, avoiding a negative entry on your credit report will benefit your financial picture.

Spouses and Children

If you're serious about degunking your credit report, you must enlist the help of your spouse, ex-spouse, and children. Here's how these family members can seriously gunk up your credit rating:

√ Spouses: If you have co-signed for any loan or credit card with your spouse, you are both responsible for the balance, regardless of who said they would pay that bill. If your spouse doesn't understand the importance of paying bills on time, there needs to be a serious discussion about financial matters and some education taking place. Having them read this book would be a good start. Your credit score, individually and as a couple, is at risk.

√ Ex-spouses: This is a very slippery slope. If you've co-signed for any loan or credit card with your ex-spouse, you are still responsible for the balance—*regardless of what the divorce settlement stipulates!* Therefore, separating your credit history and getting your name off of all loans you once had together as quickly as possible should be a huge priority. If your ex-spouse is irresponsible with credit, they can continue to damage your credit rating until you separate all credit accounts.

√ Children: If you have given your children credit cards and your finances are already gunked up, unless there are very strict boundaries about how the card can be used, it's probably not be a good idea to have them out of your possession. Almost without exception, if the parents haven't used credit well, they also haven't passed on those skills to their children. That would be akin to trying to teach someone to play the guitar when you've never had a lesson yourself. Uncontrolled credit card spending by your kids can create all sorts of problems: exceeding credit limits, exceeding the 30-percent guideline, and creating a hugely unpredictable budget. If your children don't understand how to use credit cards responsibly, their spending habits can jeopardize your credit score and gunk up your already messy finances even further.

Summing Up

In this chapter, we reviewed what a credit report is, what it reports, how to interpret it, and what you can do to improve your FICO score. A credit report is a snapshot of your credit situation at one point in time, and it can worsen or improve, depending on your actions. Your credit report doesn't lie, but it can be encouraged to tell a better truth over time. If you have a high score, pat yourself on the back. If you want to raise your score, it's as easy as following the steps listed in this chapter and being consistent about your debt repayment plan. Creating a good credit report is a long-term project. Even if your credit report is not where you want it to be now, you can change this in the same way you took off that 10 pounds that was driving you crazy—you paid attention, focused on your goal, followed some basic rules, and didn't expect the change overnight.

If you follow the guidelines I've presented in this chapter, your credit score will improve. Your score is a financial planning tool that can make things easier or more difficult when it comes to getting credit, and trying to raise it can only help in the degunking procedures for the rest of your financial life. Isn't it cool when all your planning and difficult decisions work together for a good result? I love it when a plan comes together.

Fine-Tuning Your Budget

Degunking Checklist:

- √ Make record-keeping a top priority and standardize it so you stay up-to-date.
- √ Use technology to help you keep and update your financial records.
- √ Know what documents to save for tax purposes.
- √ Look at what you buy and what you pay, and vow to get the best price on what you purchase.
- √ Set money aside and plan for major future expenditures.
- √ Learn about the pitfalls of co-signing.
- √ If you're part of a couple, find out why you should or shouldn't co-sign on credit items.

You are, by now, in the throes of managing your money. Fun, isn't it? Okay, maybe *fun* isn't the right word. How about *satisfying?* It is rewarding to be more in control of your money and to be making better decisions about where it goes and having a plan for the future that doesn't include 24 percent interest rates. You probably have the basics down, so I now want you to start looking at ways to fine-tune your budget management skills. You've graduated to bigger and better ways to manage your budget, and you know how to make your financial life more organized, efficient, and at your fingertips. You're in the majors now. The goal is, after all, to keep your budget degunked once you've cleaned it up and gotten it under control.

In this chapter you'll learn how to keep better records and track your budget more efficiently. This will help you keep even better tabs on where your money is going.

Make Record-Keeping a Top Priority

In whatever form you choose, keeping records is a very physical way to watch your money. Knowing how much you're spending, on what, and at what period of the month will help you discern patterns of spending you may not have been aware of and further motivate you to stay within your boundaries and fulfill your goals. It's tough to ignore what is happening to your money when it's in front of you on a near-daily basis, and watching your savings grow and your credit card bills shrink is a very encouraging sight.

It's easy to get distracted with all the bills you pay and all of the things you do each month. But no matter how busy you get, try to set aside some time on a regular basis to review your records and get them up-to-date. Once you get a system in place, you'll be surprised at how little time is actually needed to keep this up and running in an efficient manner. It's easy to procrastinate about record-keeping. It's probably high on your list of things to think about but never do, like cleaning out the fridge or getting rid of the grunge in the corner of the workroom. I'm hoping that once you see the benefits of having a good record-keeping system, you'll stay motivated to keep this part of your degunking procedure up-to-date.

People often don't have any idea where they actually stand with their finances because they're so convinced they're in the weeds. Some don't even open their bills and statements. This, as I'm sure you can imagine, makes a bad situation much worse. One woman I worked with brought a couple of shopping bags of unopened mail into my office one morning and confessed that she hadn't looked at anything for at least a few months. We opened everything and set up a system so it wasn't so scary for her to do it herself, and she was quickly back on track to degunking a situation that wasn't nearly as bad as she feared.

***TIP:** I know this seems elementary, but not opening your mail doesn't do a thing to help your situation. If you're laying unopened mail aside hoping something magical will happen to it while you're sleeping, you need to brace yourself and face whatever is in those envelopes. Even if you can't pay the bills right away, at least you will have an accurate view of your situation.*

In the following sections, I'll go over some more advanced degunking topics for record-keeping. Consider these ideas, and find what you can fit into your long-term financial management process. Using these suggestions will help you achieve your financial goals faster and with less pain.

Keeping Up-to-Date

You have (I hope, I hope) been keeping track of all of your expenditures and income. This section of the chapter will help you decide how to keep that information current and how to record it to make it accessible for your future uses, like tax time and when you're considering whether you can afford tickets to *The Nutcracker* at Christmas. There are two major ways to keep track of your income and expenditures—by using the technology tools available today or by using the old-fashioned paper-and-pencil method. There are also a myriad of ways within those two categories that you can personalize the process for your own uses.

Using Technology

If you have a computer, you can keep track of your numbers with any of the money management software available on the market. Quicken and Microsoft Money are two common products. In these programs, you fill in your expenses and income as if you were writing in a checkbook. One of the great features about these products is the ability to categorize your entries as you enter them. For instance, as you are entering your recent check to Target, you can, when you get to the category section of the entry, split your expense into several categories. That way, the detergent you bought is kept in a separate category from your son's boxer shorts, and the school supplies are separate from the greeting cards. If you bank with one of the larger groups (Citibank, Bank of America), you can download and reconcile your account right into these software programs. Each different account (checking, savings, investment) you have should be in your money management software because what you are saving or investing is as important to keep track of as your expenditures and income.

***TIP:* One other advantage of using a computerized system is that many of the software programs available can easily be set up to remind you to perform various actions, such as paying specific bills. This kind of feature can help keep you from forgetting to pay a bill or transfer money into your checking account. If you've been having trouble paying your bills on time because you're crazy busy, this type of feature can help you avoid paying late fees.**

Some credit cards have a download feature that will put your transactions into a checkbook format in most of the major money management software packages. In this way, you can categorize all your charge transactions in the same way you do your check transactions. If you can't download, they can be put in manually, as you do your checks, and categorized at that time.

As the month continues, you can pull up reports of your categories to see how you're doing. This report will cover all of your accounts, so if you have written checks for food and also used your charge card for food, it will count both types of transactions. Your report can show how much you've spent in any of your categories for the month, quarter, or year, or for the history of your record. It's a very good idea to monitor your expenses during the month and to know how much you have left in categories you can control. Checking mid-month to see how much is left in your clothing category gives you the information you need to know to decide whether to even step foot in your favorite store during that blow-out sale. Knowing you have extra money available in the food category gives you the freedom to fill up the freezer when chicken breasts go on sale cheep (get it?).

Breaking up your entries into categories is invaluable when it comes to your paychecks as well. When entering income, make separate subcategories for the taxes taken out of your check, and at the end of the year, check your numbers against what your company is saying was deducted. You will also have other numbers available to you that would be a pain to find, such as insurance costs for the year, how much you put into your company's 401(k) or retirement plan, and how much you gave to the United Way.

This only works, however, if you have gotten the information into the computer. Unfortunately, computers haven't reached the level where they can scan the checkbook still in your purse for transactions and add them to the ones already entered. You will need to make a firm commitment to keep all your records up-to-date. Setting a schedule to review your budget, such as every other Saturday morning, will help you keep your finances degunked in the long term.

Using Paper and Pencil

The second form of record-keeping is done with paper and pencil. I know it's amazing to the techies among us, but I have clients who are much more comfortable writing everything down on a spreadsheet than doing it on the computer. A form I like to use is shown in Figure 11-1. The form shown is based on an Excel spreadsheet and can go out as many columns as necessary to accomodate your needs.

NAME:

DAILY RECORD Month: Year:

INCOME													
Salary, Wages (Net)	Other	DAY	EXPLANATION OF EXPENSES	GIVING	SAVINGS								
			<BUDGETED AMOUNT>										
			<Year to Date OVER>										
			<Year to Date UNDER>										
		1											
		2											
		3											
		4											
		5											
		6											
		7											
		8											
		9											
		10											
		11											
		12											
		13											
		14											
		15											
			<SUBTOTALS>										
		16											
		17											
		18											
		19											
		20											
		21											
		22											
		23											
		24											
		25											
		26											
		27											
		28											
		29											
		30											
		31											
			<TOTALS>										
			OVER BUDGET										
			UNDER BUDGET										

Figure 11-1

A form you can use to track your finances.

On this form, the days of the month (1–31) are printed down the left side of the sheet. Across the top are the various categories, including income, with subcategories underneath. The budgeted amount of each category is divided up and written in under each subcategory, and the amount over or under is written in from previous months. Expenditures are written in on the day they happened and subtotaled in the middle of the month. At the end of the month, everything is totaled to see if you are over or under in your individual categories and for the longer time period within which you're working, usually a calendar year. As complicated as this may sound, it takes just a couple of minutes a day to enter your numbers and under an hour to add them together at the end of the month. It is a very good way to keep track for those who would care to do this in a way that's less technical than using the computer, and it will keep the makers of pencils and long computer paper in business.

Save Documentation for Tax Reasons

Some expenses need to be tracked for tax reasons. Medical expenses, charitable giving, and interest payments are all numbers you will need at year-end, and they can be difficult to lay your hands on if you haven't been tracking them as you go along. Think about how much easier your life will be at tax time not to have to dig through your checkbook and the medical file to come up with your medical costs for the year.

TIP: Right after the first of the year, things start arriving in the mail that are hugely important in order to get your taxes done. These could include W-2 forms, interest income statements, year-end investment statements, and your mortgage interest statement. Have a folder or shoebox ready for these documents, and keep them together and handy for when you, or a paid professional, are going to tackle your taxes. Being in the middle of the process, either at home or at an office, and not being able to lay your sweaty hands on your spouse's W-2 can make a stressful situation much worse.

GunkBuster's Notebook: Saturday Morning Budget Time

Saturday morning rolls around, and it's time to look at your monthly budget. How do you tackle this? Here are some basic steps, which you will probably personalize for your own use:

1. Gather your unpaid bills from the container on your desk.
2. Dig out your checkbooks and turn on your computer (if you're using Microsoft Money, Quicken, or some other financial program).

3. Gather any checks that need to be deposited. Make out the deposit slips, and enter the deposit amounts in your checkbook and/or financial program.
4. Gather together your receipts from the week for cash expenditures, credit cards, and debit cards. Don't forget to include your ATM withdrawal and deposit slips. Separate those that you have already put on the sheet from those that still need to be marked down.
5. Pull out your expenditure tracking worksheet.
6. Add any expenses to the expenditures worksheet that haven't yet been entered for the week. Hopefully, you have been doing some of this as you go, but if not, get them all down. Make sure to include cash and credit expenditures and those for which you wrote a check or paid online.
7. Pay bills that are due. Mark them down on the sheet, and deduct the amounts paid from your check register (either online or in your checkbook).
8. Look over your numbers. How are you doing, budget-wise? Are some categories maxed out? Will you have to carefully watch your food expenditures for the rest of the month? What bills will have to be paid next week? Be informed on how the money situation looks until the next payday.
9. Go to the bank. Deposit any checks that need to go in, and remove any cash that needs to come out. File your bank receipts immediately when you get home.

Now you can start the new week organized and ready, with knowledge of what your financial situation is currently and how it looks for the coming weeks. Feels good, doesn't it?

Change Your Spending Habits

A big piece of degunking your finances involves degunking your spending habits. One of the ways to quickly reduce how much you spend is to simply *think about* how much you're spending on each purchase. Look at prices and decide if they're fair and if the expenditure is necessary. When you remove impulse spending from your budget, you will be amazed at how much money you can save!

My thinking is that there is no pride to be had in paying more than you need to for anything. I am always amazed when people say to me, with a flip of their expensive haircut, "I never really check prices." At that point in any conversation, I break out in hives. Another heading for this section could read, "Don't Buy Diamonds at the Mall."

Look at What You Buy and What You Pay

Why pay more than you have to? If making a phone call to Best Buy and Circuit City can save you $200 on a new refrigerator, why not do that? If you know that the prices on food are substantially lower at Cub Foods than at Dominick's (or whatever the names would be in your area—I know you know!), then why pay more for the same items at the more expensive store each and every week? If you find a different place to shop that saves you even $15 per week, over a year that would add up to $780 worth of credit card payoff, or most of a week at that resort you like, or maybe 2.5 car payments. Why would you not do that if you had the opportunity?

What You Buy

By thinking about your purchases every time you reach for your wallet, you may discover that not everything you buy is essential. Over time, you will come to be more price-conscious and aware of what is fair to pay for any particular item. You can and should be aware of the span of prices for whatever it is you want or need and then compare your budget to what's available. This is not to say that the right decision is to always buy the cheapest model. When shopping for a refrigerator, for example, you will find that the range of choices will span several thousand dollars. The cheapest model will hold just enough food for one college student, but not nearly enough for your family of four. It may also need to have the freezer defrosted on a regular basis, and the $100 difference to upgrade to a self-defrosting freezer may be money well spent. Decide which features are essential to meet your real needs before you buy.

It gets more dangerous when you're looking at higher-end products. In the refrigerator example, you will need to decide how important the brushed stainless-steel finish is to you, especially if it's 35 percent more expensive than the plain white model. The latest absurdity I've seen is a refrigerator door with a TV in it (oh, please). Once you've decided on what features you need and which you can do without, you can narrow your choice down to a couple of models and then let your fingers do the typing (online) to get prices and promotions. A follow-up phone call wouldn't hurt, either, as some stores run promotions, such as free delivery, that are good only when you come in.

What You Pay

There are ways to save money on purchases that may not be immediately recognized. Calling around to get a good price on a muffler may not automatically occur to you, but that call could save you $100. Buying window treatments at Target (which usually has an especially nice selection) instead of the department store could save you as much as half on what you find. Discovering furniture at the attached outlet store can be less than half of what the item would be a hundred feet away inside the store. Waiting for an item of clothing to go on sale, which it will always do, can save you 30–50%—and it discourages impulse buying.

There is a motto here. It begins with the thought that nearly anything you purchase can be bought cheaper and ends with you being a very informed consumer and knowing what the range is for good prices on nearly anything.

TIP: Never forget the value of bargaining, especially when it comes to larger items like appliances. It is perfectly acceptable to bargain with your salesperson for a variety of options and perks. Here are some tips to save you some real money:

- √ ***Bulk discounts. When purchasing more than one appliance, ask if there's a "multiple purchase" discount. There probably isn't, but the salesperson may recognize your suggestion as an opportunity to close a deal with you if they offer an additional discount (perhaps 5–10 percent).***
- √ ***Free delivery. There may be a stated charge, but ask for free delivery anyway, especially if you're close by or can manage your schedule to take delivery at the store's convenience. It helps in this process if you can find an ad from a neighboring store that is offering free delivery. Nothing like a little competition to get things going your way.***
- √ ***Floor models. If a floor model looks to be in fairly good shape and it's the model/color that you want, tell the salesperson you'll take that one—for a substantial discount, of course (say 20–30 percent). It goes without saying that you will also get the company's warranty on the product, just as if it were new. Don't forget to ask for free delivery.***
- √ ***Discount for cash sale. If you've diligently budgeted for your appliance purchase and have the money in hand, ask if there's a discount if you pay cash.***

These are all ways of shaving a few percentage points off the ticket price of a larger item. A 10 percent discount off an $800 refrigerator is a nice chunk of change. I bet you could think of something else to do with that money other than giving it to your local appliance store. It sure would look nice as a deduction off your credit card balance, wouldn't it?

The Bottom Line

Let's say this process of shopping around and negotiating takes two hours of being online with a few different stores and a couple of phone calls. Let's say you save $200 as a result of your labors. That's $100 per hour for your work. Not bad for never leaving your desk.

This doesn't work as well if you've spent that same two hours to save 40 cents. There is a balance of time-to-result to be had here, and with time being the precious commodity it is, be cautions as to how you spend yours. Purchasing something small—such as a tank of gas—should take less work than purchasing something more expensive, such as a car or dishwasher. If you're looking for a book, for instance, spend a few minutes online to find out which retailer offers the best deal or if Amazon.com can get it to you cheaper. There's no need to make a career over saving $2.80 if it costs you an hour of time, which you could have used organizing your files.

It's not miserly to save money where you can. Don't pay more than you have to for anything, and be happy about what you save and where it ultimately goes. This isn't being cheap – it's being informed.

GunkBuster's Notebook: Plan for Holiday Shopping in the Summer

No matter how busy we get with our lives, we all know the holidays are coming. Most of us (my husband excluded) are probably aware of upcoming special occasions like birthdays, anniversaries, and other celebrations that can push us into a spending frenzy. You can save a lot of money by planning ahead and setting limits for yourself on gift buying. Don't wait until the holiday season is upon you to start your planning and shopping. It's much too easy to get caught up in the moment and spend without taking your budget into consideration. Planning for your gift expenses is like investing. If you give yourself more time, you'll get much more for your money. Consider setting up a "gift spending" account early in the year. You made out a gift list and have a budgeted amount to spend on gifts every month. By having your gift list with you, when you see a great robe in February that your sister would just love for her birthday in June, and it's on sale for $25 (down from $40), take a couple of steps before grabbing it and hustling to the checkout. Check your list to see what you've budgeted for your sister's birthday ($30), and make sure you haven't already spent your gift money for the

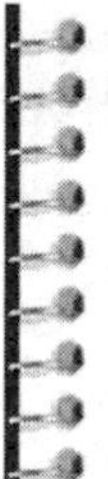

month. If these things are in line, buy the robe, put it in a box in the closet, and be happy knowing you got a great gift at a great price, and when the happy day comes, you are well prepared. Compare this to running out at the last minute and overspending for a gift on your way to the party. Chances are you wouldn't find anything as good, and it would undoubtedly cost you more.

Separate Longer-Term Spending

Most of your bills probably come monthly, but some may come quarterly or semiannually. If you pay your car insurance quarterly, for instance, you need to be putting money away for the three months preceding the bill in order to be ready for it. Some people don't have their real estate taxes kept in their escrow account, and so they need to save for those large bills. The same is true for the self-employed who pay taxes on a quarterly basis. Leaving the money in your checking account for these expenditures can be an overwhelming temptation for some people. If seeing the money in the checkbook register means to you that it can be spent, then the answer to this temptation is to get it the heck out of there for safekeeping until it is needed. Christmas will still come, even if you've spent all the gift money at the antique market, and then where will you be? The point of the following sections is to help you manage your money so that it's available when you need to pay those quarterly, semiannual, or intermittent expenses.

Create Separate Accounts for Big Expenses

To avoid the temptation to spend it if you have it, it's a good idea to open up a money market or savings account into which you can place funds for this type of longer-term spending. Every time there is a budgeted amount to be set aside, move it out of checking into this account. If it is a money market account and checks can be written on it free of charge, then the rest is easy. When the bill is due, write the check. If it's a savings account, transfer the money into checking at the proper time and write the check then. Online banking makes this transfer nearly effortless (and usually free), and because banks are tirelessly competing for your business, your bank either already has online banking or will be pressured into getting it soon.

Planning for Future Expenditures

I've mentioned before that cars die. The actuary rate for the death of cars is right around 100 percent, and strangely enough, it is the same for people, microwaves, and your water heater. You can't, without becoming annoyingly compulsive, figure out when everything in your world will need replacing, but you can make some basic allowances for how long things may last. Your car can go for well over 100,000 miles if it's taken care of, and an air conditioning unit should last at least 15 years. If yours is 10 years old, the time to save for a new one is now, so that when it quits working when it's 90 degrees and humid, you can smile through your perspiration. If your mechanic is sighing and shaking his head when working on your car, you should have been saving for a different one long before now.

Create a List

There are some standards you can count on. The day you buy a car, it's time to start saving for a different one. In the perfectly degunked world, you have paid cash for this current car and can put away what would have been your car payment for the next one. If you are making payments, you still need to be thinking about its replacement, and as soon as you are able, and absolutely as soon as it's paid off, begin saving toward the demise of what you're driving now. With other things in your home, like a faucet or the toaster oven, the expense would go under the category of "home repairs" unless it is for a major item you know is up for renewal, and then it can be saved for in its own savings category.

The big goal is not to be surprised. You knew the furnace was 20 years old. You knew the warranty was for 18 years. You don't get to be shocked when it quits working. You just have to be prepared to, somehow, pay for it.

Don't forget, if you get caught short, you have an emergency fund. Although you will have to beef it up again once it's depleted, it can be used for the things that sneak up on you until you get more knowledgeable about what can go kaput, and when.

TIP: Have a list of anticipated major expenditures, and add money to your emergency fund with the thought of being able to fix the things on the list. It might include the following items:

- √ ***Roof: Most last 10–20 years. How old is yours?***
- √ ***Major appliances: Estimate the age of each, including items such as water heaters and pool pumps, and guess when they're going to go. Murphy's Law dictates that these units will die at the worst possible time: my stove quit working on Christmas morning when I had two shifts of family to feed.***
- √ ***Automobiles: Cars are now engineered to run at least 100,000 miles. Consumer Reports, or another comparison-type publication, may be able to help you estimate when yours is going to die.***

- √ ***Heating/cooling systems:** These units last anywhere from 10–25 years, depending on the quality. If you live in an area of severe weather, you absolutely need to plan for this expense.*
- √ ***Plumbing/electrical:** If you live in an old home, you may know that major plumbing or electrical work may be required at some point. Hopefully, you worked that into your monthly expenses when you purchased your home, but if not, plan for it now.*

Make Saving a Goal-Oriented Activity

Saving for future expenditures can be fun. It can strengthen and reinforce your goals, your values, and your family, and when your family provides support for a savings plan because they recognize it as a benefit for them all, it doesn't become such a chore. I have friends for whom spending money on clothes or going out to dinner is verboten because it is much more important to them to provide exciting opportunities for their family to share. One year, they went rafting in Colorado, and the year after that, it was hiking somewhere I would never go, but they had a great time. It is well worth it for all of them to give up some things in order to save for these trips. Is there something you are willing to sacrifice some current pleasures to get?

Saving for vacations, an engagement ring, or a convertible can keep you within your budget for current spending and keep you out of debt from impulse buying. If you remember your goals, you won't tempt yourself into spending money you don't have, and when you pick out a ring (not at the mall), you'll know you won't be still paying for it on your fifth anniversary. And, looking at a previous section in this chapter, you'll know you got the best deal for what you did buy. Aren't you proud of yourself? You go, informed consumer.

Avoid Co-Signing

All of us, at some point, will probably be asked to co-sign a loan for someone else, be it a friend, child, or other relative. This is almost always a bad idea.

***CAUTION:** If a person needs a co-signer, it is because they either have little credit or poor credit. In either case, it puts you at risk for being responsible for the loan in full. That is what you are promising as a co-signer: you are responsible for the repayment of the loan if the first signer defaults, and if you don't make a payments on time, it goes on your credit report as a late payment, lowering your credit score. Even if the payments are made on time, it reduces the amount of other credit you can receive because you have signed on to be responsible for this debt until the loan is completely repaid.*

A request for you to be a co-signer is usually made with the best intentions from the person asking. If they have no credit, they promise they will make all the payments as promised. If they have bad credit, they promise they will be better at it this time around. In either case, there is no history to count on the payments being made. If you are tempted to say yes, make certain that you will have the money available to make all the payments on the loan if need be.

If you are considering co-signing a loan, there are a few things you can do to hedge your bets on the principal borrower being able to make the payments. Pretend you are a bank. Have the borrower get their credit report. Look over all of the financial dealings for the past year. See if other recent payments are being made on time and if their report shows a good history of debt repayment at any time. Ask to see their budget, and have them explain how they expect the payments will be made. This might be a good time to either introduce or help them reinstate a budgeting plan. If they mumble about privacy, it would be appropriate to mention they came to you for help and you are protecting yourself.

This is not only good money management for you, it is a good example for the person wanting you to accept responsibility for their actions. Whether you say yes or no may very well depend on their past performance and their willingness to accept some new or further direction on their budgeting practices. Don't use this, however, to become their own personal money police. Co-signing does not give you the right to oversee every penny they spend—and to comment on their financial practices at family gatherings.

CAUTION: Avoid co-signing if you can, and if you choose to do it, protect yourself as much as possible.

Advice for Couples

The decision of whether to join your credit is as serious as deciding to join together as a couple—the implications can be far reaching and involve the ability to honestly communicate about money, credit, finances, and real estate ownership. Co-signing situations can quickly go bad, and many a relationship has been trashed by the broken promises of one party negatively affecting the other's situation. This can be a devastating situation for couples, regardless of whether you're married or not or have children or not. Financial stress can poison a relationship, so the clearer a couple is about its finances—who is to pay what bill and when, who controls the money, and what kind of expenditures are allowed—the healthier the relationship will be. When it comes to degunking a couple's finances, they will need to make some hard decisions about five separate areas:

1. General banking
2. Real estate
3. Bill paying
4. Credit usage
5. Investments and savings

Each of these areas can contain mine-fields of problems. The upside is that some of these areas also represent opportunities to build an asset base and financial security for the couple's future.

General Banking

Deciding how to do your banking as a couple—whether individually or jointly—is an important discussion to have. Many couples I know do everything jointly, but I also have happily married friends who have kept their finances completely separate. If you are deciding to commingle your finances, you must realize this is a serious step and it should be discussed thoroughly. It is vitally important for both parties to know everything about the other's finances before committing to a relationship. Nasty surprises of this kind ("by the way, I have $20k in credit card debt…") can cast a large shadow over a honeymoon in Hawaii. It doesn't mean you can't marry someone with finances worse than yours, but it does mean it should be out on the table early in the game.

Although it is certainly not your intention (and wasn't for the 53 percent of couples that divorced last year), marriages and relationships end. There will be a great deal of cleanup to do concerning your finances if this happens. In most cases, neither member of the couple is happy with what is left, and both take a financial hit.

Real Estate

It will be important to discuss how you are going to own real estate (home or business) as a couple: sole ownership, joint tenancy with right of survivorship, tenancy by the entireties, or tenancy in common. Each of these options has its benefits and downsides. You should investigate each option thoroughly and discuss them with your other half. Married people do have certain rights that nonmarried couples do not, so nonmarried couples will need to address inheritance and dissolution situations through legal documents. The most important piece of advice I can give you is to talk about the situation with your partner, read up on what your options are (there are a ton of good real estate books out there), and talk with your attorney if you are serious about purchasing property together.

Bill Paying

A good discussion to have long before becoming a cohabiting couple is who will be responsible for the day-to-day financial matters. Who will pay the bills? Who goes to the bank? We had been married about a minute and a half before my husband relegated this responsibility to me (we had discussed it previously, but he made it into a bit of a weird ceremony), and it has worked out very well for us. I actually care when the bills get paid and that the checks get deposited. He has had some "selective amnesia" on this front and now can't remember where the bank is, or what one does there, but that is a different book. The key is to have some understanding about who is going to do what, akin to the "who cooks, who cleans, who mows the lawn" discussions. Domestic disputes about money or bills can get mean quickly. Decide from the onset who's responsible for what. This decision is usually made out of preference—usually there is one partner or the other who either cares about this subject more or likes it better than the other. If situations change—one partner decides to stay home to raise a child, for example, or a spouse loses a job—you may have to change the arrangement to fit new living situations. Having a good set of ground rules and expectations, however, is a great place to start.

Credit Usage

Credit usage is different from bill paying. Other family members—children, parents, or other relatives—might be using your credit, so it's important to be clear on what the terms of use should be.

> **STORY:** You've recently married a man who has a teenager. Your husband's child has always had one of his father's credit cards. You have now assumed the responsibility for paying the household bills out of your joint checking account, and you notice that the child has a $300 monthly bill for online services. Are you expected to pay for this out of your salary? Does your husband pay for this separately? What about the child? Wasn't his credit card for emergencies only? There are many questions that can be discussed as the result of this situation. Don't be shy about discussing such issues with your spouse. Unresolved resentments can be nurtured by not having these talks, even if they become arguments, and you need to come to some agreement over these types of situations.

If there are no children, you and your spouse still need to discuss credit usage—whether you have debt, how much debt is acceptable, and what your goals are for your debt situation. Similarly, this type of discussion should include any car loans, equity lines of credit, installment loans, monthly services, or mortgages.

Investments and Savings

One of the great financial pluses about being in a couple, if both of you are working, is that you have the opportunity to build an asset base more easily than single people. You presumably share living and housing expenses, so there are economic benefits there. But, with two incomes, you can also leverage that earning power to invest and save more aggressively. Regardless of whether you are investing in the stock market, buying and selling real estate, or simply putting money away for a mutually held goal, coupledom can be a situation that can help build financial stability quickly—if both parties want similar financial results. If you both share a fascination for the stock market, have a knack for fixing up old houses and reselling them, or possess a passion for eBay auctions, you can make big strides in meeting your financial goals. Talk with your partner about how you want to save and invest, how much you want to put away, and what your financial goals are (both as individuals and as a couple).

Summing Up

In this chapter, you've taken your budgeting process to the next level. You've learned how to standardize your record-keeping so you keep your records up-to-date and how to use technology to help you manage your financial records (even though the pencil-and-paper methods works just fine too). I've talked a little bit about saving certain documents for tax purposes. You should know now that one of the most important ways to keep your finances degunked is to look at what you buy, what you pay for your purchases, and how to get the best price on everything you need. You've learned why it's important to set money aside and plan for major future expenditures and why, if you are ever tempted to co-sign for a loan or line of credit, you should rarely, if ever, do it. I've also covered the five major areas that couples need to talk about if they're serious about staying out of financial trouble—and maintaining a harmonious relationship!

The point of fine-tuning your budget is to get closer to your goals. None of this is done for sport, and all the steps you take toward further organization will help you optimize the good choices you're making. By becoming an admirable record-keeper, an informed consumer, and a planning expert, you are taking the money you have and putting it to the best possible use in line with your long-term goals. This is a good use of your time and resources and will serve you well in your long-term degunking process.

Investments and Savings

Summing Up

Degunking Other Expenses

Degunking Checklist:

- √ Save on vehicle purchases and maintenance.
- √ Comparison shop online for everything.
- √ Decide how many shoes are enough.
- √ Degunk your gift-giving habits.
- √ Align the holiday shopping expectations in your family.
- √ Budget for vacations or long weekends.

Chapter 8 got you in the mood to sit down and take control of your household expenses, and Chapter 11 showed you how to further fine-tune your budget management skills. In this chapter, you'll get to expand those skills and apply them to other expenses as well. Gunk can happen quickly when you start talking about cars and clothing and gifts and vacations. Without planning and good decision making, you can zing yourself in the heartbeat it takes to say "yes" when you should be saying "not now".

Drive Time

Let's start by looking at how you can keep your car costs down. This is an area where many people spend more money than they realize, and more than they can afford. Our cars come loaded with expenses that we often forget about:

- √ Finance charges, late payments, and extra loan fees
- √ Taxes
- √ Insurance
- √ Maintenance
- √ All the extras—gas, car washes, detailing, and those hub caps that spin around

If you're thinking about getting rid of your current car and purchasing another, the first thing you should do is take a quick look at the expenses incurred by the car you now own. Your Monthly Expenditures sheet should help here, as you should have numbers down for payments, gas expenses, insurance, and maintenance. Reviewing what you're currently spending will help you understand what would change by getting a different car and help you decide what you can afford. The last thing you want to do is to walk on a car lot without knowing your limits. Car loans (and the dealers who sell them) have really gotten out of hand in recent years. The dealers are so anxious to sell you something that they will often finance a car for a longer period of time than in previous years. They do this to entice customers to buy more car than they can truly afford, which makes for a twofold problem. First, if you can't afford the car, it doesn't help to finance it for a longer period of time. That only insures that you'll be paying interest longer and will make the loan company happier. Second, by stretching out your payments for longer periods of time, it almost always means you will be "upside-down" on the car for the life of the loan, meaning you will owe more than the car is worth. If, by chance you need to sell the car during the life of the loan, you will owe more on it than you can sell it for, and you will have to make up the difference out-of-pocket.

I know I've said this before, but an auto purchase is not a good investment, like your home. It doesn't raise your net worth, and cars depreciate considerably each year. You'll want to be especially careful about how you decide when and why to make that change.

Do You Really Need to Replace Your Car?

Replacing your car by purchasing a different one can quickly gunk up your finances. By and large, the cheapest car to drive is the one you already own, so think carefully about why you are considering a vehicle purchase:

- √ Are you tired of your car?
- √ Does it need a major repair and you don't know if it's worth putting money into it?
- √ Is the mileage climbing to the point where you think it's going to start breaking down?
- √ Does your monthly car maintenance bill look like a new car payment?

Only you can decide if purchasing a different vehicle is a good idea, but if you must, check out the guidelines in this section before making an auto purchase.

TIP: Cars are depreciating assets, and the only way to get your money out of them is to drive them as long as you can. Regular vehicle maintenance is one way of insuring that you avoid huge, unexpected repair bills in the future. If you shop wisely and buy a top-rated vehicle, it will last you that much longer and will have fewer repair bills. (See the section "Look Online" for advice on how to research, comparison shop, and price cars online.) Try to avoid buying today's trendiest car, especially if the car doesn't really fit your needs.

The Leasing Option

Leasing is a losing proposition for everyone except the dealer. Making payments on a car for four or five years and then having to give the car back is an amazing scam. I'm sure the dealers wished they had thought this up with the Model T. Even more astounding is that if you go over your prescribed mileage limit in your leasing contract, you may have to pay another few thousand dollars when you turn the vehicle in, as well as being docked for any nicks or bumps the car picked up in its travels. You have now made a down payment, made payments for years, paid penalties, made repairs, and still don't own anything.

CAUTION: One problem with leasing is that the law doesn't require car dealers to disclose their calculations, and thus you likely won't know what you're really paying for in your lease. I've worked with many clients over the years who got themselves into leases only to realize a year down the road that their leased vehicle ended up costing them much more money than they ever expected.

When I have questioned people as to why they decided to lease, two main points are voiced:

- √ The payments were lower on a lease than a purchase. The problem here is that while the payments may be lower, you still aren't left with anything at the end of the lease. In the short term, you get the use of the vehicle. In the long term, you get nothing. It is akin to renting a car for four or five years.
- √ For what they could afford, they could lease a higher-priced car for the same price as a lower-priced car's purchase payment. In other words, they leased in order to drive a car they could not afford to purchase. These individuals saw a vehicle as a physical representation of their self-worth or self-image. A good question to ask is why it's important to have such a status symbol.

In either case, leasing is a bad deal. You are getting taken, and it is with your approval. Change your expectations to fit what you can afford, and purchase instead of lease.

If I still haven't convinced you that you shouldn't lease (and you might be feeling this way because you don't think you can afford to purchase a car), here's what I'd like you to do. Hold off leasing the car of your dreams for six to eight months. It's likely that you can keep the car you have now going for that time period, at least. Put any money that you would spend on a car lease over this period into a savings account. At the same time, try to improve your credit score some by following the degunking techniques in Chapter 10. When the waiting period is over, you might find that you'll have enough money saved up and your credit score is good enough that you can purchase a car instead of having to lease one. And when you go to purchase, seriously consider a quality used car, as I'll discuss shortly.

Comparison Shop

When you buy, the key is to shop until you drop—until you drop the phone, I mean. Comparison shop, and do it by phone. If you are buying from a dealer, tell the salesman what you're looking for, and mention you are getting cost comparisons from at least three other sellers. Tell him to give you his best price, because it's the only one he gets to give you. It's amazing how much of the car buying game disappears when you are not facing the salesman in that little cubicle with the car you are considering in your line of sight. There is no such thing as a once-in-a-lifetime offer. There are different cars on the new and used market every single day. If you don't get this one at the price you want, wait. Another one, with a hungrier seller, will come along.

Look Online

Another way to shop for a car is to use the Internet. Shopping online can be very helpful when looking for a car. I did a search recently for a car we were looking for and found quite a selection (including the one we bought) at dealerships within a 30-mile radius to where we live. I sent e-mails to get more information, the salespeople answered my questions, and we only went to a few dealerships instead of tramping around up and down "Car Dealer Row." We got a great price, bargained before we ever left the house, got extra features that were part of the Internet deal, and certainly had a less painful experience than walking into the dealership cold. I still detest buying cars, but you can take steps to make the process better than it used to be.

TIP:* *One of my favorite sites for car shopping (well, "car fantasizing" is more like it, since I hope my current vehicle lasts another decade) is* www.edmunds.com*. This site has Blue Book values for all cars, so I can see what my current vehicle is worth as a trade-in. It also has invoice and option pricing for virtually every car made today. This site can help you research new and used car prices, get free quotes from nearby dealerships, bargain with salespeople, understand car-dealer terminology, and explore various reader discussion groups. If you are mystified by the process of buying a car, this site will help eliminate a lot of that confusion. So, when you actually walk into that dealership, you will be prepared for all the lines the salesperson can, and will, throw at you.

New or Used?

Buying new, as I'm sure you are aware, is the most expensive way to buy a car. The immediate depreciation on a new car can put you upside-down (you owe more than the car is worth) immediately if you are borrowing most of the money to buy it. This is money you will never recover. It is much more advantageous to buy a car that is a few years old if you are looking for something in the "newer" range. In either case, there are multiple sites on the Internet to check for what a new or used car is worth, and these sites can be used to your advantage in making a deal.

Let's say that you finally decide to replace your 10-year-old Toyota with that Lexus you've had your eye on for years. And why not? You deserve it. You've kept your current car as long as you can and you just got a promotion at work and a sizeable raise. It certainly would be nice to drive around the neighborhood in your shiny new luxury car with leather interior, a working stereo that still has its knobs, and tinted windows. Away you drive to the only dealer in town....

Before you show up at the dealer wearing a sign that says, "I'll buy any new car you can sell me," do a little math. You need to understand how much money you're wasting by purchasing a new car off the lot instead of a used (pre-owned) vehicle. Buying the new Lexus could cost you $50,000 or more (as much as I paid for my first house), and you will likely need to finance it for five to seven years (ouch!) unless you have the money sitting in the bank. This wonderful good-smelling car probably looks like it's worth every cent, but the real truth is that it will depreciate at least 20 percent per year over the next two years. If you were to purchase a pre-owned model that was just two years old, you might be able to pick one up for $32,000 to $35,000. The kicker is that you'll not only save money ($18,000) because of the purchase price differences, but you'll save another $4500 in finance charges, taxes, and insurance. Notice how the pre-owned model can save you approximately $22,500. If you had to earn this money (before you paid income taxes), you would need approximately $30,000 to cover the difference between buying a new car and buying a pre-owned car.

Let's go one step further. If you have no debt to pay off with your huge raise and your finances are completely degunked at this point, then put all of your raise in a separate account to save up for the Lexus. When you have enough, pay cash. No finance charges, no fees, no muss, no fuss. This is, by far, the best way to buy a car.

TIP:* *If you are shopping for a car, you may find that there are a lot of three-year-old vehicles available. The standard term of most leases is 36 months, so many of those cars are returned leases, and most are in good shape. The Blue Book value of a car takes a big dip after three years, so looking at cars this age is a good idea. If you keep in mind that most vehicles today are engineered to last 100,000 miles or 8–10 years, the purchase of a 3-year-old vehicle is probably a good investment.

Now that vehicle pricing information is easily accessible, there is no reason to go to a dealer without real-time knowledge of a reasonable asking price for any car. Buying a newer car from a dealer can also net you a warranty if they are very sure of the car, which is a comfort when buying a used car. Many dealers also offer longer-term "certification" in the form of a drive train warranty lasting as long as if the car were new.

***Caution:* Buying from a private party can be cheaper than buying from a dealer, but make sure you can take the vehicle to your mechanic and have it checked out. There is little recourse in a private sale if the car turns out to be a lemon, and having to sue someone is a lengthy and expensive business. A trip to the mechanic is a small price to pay to find out the shape the car is actually in and if it needs work. This information can become a bargaining chip in the negotiations.**

Vehicle Financing

In the area of vehicle financing, it is common to take the easiest road. People without the full cash price in their bank accounts often buy from a dealer because it's more convenient for the dealer to arrange for financing. This is almost always a bad deal for the consumer.

Before you step foot in a car dealer showroom, make some phone calls to your bank to find out if you qualify for a loan and the best terms they will offer you for a car purchase. Check with your credit union through work, or check with a friend who just bought a car to find out where they got their financing. Check online at sites such as **www.eloan.com** to see what kind of interest rate you can get.

***TIP:* Don't walk into a vehicle dealership unless you have prearranged financing. Even if you find out that the dealer has better terms, having a financing deal in your pocket beforehand is a huge bargaining chip. This is one way of making sure that you get the best financing deal overall. When you're sitting in front of a car salesperson waving your preapproved check, they are going to be much more willing to bargain with you on terms and pricing. Car dealers hate it when a customer walks out the door and a sale is lost—especially if that individual has a check in hand.**

Car buying is not a fun experience for most people, and it is tempting to buy something quickly just so that the horrible process can be over. To do well on an auto buy, you need to carefully research models, options, and financing; this process shouldn't be an emotional or impulsive purchase, and it shouldn't be done in a single day. Take your time, do your homework, and walk out knowing you got the best deal possible, with financing, if you need it, to fit your budget.

Vehicle Maintenance

One of the areas where most people can save a few dollars is in vehicle maintenance. Dealerships try to position themselves as the best places to go for service. I have found this to be blatantly untrue. They are the most expensive places to have your car serviced, and they certainly haven't cornered the market on quality. For routine oil changes, for example, there are several national chains (Pep Boys and Auto Zone, for example) that can do this type of simple maintenance quickly and cheaply. Why pay $75 for this service when you can pay $25? Another choice is to find a mechanic in your area whose prices are competitive and take your work to him. There is a lot to be said for having someone who knows your car, and by continuing to check prices when you need work done there, you can be sure you're getting a good deal. If they quote a repair that is much higher than you believe it should be, don't hesitate to question them, and bring in competitive pricing from other shops.

CAUTION:* *When you purchase a new car, there is a warranty attached. Check to see if the manufacturer requires you to receive "authorized service" from the dealership so that the warranty is not voided. With certain expensive European makes, this is the case. If dealer service is not required, don't use the dealership to maintain your car. There are plenty of qualified mechanics out there who can provide the same (or better) quality of service. Even if the warranty stipulates dealer service, there may well be small print that says, "or other authorized service providers." Although the dealership will certainly try and keep all the money in-house, it is very possible your mechanic, as long as they're not doing the work in their driveway, can be considered an "authorized provider."

When you're faced with major-service milestones, it's important to make sure you have a reputable and experienced mechanic servicing your vehicle. Check around your neighborhood, and ask friends who they use for car repairs. You can get information online and through the Better Business Bureau as well, but be sure to speak to some actual people for a recommendation to find a mechanic that meets your requirements.

Don't Play the Fashion Game

Out of all the things we buy on impulse, clothing is probably at the top of the list. We all need clothing. I know for sure that my city has an ordinance against running around naked. The problems happen when we don't know when to stop. We stuff our closets with clothing, buy new items for every season, and have wardrobes fit for royalty. How much is enough? There are seven days in a week. You need to be dressed all seven of them. How many shirts, pants, suits, and (take a breath) shoes does one need to fulfill the requirement of dressing every day?

Everyone needs a clothing budget. When people are severely gunked up financially, the first thing they think about is reducing the clothing they purchase. It is, however, not realistic to think you will never need clothing again, and it's even less realistic to expect that your growing children will somehow fit into last year's winter clothes this year. The challenge for your clothing budget is *balance:* how do you balance your family's clothing needs with the reality of a limited budget? I have a few (okay, many) thoughts on this subject that I hope you will consider. Read on.

Degunking Your Closet

The first thing to do in this organizational process is to go through your closet (and the closets of your family) and separate out everything that no one wears or that doesn't fit, is damaged or worn, or is sentimental and you can't bear to throw out. Start a shrine box for the sentimental items and get rid of the rest, either by having a garage or yard sale or by donating it all to a worthy cause.

***TIP:* My rule of thumb is, if I haven't worn it in the last two years, I get rid of it. If you adopt this policy, harsh as it may seem, you will discover a few things:**

- √ ***You have a lot of clothes that don't make practical sense. This will force you to think about the utility of future clothing purchases and what you really need.***
- √ ***You keep old clothes for sentimental reasons. Your mother's wedding dress or your father's felt hat may be important keepsakes, but you should limit how much of this stuff takes up space in your closet.***
- √ ***You have several (or dozens, as my husband recently insinuated) pairs of shoes that you neither need nor use. The wear-it-or-give-it-away rule applies to shoes too, I am very sorry to say.***
- √ ***You save your children's and grandchildren's clothing. Are there people who might be able to use these items now—such as your local women's shelter or the Salvation Army?***

By degunking your closets of this type of clothing, you will free up a lot of closet and storage space. By donating these items, you will get a tax deduction and benefit someone who needs your castoffs much more than you do.

Once you can see what you actually have, you can determine whether you possess enough for your needs. Is it still too much? Now is your chance to change your habits if your clothing budget has been close to the National Debt and time to take a realistic look at your needs as opposed to your wants. By doing this, you can put your clothing spending into a more reasonable bracket and have a more organized closet, all in one swoop.

Shop Smart

For most of us, the answer is buying less, not more. For some, however, a new job necessitates different gear, and money you don't have needs to be spent to outfit you in steel-toed shoes, business-casual wear, or as my son recently requested, a tuxedo shirt to wear at the pool hall where he has to dress up on the weekends. In these cases, there are venues to shop where you can get a lot for a little. Resale shops can be a bonanza for all members of your family, and as in the case of a new car, someone else has taken the big hit to buy it new. If you buy it used, you can get it for pennies on the dollar. There are resale stores scattered all over the country (at last count, we had five in our town alone), and they're not just for those financially challenged. Venture in to a couple, and take a look. You might be pleasantly surprised.

Kids' Clothes

As anyone with children knows, kids' clothes aren't cheaper just because they are smaller. Major clothing retailers have sky-high prices for stylish little sundresses for one-year-olds and nautical-themed raincoats for toddlers. Without a reasonable budget for your kids' clothing, you could easily gunk up your budget just by outfitting them for Easter.

My advice on buying clothes for children is to think "reasonable" when it comes to outfitting your kids. Babies simply don't need expensive sleepers, and the excuse that pricey baby-wear is "better constructed" doesn't hold much water (unlike their diaper) when they wear it for only a few months. As children grow and become more demanding about brand names and styles, it is a good idea to give them a clothing budget for the year and let them help choose what they want with the thought that there is finite amount of money that will be spent. This gives kids in our culture, who have pressures to wear what everyone else does, a wake-up call about what clothing costs and provides them a head start for making good decisions when they leave your home and have their own charge card.

Shopping for Our Pets

I'm an animal lover (my dog is better than your dog), but I have to say that some clients go completely overboard when it comes to their pets. While it's important to recognize that pet care is a budget item, and good pet care is your duty and responsibility, that fur-trimmed raincoat for your schnauzer probably isn't an essential item. Do you buy a "vet recommended" food for your pet when a less-expensive brand has the same nutritional value? Examine your budget for your pet expenses and see if there is any gunk in there that can be eliminated.

Buy Only What You Love

One of the big lessons of shopping is that we all need to be more judicious in our purchases. What this means, primarily, is to eliminate impulse shopping and consider our purchases more carefully. In order for this to happen, you'll have to start with a budgeted amount. To make your money work best for you, the next step is to not buy anything you don't absolutely love.

Although I believe this is a good test for anything you buy, it is especially true for clothing. If you are a clothes person, you probably have something in your closet you recently bought on sale because it was too good a deal to pass up even though you really weren't all that taken with it. So there it sits. You may wear it a couple of times before deciding it was a mistake, but it was a waste that could have been avoided if you had made sure it passed the "I love it" test before you bought it. We end up wearing the same things consistently because they passed that test to begin with. Often, we can do with less if we are really fond of what we have. Make absolutely sure you truly like what you decide to buy.

Menswear

Men's business clothing has changed dramatically over the past 10 years, and many men now need standard business wear as well as "business casual" dress. In the 1980s, the uniform for men was coat and tie at most offices. In the 1990s, the trend moved away from the more formal attire. Now, there's a trend back to coat and tie. If you change jobs, there's no telling what the standards are going to be at your next company. There's nothing like needing two separate wardrobes to gunk up your clothing budget.

For those of you in that position, check out the T.J. Maxx type stores in your area. They usually carry a great selection of dress shirts, ties, and casual shirts and pants for the man who needs to look snazzy. If you like brand names, these stores are commonly stocked with familiar designer names at a fraction of the regular price. Depending on where you go, they may also have a decent selection of sport coats and dress pants as well. You can build a workable wardrobe over time that can be much less expensive than you would get shopping at major retailers and pick up some nice inexpensive socks at the same time.

Taking these steps on buying (or not buying) clothing can put a pile of money back in your budget, which could go a long way to helping you reach your other financial goals. Really, what's more important: another pair of shoes or getting out of debt?

Gift Gunk

Happy Birthday, Anniversary, Mother's Day, Valentine's Day, Sweetest Day, Grandparents Day.... Gift giving is big business, both personally and financially. We give a lot of gifts, and when working with clients, I find that it is the line item on the budget that shocks them the most. Adding up the total of your gift list can be an eye-opening experience, and these buying patterns can also be difficult to change. For a great number of people, gift giving is a part of life-long tradition, and changing it can be like asking them to remove a kidney.

Be a Good Gift Giver

Being a good gift giver can be a gift in itself. Take a look at the gift list you made in Chapter 4. Who on your list may not want or need the gifts they receive from you? It has been my experience that people in later years have more stuff than they need, and often a less-expensive but more personal offering—a drive to look at Christmas lights and a piece of pie at the local pie shop instead of yet another designer golf shirt—is much more appreciated. Babies are another prime example: how many toys or adorable outfits does a 10-pound human need? They don't know or care what you got them or how much it cost, so this gift is really for the parents anyway. How about starting a college account instead of adding to the overflow of Fisher Price plastic piling up? Be creative with your gift giving, and know that even if you have lots of money to spend on gifts, it's not always the wisest thing to do.

Think of gifts you've received in the past year. How many of these did you actually enjoy, need, or want? How many could you have done without? So often, gifts are given that aren't a good fit for the receiver and are almost immediately banished to the back of the closet or the garage sale pile. Take notice of gifts you really liked this past year, and I'll bet you'll find it wasn't the highest-priced item but the most thoughtful gift that you remember. Use this information to become a better gift giver, and understand that price is not the most important ingredient of giving good gifts.

Plan to Spend Less

For those who need to cut in this area, make known your intentions to those who will be affected. Mentioning long before Christmas that gifts will be less expensive than in the past will free up others to spend less too, and there could well be family members not as gutsy as you are that will be grateful for the reprieve. (See the GunkBuster's Notebook next on how to align expectations for holiday shopping.) The same is true for birthdays and other gift-giving occasions. For people who do not take your announcement well, that's unfortunate. The truth is, the amount you spend on a gift has nothing to do with the love, care, or feeling associated with giving.

Shop throughout the Year

A good way to lower not only what you spend on gifts but your stress level is to keep a gift list with you as you go about the rest of your business. Collect the gifts you'll need all throughout the year, and when the time comes, the gift will be there. I keep an area in a closet where gifts get put all year long, and when the birthdays of my sisters-in-law come in March and October, I nearly always have their gifts already purchased, and almost always I've purchased them on sale. I bet you see things for friends and relatives all year that make you think of them. Purchase them as you go along, with your monthly budgeted amount for gifts, and be much more prepared for the holidays than in years past. This won't work for everyone as children's sizes change quickly (along with their taste), but for the people on your list that this will work for, keep an eye out for good gifts as you do your regular shopping.

Avoid Last-Minute Purchases

Gunking in gift giving can occur when the occasion in question is tomorrow, you have 10 minutes to shop, and the only thing even slightly appropriate is well above your budgeted amount. At that point, you may feel you have no choice but to overspend. This is a situation that could have been prevented. So little in life comes with only one choice. Your choices in this case might be to find a bit more time to shop or make apologies to the recipient about your lack of a gift and deliver it in the next couple of days when you've had more time. A gift certificate is always an option, and although not very personal, it may well be just what the recipient would like best. That is the point, of course. Giving a gift is for the receiver and not for how good or not good you will look as the giver.

Make decisions on gift giving on the basis of what you can afford, and rearrange your spending to fit your budget. Now is the time to get better at this part of your spending. You will be happier and more balanced financially for it.

GunkBuster's Notebook: Align Your Holiday Shopping Expectations

Every year, when the holidays roll around, it may seem as if everyone has different expectations about what they should buy and for whom. If you have a large family—and even if you don't—it's important to get all the major parties to discuss together how to shop for the holidays. This is especially important if some members of the family are having economic difficulties. There's nothing worse than knowing you're having Christmas dinner with the "well-off" brother who buys presents for everyone and feeling obliged to rack up a bunch of credit card debt to save face in the gift-giving department.

In these challenging economic times, most people understand that times can be tough. Lavish gifts aren't always appropriate; in fact, *lowering* the bar on expectations is often a good thing when it comes to gift giving, as so many of us have more "stuff" than we need already. Here are some suggestions for aligning holiday shopping expectations with the members of your family:

√ Plan for the holiday season. Start discussing what the expectations are for the holidays in the summer. This can begin with a conversation at a family gathering or with your family members individually. If you are degunking your budget, explain that you are making some changes and will be making changes in your gift giving. Mention as well that you would rather your siblings didn't spend a great deal of money on you, either, and would so appreciate their respecting your boundaries. This is not only for those to whom degunking is a necessity. It is very possible that different gift-giving habits would be best for your family even if everyone is doing financially well. Discuss and decide on a gift-giving policy. This can be as restrictive or open as you need it to be. I know a family of adult sisters who all chip in to give to a charitable cause every year as their gifts to one another. At Christmas dinner, they decide which organization will receive the money. Often, families will do grab bags or just give to the children. This is a thought, but the truth is, most kids get so much over the holiday season they lose track of what they've received or where it came from. Keep in mind that there may be people who don't like the new ideas and fully intend to keep things as they were. That is their choice. Your responsibility is to decide what is a good choice for you and stick to your guns. Broadcast your plans. Once you've decided on how your family is going to celebrate (and shop for) the holidays,make sure everyone knows. Children, grandparents, and friends need to be included in these announcements. If you've decided on a $10 limit for all gifts, it's essential to get the word out. If you've decided on a "no toys, no clothing" policy, make sure everyone understands why, and know who agrees and who doesn't. Our family put a strict limit on the number of gifts and the cost for everyone involved. It was a good lesson for my children about having enough, and it saved us all from a holiday shopping nightmare.

√ Align expectations. If you follow these steps, you will have aligned everyone's expectations on what gifts they will be receiving from you. If they choose to go along with the new program, it can be a budget gunkbuster for them too. If not, there may be some tension, but you will still be on track with your goals, and will have done everything possible to inform those involved of your plans.

Use the Internet

The Internet has given us unlimited places to shop and the opportunity to check prices against each other with a click. It is a good idea, when buying nearly anything, to check online to see if it can be had for less money.

eBay is a wonderful resource. My daughter requested a lotion I had never heard of last year for Christmas. I found out it came from England, was not available in the States, and would have cost a small fortune to get a bottle across the ocean. For sport, I checked eBay, and there was a bottle for sale that, when I won the auction, cost less with shipping than shipping alone would have cost to get it here from England. It was a good thing for my daughter as I would not have bought it had I not found it cheaper, and everybody won—the seller, my daughter, and me—as it became a gift I didn't have to hunt down. When a friend turned 50, all of her closest friends and family got together and got her the fancy dishes she liked, with the serving pieces to match. I got them all on eBay, and it cost about one-half of what it would have had I driven over to Marshall Field's to get them.

Check around before you buy. Many Internet sellers don't have an actual store, so their overhead is tremendously lower than it would be if they did. As a result, they can sell to the consumer cheaper. The litmus test becomes how much less you can get it for online once you include shipping. The Internet sellers who get my business are the ones who have very reasonable or, in some cases, no shipping costs.

For major holidays, some stores run "no cost for shipping" promotions. This can be a great deal. Not only do you not have to go out to get whatever you're buying, it doesn't cost to get it to you. When something you would normally have to do ends up not costing you time or money, it's a good thing.

CAUTION:* *Always check and compare shipping costs, not just the retail price. For example, on Amazon.com, you may have noticed that some books in the "nearly new" category are priced lower than Amazon.com's price but have higher shipping charges. If you buy from a non–Amazon.com affiliate, your total price may end up being nearly the same as if you had purchased the product through Amazon.com. Buying from a private party on Amazon.com may include two downsides: (1) you're not guaranteed by Amazon.com that you will be satisfied with your purchase, and (2) shipping time may be much longer than with Amazon.com. Similar situations exist with many other online retailers, so always check and compare shipping costs before making an online purchase.

Amazon.com, and other similar companies, have carved their niche with new and used books. This can work out well for you in two ways. You can buy cheaper, as Amazon.com often runs discount specials on a great deal of its stock or there may be a used book costing a fraction of what the new ones cost. And you can sell books you no longer want or need on its Web site. When I first looked into doing this, I wondered why Amazon.com would let me do that, as it must take away from its business. It turns out Amazon.com isn't dumb. It takes a cut from the sale of the book, the payment arrangements, and the shipping costs. In this fashion, it can make as much money from the sale of my book as it would from a new one. It is still a win for me, however, as in most cases, I can get more for my book on a Web site of that kind than I could selling it in the garage sale.

If you decide you want to try this out, all of the Web sites (Amazon.com, Half.com) will guide you in how to go about doing it. Go to "sell yours here" and screens will pop up for the condition of the book and your selling price. To decide what price to place on it, go to the list of used books available and price it slightly under what one in the same condition is going for.

A good rule of thumb is that if you can't sell your book for more than $5 on a Web site, it's probably not worth your time to pack it and ship it.

Budget for Vacations

Don't take a vacation impulsively if you can't pay cash. Vacations are nonmaterial, and not only do they gunk up your finances, they can be psychologically harder to pay for since they're not something you have in hand. The crummy T-shirt and some snapshots may be all you came home with, and still paying for a vacation you took three years ago can get very old, very fast. It will also put a big hump in the road of reaching your financial goals. If you want a vacation, make it a line item on your balanced budget, save up for it, and then go and enjoy yourself completely.

I know a couple who love to travel, and they routinely put $300 per month into their travel account. They have little debt otherwise and always find ways to put aside their travel money. You may think that saving $3,600 a year for travel is goofy. That's fine. What are you saving for? The point is to make your budget and savings goals an extension of your values and work at it.

TIP:* *Even if you can't afford an annual overseas holiday, try to put away $50 a month for some time away. That will give you $600 at the end of the year to use as you choose. If you and your spouse save double that amount, you could have $2,400 every two years for a trip with (or without!) the kids. A nice two-week vacation can be a rejuvenating and relaxing time—especially if you avoid the temptation to check e-mail or call into work every few days to see what's happening.

Summing Up

In this chapter, I talked about different areas in your budget that can be degunked. When it comes to vehicles, there are many ways to save money on purchasing and maintaining them. You should probably also look at your closet and rethink your clothing buying habits. Gift giving is a huge sinkhole for most people, but if you plan your gift giving, chances are you can save a bundle in this area. And, while many people think of a vacation as a luxury, it can be affordable if you budget for it consistently. Don't forget that comparison shopping online is the best way to find out what the best price is for all of these items.

Making changes in your shopping habits can be hard. No one is saying it isn't, and I'm certainly not telling you it will happen without making difficult choices. The point remains, however, that the goals you've set are there for a reason, and the lifestyle you are now living may have become a deterrent to your goals. You now have practical information to help you spend your money in a wiser fashion. Buying more than you need, or spending more than you have to for any item, can carry heavy consequences, both emotional and financial. When you change the way you spend, and these changes become habit, you will be amazed at what you don't miss and will happily wave goodbye to the guilt of spending more than you can afford.

Degunking Your Taxes, Benefits, and Insurance

Degunking Checklist:

√ Make the tax system work for you.

√ Adjust your withholding and plan for your tax refund.

√ Learn about which tax deductions you can take.

√ Learn how certain pre-tax deductions can help your budget.

√ Consult a tax professional to get advice on complicated returns or running your small business.

√ Know your employee benefits.

√ Buy only the insurance that you need.

Thinking about your taxes, employee benefits, and insurance may not get much of a slice of your time pie, but they should. These are areas where there are opportunities for you to save money and increase your tax deductions. While most people don't relish the idea of learning about the often hard-to-understand language of taxes, benefits, and insurance, it will behoove you to spend some time getting acquainted with their terminology and functions. The funds you spend in these areas, after all, are your hard-earned money. Ignoring these important concerns can cost you cash.

A lot of people only think about taxes in early April, when they are going nuts preparing their tax return. Most of us only think about our employee benefits once a year when our human resources department asks us to fill out our annual W-2 forms and update our insurance and deduction information. We seldom think about our insurance, except when renewing a policy. Even with policy renewals, your insurance company is happy to do that automatically so you don't even have to think about it then.

The problem is that if you aren't keeping an eye on your tax situation, the news you get when you file may not be cheerful. Not fully understanding your employee benefits can cost you money you can't afford or may cause you to pass over investment opportunities that would be detrimental to miss. Neglecting your insurance needs can either cost you money or leave you underinsured, neither of which is good. In any case, these three areas probably contain a certain amount of gunk for you, and it's time to clean up and degunk these expenses. In this chapter, I'm going to show you where to find hidden money in your tax, benefits, and insurance decisions that you can reallocate to better uses. I'll try to make it as painless as possible. Honest.

Make the Tax System Work for You

I know that the idea of making our tax system work for you seems like a dream. Your thought may be that only high-priced attorneys and accountants can do this, and they do it only for their fabulously wealthy clients. I am here to tell you that there are some easy steps you can take to degunk your tax situation each and every year. It will take a little time on your part, but the rewards can be substantial. The areas on which most working people need to focus are tax refunds and deductions. Both points will be covered in the following sections.

Plan for Your Tax Refund

One of the easiest ways to degunk your taxes is to plan for your tax refund. Most people think of their annual refund (if they get one) as a big pile of money the government was nice enough to send along just because they were good this year. Not. This is money that you overpaid the government. The idea behind payroll withholding is to give employees an easy way to pay taxes throughout the year so they're not hit with an income tax bill all at once. The money that makes up your refund was actually yours all year, but because of what you decided (and filed with your employer) to have withheld, you gave the government the right to keep it, make money on it, and give it back to you at its convenience.

Don't Blow Your Refund

I contend that you shouldn't look at your tax refund as a "bonus." This was covered in Chapter 6 (degunking your debt), but a tax return isn't money you found on the street and can then use for a major shopping spree. You've got debts, right? You have kids to support, right? You're trying to save for a house, right? So don't blow this refund on something that won't help your long-term financial picture. Here are a few places where you can put that refund so it will help you in your long-term degunking plan:

- √ Use it to pay off one or more debts. Remember the debt payoff worksheet you developed in Chapter 6? If your refund is big enough, you can make a dent in your personal debt by applying the refund directly to the balance you are currently paying off.
- √ Contribute to a savings account for another financial goal, such as a down payment on a house, your kids' college funds, your home emergency fund, or a family vacation.
- √ Put it in a savings account for next year's IRA contribution, which will be tax deductible.

Don't blow your refund on something frivolous. Think about your financial plans and apply that check where it will do you the most good.

Tweak Your Withholding

The easy way to tell if you're withholding too much from your paycheck is if you get a big tax refund every year. As I mentioned earlier, this isn't a wise way to manage your money, regardless of how good it feels to get a big check in the mail.

***TIP:** If your annual refund is more than a few hundred dollars, you're not claiming enough exemptions for tax purposes. Adjust your withholding by going to your employer's human resources department and filling out another W-2 form to increase the number of exemptions you're taking.*

Under-Withholding

If you go nuts with exemptions, you could end up owing money at the end of the year. If this is the case, the government can impose fines and penalties if you under-withheld and owe a substantial amount of tax. It certainly seems colossally unfair that the government can hold your money and not pay you interest but if you don't pay the government on time you get to pay a fine, but that is the deal. Go figure. You don't want to be in the situation of having to cough up a check for the IRS and being levied additional fines. Talk about adding insult to injury!

***TIP:** If you are concerned about not withholding enough for your taxes, use the worksheet on the back of your W-2 form to calculate how much money you should have withheld from your paycheck. If you are confused by this form, ask your human resources representative or an accountant for help in deciding how to best manage your exemption status.*

Get Your Withholding Just Right

The goal for your withholding is to withhold only enough to cover your taxes and get a minimum refund. Don't treat your tax refund like a savings account. Although it might seem easier to get a hunk of money in the beginning of the new year, this is not a foolproof way to end up with extra cash to pay off your Christmas bills, and it shouldn't be counted on to boost your first quarter earnings. The point is to keep control of your money as you earn it and not hand it over to the government to hold for you. The best way to treat the money you earn is to try to get it in your hand as you go along and then be disciplined enough to use it in a way that helps you reach your financial goals. If you plan to use your refund to pay off your credit cards, why not pay them off throughout the year? That way, you're paying more toward principal in your monthly payments and less in interest. This will help you pay down that debt faster.

Apply Your Earnings toward Your Goals

The point here is to actually get the money you earn and put it to use as it becomes available. You have certainly learned some discipline over the course of degunking your finances, so I think you're ready to take the money that would have ended up as a refund and apply it to your financial goals. Pay off debt, bank it, or use it to go to the Cayman Islands and see the stingrays—whatever fits with your financial goals.

Learn about Deductions

An important way to degunk your taxes is to learn about deductions. You are probably entitled to more deductions than you are currently taking. I'm not expecting you to learn the tax code, but it is important to know about common deductions available to most taxpayers.

Let's begin with a definition: a deduction is simply a decrease in your gross income. Deductions fall into two broad categories: pre-tax and post-tax. A pre-tax deduction means that the deduction is taken off *before* your income is taxed. A post-tax deduction is an amount that is taken out of your paycheck *after* you've paid taxes on your income. What's the difference? It can be substantial.

Pre-Tax Deduction

Generally, a pre-tax deduction is a very good thing. A pre-tax deduction reduces the amount of income you earn, as far as the IRS is concerned, so it reduces the amount of taxes you pay. Sound good? Here are some examples of pre-tax deductions:

- √ 401(k) contributions
- √ Medical savings accounts (employer sponsored) to pay for your family's medical care
- √ Child-care savings accounts

These amounts are deducted from your paycheck before you are taxed. Let's look at an example of someone who receives a $2,000 paycheck every two weeks. Table 13-1 shows the difference in spendable income after making deductions for savings and medical expenses. In the pre-tax example, the employee has taken advantage of the employer's 401(K) plan and a medical spending account. The post-tax example shows what happens if the same employee doesn't take advantage of those benefits.

Table 13-1 How your income is affected by deductions.

	Pre-Tax	Post-Tax
Gross Pay	$2,000	$2,000
pre-tax 401(k)	-$200	
pre-tax medical	-$100	
child-care account	-$100	
Net Pay	$1,600	$2,000
Tax (15%)	-$240	-$300
Take-Home Pay	$1,360	$1,700
Post-tax savings account		-$200
Post-tax medical expenses		-100
Post-tax child care		-100
Spendable Income	**$1,360**	**$1,300**

In the post-tax example, the employee, instead of using the employer's offerings, put money in the bank, paid for a doctor's appointment out of their check, and paid the child-care provider with a check. The post-tax person ends up with $60 less of spendable income than the pre-tax person. Keep in mind that this figure is *per paycheck,* so over the course of 26 paychecks, the pre-tax employee would have $1,560 *more* spendable income per year just because this person took advantage of the employer's pre-tax benefits. That's a nice sum to apply toward debt repayment or other savings. Notice that the pre-tax option also pays less tax ($240) than the post-tax option ($300).

Generally, any pre-tax deduction that you can make is a plus. It lowers your tax base and gives you a tax-free asset.

Post-Tax Deduction

A post-tax deduction is an amount that is taken out of your paycheck after taxes are deducted. Here are examples of these:

- √ Employee stock purchase plans offered through your employer
- √ IRA contributions
- √ Charitable contributions that you might make to your local church or synagogue

A post-tax deduction is a way to lower the amount upon which you have to pay taxes at the end of the year. The impact of a post-tax deduction might look something like the one shown in Table 13-2.

Table 13-2 The impact of making a post-tax deduction.

	With Post-Tax Deduction	Without Post-Tax Deduction
Take-Home Pay	**$24,000**	**$24,000**
IRA contribution	-$2,000	$0
Church donation	-$1,000	$0
Taxable Pay	**$21,000**	**$24,000**
Taxes (15%)	-$3,150	-$3,600
Spendable Income	**$17,850**	**$20,400**
Reduction in taxes	**-$450**	

In this example, the individual who made contributions to their IRA and local church realized a tax savings of $450. This individual had to spend $3,000 to get that savings, but they also gained an asset (increasing his IRA balance by $2,000) and felt good about helping their church (priceless).

While the government, in its inimitable wisdom, has given us some ways to decrease our tax liability, they don't always make it easy to know what these loopholes are. To that end, you need to get educated about what you are allowed to deduct, as a private person, and to use these deductions to your fullest advantage.

Applicable deductions include medical expenses over a certain amount, child-care expenses, charitable giving, interest on mortgages, and interest on education loans. There are books written every year on what deductions you can take and what rules change for the current calendar year. As each state has its own tax rules and the federal laws change every year, I will not spend time going over every possibility here. Get the current tax software, buy a book on the subject, or have a long discussion with a tax professional in your area.

Consult a Tax Professional

If you have gunked-up finances, the last thing you probably want to think about is spending your hard-earned money on yet another bill. I will say, though, that unless you are comfortable with numbers and reading tax preparation materials, you should consider consulting a tax professional. A one-hour consultation could be well worth the fee. Tax professionals are, believe it or not, eager to help you out of your tax mess. They will try to ensure that you pay as little tax as possible, and they'll make certain your forms are filled out correctly as well.

It can be well worth paying someone to do your taxes if you have no interest or time to do it on your own. Sometimes, letting the experts do what they are trained to do can pay for itself in the long run. However, with the current availability of computer software, it is much easier to do your taxes on your own and be accurate. The key here is to compare the cost of the software with the cost of getting your taxes done and make a decision based on real numbers and your history with this kind of task before purchasing anything. Be advised that the federal tax software is separate from the individual state software, so you will need to purchase both.

Keep Good Records

You've heard this before, but I'm going to say it again. A surefire way to make your tax person fond of you is to keep accurate and complete financial records. This is one of the first steps in any financial assessment process, and walking in with your numbers nicely organized (as opposed to carrying a shoe box full of receipts) will put a happy smile on the face of your accounting professional. Keeping good records of everything will make getting the deductions you are entitled to much easier, and the less time you spend with the tax person, the less it will cost you.

If You Owe the IRS

If, by chance, you owe money to the government, there are a couple of things to note. The most important thing to know is that you must pay this bill. You will be found. We live in a numbers-generated society, and your numbers will tell on you at some point. You need a Social Security number to get a job, and through those records, the IRS will come knocking. You can't claim IRS debt on bankruptcy, so that won't get you out of it either. The best way to deal with IRS debt is to contact the IRS, negotiate down the total of what you owe, set up a payment plan, and pay it. If the dollar amount is very high, consult an attorney who has experience dealing with the IRS.

Don't let this situation keep you from attaining your goals. Treat it like any other debt, and pay it off.

TIP: If you owe the IRS money, treat it as you would any other creditor. Call and talk with a representative. As with any other creditor, it just wants its money. The IRS will often work out extended payment plans with low interest rates. They know they can't get blood out of a turnip, so they'll do everything they can to work with you. The thing not to do is avoid the IRS, because they will not go away.

Audits

Just the word *audit* sends shivers down most people's spines. If the IRS notifies you that your tax return is being audited, don't panic. Sometimes a simple explanation of a minor problem is all that's needed; sometimes, it's more in-depth than that. In any event, the first call you should make is to the tax professional who prepared your return. That individual should stand behind their work and help you through the audit. If you prepared your own taxes, then it is up to you to deal with the IRS directly or hire an accountant to assist you through the process.

TIP: Some of the larger accounting firms offer "guarantees" or "insurance" policies on their tax preparation services. These can be a good idea as the additional fee for this service covers the costs of an audit and you will have the benefit of an accountant representing you every step of the way. If you have a large or complicated tax return, this is often a good investment. If this is offered with your return, be sure to read every word of the agreement, and know what you will get for your money in the case of an audit.

The good news about audits is that the IRS tends to go after high-income people. Unless you're making over $100,000 a year and have a mile-long tax return, you probably needn't worry about an audit.

Small Business Deductions

There is something nearly ethereal about the thought of being an independent business person. People get cheerful when they talk about making their own hours, being the boss, and making tons of money. What may not be understood immediately are the difficulties of making a business profitable and some basic principles of financial management and taxes. I have worked with dozens of clients who have small businesses, and there are many common issues that come up.

Planning to Start a Business

It's essential that you do extensive planning before starting your own venture. Before opening the doors on a new business, it is imperative to have funding. As a beginning number, make sure you have at least 6 months (and preferably 12) of your total expenses in the bank before even thinking of opening. Many businesses fail because new business owners think that there will be money to take from the business nearly immediately. This is not usually the case, and undercapitalization is the first reason businesses fail. Even if your business makes money in the first year, there will be expenses you never saw coming that will eat up profits as quickly as you can make them. Consider self-employment tax, for starters. Instead of paying the 7.5 percent that you now do for Social Security, you will be paying, as the business owner, the full 15 percent necessary by law.

Personal vs. Business Expenses

One of the things a tax professional will tell you, before you start your business, is to keep all business expenses completely separate from personal expenses. Keep a daily expense sheet, just as you do for home expenses, and have any credit card purchases on a card separate from your home account. This will make auditing and tax preparation much easier, and it will help keep you reality based when it comes to what you are actually spending and making.

CAUTION: Do not use personal or retirement savings to start a business. It's important that the money you use for a business venture are funds you've set aside specifically for that purpose. Don't jeopardize your family's home or your retirement savings on a venture that may or may not succeed. The media tells stories of people who have maxed out their credit cards to fund a business and have made a million. They tell you these stories because it's so unusual. What they don't talk about are the thousands of people who put up their home as collateral for a new business—and lost it. Don't put yourself in this position.

Home Office Deduction

There are unique deductions for small businesses. Again, the rules change constantly, but there are some you can count on. The home office deduction is one of them, but it's important to remember that the IRS has very specific requirements of what constitutes a home office.

If you have space used *exclusively* for the business, the costs associated with that space can be deducted. (The desk in the corner of the guest room doesn't make that room a business office, by the way.) If your Creative Memories supplies take up an entire room (which wouldn't be hard), that is a possible deduction. If you have a room that ends up being dedicated to your home-based business, then a portion of your mortgage (or rent), electricity, cleaning, and home upkeep bills can be deducted from your income. Again, check with the IRS or your tax professional in terms of what specifically can be deducted.

Other Deductions

There are other tax deductions you can take as part of a home-based business. This isn't the place to go through them all, but I will mention a few:

- √ Mileage. Keep close track of the mileage you put on your vehicle for business purposes. That can be a huge deduction at over 30 cents a mile.
- √ Licenses. If you need a license or education to perform your job, those fees are deductible.
- √ Health insurance. These expenses are deductible for small business owners who are self-insured.
- √ SEP-IRAs. This is an IRA that a small business can set up to benefit its employees. The contribution limits are very different from regular IRAs, so check the laws on this deduction.

Tax laws change from year to year, and a local tax professional who makes it their full-time job to save small business owners money can be worth their proverbial weight in gold. My guess is you don't have the time or inclination to know everything there is to know about your taxes, so find someone who does. And, for goodness sake, don't keep your receipts in a shoe box.

Know Your Employee Benefits

It's important to know what you already have in the way of benefits or insurance simply by virtue of where you work. If the company hasn't made you aware of what is available to you, truck yourself down to Human Resources and find out for yourself. There are some benefits that are fairly universal from one company to the next and those that are distinct to the public or private sector. I will outline those that are either common or required by law and leave it up to you to get more information from your employer as to the various flavors of benefits it provides. You might be in for a pleasant surprise.

It could be that your employer is providing you with benefits you haven't had before. Part of your job is to make yourself aware of which benefits your employer is providing and be sure you are using the benefits provided to their fullest potential.

Full Time vs. Part Time

Some of these perks are only available to full-time employees. Although some companies are making health insurance available (at a price) to part-time employees, providing benefits is very costly, and most companies cannot afford to provide them to everyone. Separating the full-time from the part-time employees is a natural line by which to gauge who gets benefits and who doesn't. For some companies, keeping most of their employees working less than 40 hours per week is a way to avoid paying benefits.

TIP: ***One of the first things to find out about a company you are interested in working for is what their policy is on company-paid benefits such as health insurance. You need to find out whether their plans fit with your particular needs. Finding out you will never get full-time hours when you are the sole provider of health care benefits for your family is a good reason to go elsewhere to work. The time to ask is before you accept the job, not after.***

Health Insurance

For full-time employees, there are a few benefits that are standards, but usually there is health insurance available for you and any dependents. Gone are the days of free coverage, but the cost for health insurance through your company is usually much less than being self-insured. It is important, however, to find out about the different plans available to you and to choose according to your needs and preferences. The difference between an HMO and a PPO is not just the amount you may pay for any given procedure, but where you have to go to have it done and the range of doctors from whom you can choose. A PPO will cost you more than an HMO, but you may have more choice of providers. What is more important to you? Are you attached to your doctors but they aren't a part of your network? How much are you willing to pay to keep your pediatrician or the doctor who removed your appendix? Ask these questions before committing to a plan, and as you may only get to make a change once a year in your coverage, make sure it's something you can live with for that long. Other questions to ask include the coverage of preexisting conditions and the wait time between getting hired and when your coverage begins.

TIP: ***Many companies offer "cafeteria" benefit plans, meaning they will give each employee a dollar amount of free benefits, and with that amount the employee chooses which benefits the company will pay for. Any additional benefits offered in the cafeteria plan will cost you money, usually in the form of a deduction from your paycheck. Keep in mind that company rates are usually much lower than paying for these benefits on your own. Take advantage of whatever benefits you must have (and can afford), even if they cost you a bit.***

Life and Other Insurance

Life insurance is another common benefit. Often, the amount of life insurance is a multiple of your yearly income, usually in the range of one to five times your annual salary. It may be possible to purchase additional life insurance for your dependents. Disability insurance can usually be purchased for the employee, and dental insurance is often available for a small premium. Some companies even offer low-cost vision examinations and reduced-price glasses and contacts, usually through a particular provider. Decide which of these insurance packages is essential for you and your family and pass on the others.

TIP:* *Dental insurance, while offered less often than in years past, is usually a great deal for families with children. If it's offered as part of your company's benefits, seriously consider it.

Pensions and 401(k) Plans

Traditional pension plans are seldom offered these days, but some large and well-established companies do have them. These plans are sometimes called "defined benefit plans" in that they tell you how much you will be paid when you retire. There is less risk with these plans, and the amount is not dependent upon how much you can save. If well run, they can be a gold mine for retiring employees. That being said, you shouldn't rely solely on your traditional pension plan to fund your retirement. In today's economy, it's important to have other sources of income. (See Chapter 9, "Degunking Your Savings and Investments," for more on this topic.)

TIP:* *If your company has a pension plan, it is very possible that further life or supplemental health insurance is available through the administrators of that plan. This would apply to the employee and their dependents and does not usually require a medical exam for approval for any applying member. This could be a huge benefit for a hard-to-insure member of the family. For companies that allow part-time employees to enter into their pension plan, these extra insurance benefits would be available to them as well.

401(k) plans are often called "defined contribution plans," as their value is determined by how much you contribute to the plan. As I've mentioned in other parts of this book, 401(k) plans can be a very good way for you to build up your savings for retirement *and* save money on income taxes. You should definitely participate in these plans, if at all possible, at least to the amount of the company match.

Medical Savings Plans

Medical savings plans (sometimes called Flexible Medical Savings accounts) can save a small fortune for those who have medical expenses not covered by regular insurance. An employee can put aside, pre-tax, up to $4,000 per year for medical expenses. Then, as the money gets spent, the employee puts in a request for reimbursement from the account. Although the list of what constitutes a "medical expense" is determined by the government, it's surprisingly large. It includes false teeth, smoking cessation programs, medically required air conditioning, contact lenses and glasses, and special education, none of which is paid for by your insurance plan. The full list of eligible expenses should be available at your workplace.

CAUTION: The government is not dumb when it comes to medical savings plans. You may not claim these reimbursed expenses as a deduction on your taxes since they have already been paid for with pre-tax dollars. You may either use your flexible spending account to pay for them or take them as a deduction, but never both.

Another plus with medical savings plans is that the money doesn't actually have to be in the account before it is used as reimbursement. You are required by law to predetermine the amount to be deducted per year for these plans; this amount cannot be changed. Therefore, after the first employee contribution of the year, the entire amount can be requested as reimbursement. The employee can then make the rest of the per-paycheck contributions to refuel the account. Another detail to remember with your flexible spending account is that any money left in the account at the end of the year is lost—it's a use-it-or-lose-it plan. Be sure to have as clear an idea as possible of how much you will need for this account during the year.

I have a friend with a chronic illness who uses this plan to keep more money in her hand during the year. Although the $4,000 cap doesn't come close to paying out her tons of noncovered expenses, she can do that first chunk pre-tax and use the rest as deductions on her taxes at the end of the year. It is also a very popular way to pay for orthodontia with pre-tax money.

If you know you have a medical expense coming in the next year that will be costly and won't be paid for by your insurance, this is a great way to use pre-tax dollars to pay for it.

Child Care

Money for child care, up to $5,000, can also be set aside pre-tax. Unlike the medical spending account, these funds must be actually in the child-care account before you can be reimbursed. This type of account follows the same IRS rules as the flexible spending account in that money used from this account cannot be taken as a child-care deduction on your tax form. Any money over and above the $5,000 can be fully deducted.

Retirement Health Service Plans

Getting more common in the public sector (government and municipal jobs) are Retirement Health Service plans. These plans are specifically for medical costs and insurance premium payments, and the money is set aside pre-tax during the working career of the employee. Once retirement has taken place, no more money can be added to these accounts.

The plan is quite specific as to how much and which money can be used to build this account, and it may not be used until after retirement. Unlike a flexible spending account, the employee can treat this money like a retirement account in that it can be divided up into different investment vehicles. The benefit is that the money is not taxed as it leaves the account. It stays pre-tax, and there are no penalties for removing it for eligible expenses after retirement. This type of plan is mostly limited to jobs where the government or a municipality is writing your check.

GunkBuster's Notebook: How Much to Budget for Pre-Tax Plans?

A big question people ask when they first encounter the myriad of pre-tax and post-tax plans offered as part of their company's benefits is how to figure out how much to put away per individual plan. In this notebook, we'll work precisely on that problem.

Let's first start with some assumptions:

- √ Your income will not change in the next year.
- √ You have worked out your budget (in Chapter 3) and know how much you have for child care, medical expenses, savings, and other expenses.
- √ You do not anticipate any big changes in your life during the next year, such as divorce, buying or selling a house, or the addition of a child.
- √ You have good financial records for last year's expenses.

When it comes to your 401(k) contribution, if you have budgeted $100 per month to put into retirement savings, this is the place to put your money. If at all possible, try to maximize on your company's matching plan in your 401(k). If you can't afford to do this now, at least set out this amount as a goal. For example, if your company matches you 50 cents for every dollar you contribute to its 401(k) plan up to 6 percent of salary and you can only afford a 3 percent contribution this year, that's fine for now. Next year, plan to contribute 4 percent, and so on, until you've reached the 6 percent mark.

As for child care, find out how much you paid (in total) for child care last year. If you do not anticipate this amount to change, assign that amount to be deducted from your paycheck for your child-care account. Always make your best guess in these situations because this deduction amount cannot be changed once you've decided on it.

When it comes to medical expenses, it's important to work with known information. Tally up everything you spent out of pocket (expenses not covered by insurance) on health care last year. Don't forget your medical plan's deductible amount, and make sure that number will be the same this year as last. If you are unsure, err on the side of being conservative and withhold a bit less than you think you'll need. You will still receive some money tax free on this account, and you won't lose anything.

Next year, look at these deductions and assess whether your selections were appropriate or off base. If you burned through your medical savings plan before June, you should consider withholding more funds next year. If you ended up with a surplus in your child-care account, revisit the amount that's being deducted for that purpose. And, if you found you started accumulating more money than you expected in your bank's savings account, perhaps you should consider contributing more to your 401(k) plan at work. It's all about trial and error, but make sure you're working with the best possible information before making these important deduction decisions.

Other Benefits

There are many other benefits that may be offered by your company. Many of these benefits, if available, can help you degunk your finances by helping to pay bills, increase your savings and investments, or improve your quality of life.

Employee Assistance Programs

Some institutions offer counseling, legal, or budget help to their employees through outside organizations, usually at little or no cost to the employee. Often called Employee Assistance Programs (or EAPs), these plans can be a huge benefit. Before signing up, though, make sure you understand the relationship between the outside provider and your organization and what the confidentiality agreement is. Most EAPs are very conscious of the confidentiality of these issues, so they take great pains to make sure that your company isn't privy to the details of your personal problems. If you need professional help and can't afford it, EAPs can be a great benefit to you and your family.

Employee Stock Purchase Plans

Some companies offer the benefit of allowing employees to purchase company stock at a discount, if it's done through regular payroll deduction. They usually offer the stock at around 15 percent off the current trading price. The reason they require regular payroll deductions is so that employees cannot time their purchases of stock to key product launches or other opportunities that would create an unfair advantage. If you believe in your company's future and think its stock will do well over the long term, these types of stock purchase plans can be very beneficial. Be sure to discuss any decision to buy your company's stock with your family and financial planner.

REALITY CHECK: Acquiring stock in the company you work for is a good way to build up investment savings over time. You should, however, be careful about putting all of your eggs in one basket. If you don't have other investment programs set up, you could end up with all of your investment money in your company's stock. If your company falls on hard times, you could lose your job and your investments. If you don't think this is possible, consider the unfortunate people who worked for Enron a few years back.

Adoption Benefits

Some companies offer financial assistance to families that adopt children. This is a rare situation, but I've seen companies that offer a $5,000 one-time payout to assist in the adoption of a child. If adoption is something you've been thinking about, this type of employee benefit could be a tremendous help to your budget.

Tuition Reimbursement

If you work for a company that provides tuition reimbursement and you are inclined to further your studies, this is a great way of degunking your education budget. Some companies will pay for the cost of books and tuition up front, while others will reimburse only when you submit a grade report. Either way, if education is part of your long-term planning, this type of benefit can be exceedingly helpful.

Health Clubs/Weight Loss

A healthy employee is a better investment for a company. Illness impacts health-care costs, time away from work, and overall productivity. To the end of promoting health for their employees, many employers have offered incentives in the form of health-club benefits or weight-loss programs. The bottom line for the company is that if these programs help you and your family stay healthy, it will spend less money on health-care costs. The benefits to you will span much further than that, including better health, improved self-esteem, and the respect of your employers.

Company-Specific Benefits

Companies often offer free or discounted services to their employees and their families. For example, if you work for an airline, you probably receive discounted airline tickets. If you work for a brokerage house, you may receive free investment accounts and advice. And, if you work for a restaurant, you probably receive at least one complimentary meal per shift. Wherever you work, you should find out what company-specific benefits you can receive. However small, these benefits may contribute to degunking your budget.

Do Insurance Right

Apart from employer-sponsored insurance, you should decide on the types and level of insurance that you need to have. Choosing deductible amounts and whether or not to do term or whole life is a little like painting the bathroom: performing the work is such a pain that it's a pleasure to think you won't have to do it again for years. The trouble with that is that situations change, and in the time it takes for the bathroom to need fresh paint, you could be in a different stage altogether in your crazy, wild ride of a life.

Insurance is a form of protection. Bad things are probably going to happen in some form to you or people you love. Insurance is necessary, but as with anything else, you can go overboard on what you purchase. How you decide how much insurance to buy will be based on your needs and your available resources. Have a basis for the decisions you make, and make them within your financial parameters. Keeping this in mind, there are five major areas of insurance that you should consider:

1. Health
2. Automobile
3. Life
4. Home
5. Disability

You may not have to purchase all of these types of insurance right now—some of them might be employer sponsored, and you might not need some of the other types. Still, it's important to know how to think about these types of insurance.

Self-Insured Health Plans

If you don't have health insurance through your employer, it's a darn shame, but it's not the end of the world. There are more policies available now for individuals, and although they may well include a larger deductible (what you pay before insurance kicks in), these plans will still protect you and your family from financial ruin in the event of a catastrophe. The sad fact is that many people have little or no health insurance. It is imperative to get some kind of insurance for you and your family, if at all possible. You're a walking financial time bomb without it. A broken leg can cost you $20,000, and a major illness or surgery may be many times that amount. Be covered, even if it's only for the bigger issues (hospitalization or accident). Don't put yourself in the position where an appendectomy will kill your credit or where you're afraid to get the care you need because of the cost.

***CAUTION:** A major cause of bankruptcy in this country is caused by unforeseen and crushing medical bills. If the sole wage earner in your family is seriously injured and there's no medical insurance, the medical bills won't be classified as "gunk," they'll be a disaster.*

Medical insurance policies are offered through regular insurance companies, and there are a variety of different plans and deductible amounts to choose from. There are numerous insurance brokers around who can help you, even if you're on a limited budget and think you can't afford insurance. Understand that if you have children, the premiums will increase, and if you need maternity coverage, your premium will nearly double. My suggestion is to get catastrophic medical insurance, which is insurance with a high deductible and no maternity coverage that will at least cover you in the event of a trip to the emergency room.

Automobile Insurance

Automobile insurance is required by law in the United States. If you own a car, you must have insurance. It's important to note that auto insurance follows the car, not the driver.

***CAUTION:** If you are driving a friend's car and get into an accident, your friend's insurance rates will go up, not yours. That's not a real friendship builder. Also, if someone other than the insured driver is driving and there is an accident, the amount of coverage may be less than if the owner was driving. The moral of this story is to not drive anyone else's car if you can help it, and make sure they understand what happens if there is an accident.*

States can set their own minimums for coverage, but a running standard is that you must carry at least the following:

- √ $20,000 in medical coverage for people involved in an accident with you. This amount is per person in a single incident.
- √ $40,000 total in medical coverage in a singe incident. So, if there were four people in the other car, they still only get $40,000, which negates the $20,000 each if there are more than two people.
- √ $15,000 in property damage coverage for a single incident. This covers the other car, the lamppost you hit, and the car you sideswiped on your way to the lamppost.

I hope it is immediately evident to you that this coverage is woefully short. I know the state had to start somewhere, but this would cover only the most basic in medical costs and property damage. The other party and the other insurance company would legally come after you personally and would sue you for the remainder of costs. More standard coverage amounts would be $100,000/$300,000/$50,000, and as medical costs and car replacements continue to get more expensive, coverage amounts can go up from there. The moral is to be covered, but be covered much above the minimum. There's no need to lose your home over a car accident.

If you need to reduce the amount you pay for insurance, shop around for cheaper rates. You can also make your deductibles higher and lower the amount of coverage you have. While this means that you will need to come up with more out-of-pocket money if there is an accident, by raising your deductible and lowering your coverage you can save on your total cost of insurance.

Life Insurance

Everyone should have at least enough life insurance to pay for their funeral. When checking on funeral and interment costs recently, I was astounded to find that a traditional funeral and burial can cost in the neighborhood of $15,000, and that doesn't include the luncheon. That's probably not a burden you care to leave to your family.

The next question most people ask is about the purpose of life insurance and how it is designed to work. Life insurance is intended to replace money that won't be forthcoming if someone dies. As your financial needs change as you get older, so will your need for life insurance. For the parents of a young family, the need for life insurance is huge. What would it take to replace their earnings until the children are out of college? As the family grows older, the need for insurance changes. When the children are out of college, and hopefully providing for themselves, the question is different. If one partner dies, how much would be needed to keep the other partner in the same lifestyle? It is a sad thing when a partner dies and the other is forced to move for lack of money. Do you need enough insurance to pay off the house? For a single person, who is in charge of your final arrangements? Is there someone whom you would like to benefit on your death?

The younger and healthier you are, the cheaper your insurance will be. Actuarially, people die on a schedule, and life insurance is priced per that schedule. If you buy it when you're young, and get a guarantee of consistent premiums for a set number of years, you will do better than if you wait until you're older.

Term vs. Whole Life Insurance

There are two basic types of life insurance: term and whole life. Buying term insurance is buying insurance only. The only benefit is if you die. Whole life is a combination of insurance and an investment vehicle. In my opinion, you will do better separating these two functions. Invest in the ways previously discussed (see Chapter 9), and buy term insurance to protect yourself and your family.

TIP:* *Saying no to life insurance is appropriate under certain circumstances. If you are single, have no dependents, and don't have to worry about caring for anyone else, then you can probably pass on buying life insurance. If your family relies on you for income, or if you have a spouse, children, or other family members who need assistance from you, you should consider buying some type of life insurance.

Home Insurance

Deciding to insure your home is an important choice. If you're a renter, you might want to consider renter's insurance. It is usually very inexpensive and can protect you against theft, fire, or other disasters. If you own a home, your mortgage company requires that you have insurance on your home before you can receive a mortgage. Think seriously about the terms of this insurance. Your home, after all, is probably your most important asset. Keep it safe. Revisit the terms of your home insurance at least every few years in case the value of your home or its contents changes. In some states, home values have increased significantly over the past few years, and if you haven't reviewed your policy in some time, you might be underinsured.

Disability and Long-Term Care Insurance

Disability and long-term care are other insurance possibilities. Disability insurance is getting more common for one-income families and for the self-employed. Based on how much money you need to live on per month, you purchase insurance to pay you that amount for a set period or until you turn 65. Again, to make this less expensive, there is a waiting period before the benefits become active, anywhere from 30 days to a year. The longer your waiting period, and the shorter time the benefits pay, the lower your premium.

Long-term care insurance would pay for care in your home if you become unable to do two out of the six listed activities without help. The activities are bathing, continence, dressing, eating, toileting, and transferring (moving from place to place in your home). The point of this insurance is to hold on to independence for as long as possible, and for some people, being able to stay in their home is their line in the sand.

Summing Up

Taxes, benefits, and insurance may not be the most fun subjects to ponder, but they are a necessary part of life. These are sources of potential gunk, and if you are serious about degunking your financial life, it will be important to spend some time educating yourself about these areas. Tax law can be a jungle, so if you're not comfortable using tax preparation software, consult a tax professional to help you find the deductions to which you're entitled. This is especially important if you have a complicated tax return or run a small business.

Another area where there can be financial gunk, as well as substantial opportunities, is your employee benefits. It's your responsibility to learn what your benefits are and how best to use them. If you work for a large company, you may be surprised to find some very attractive benefits that can help you save, help you manage your expenses, and improve your quality of life. Related to all of this is your insurance situation. If you are covered by employer-sponsored insurance plans, you are fortunate, but there is most likely a cost associated with this insurance. Even if you have lavish job benefits, you will still have to purchase home or renter's insurance, as well as disability and life insurance. Be sure you know what your options are.

All of these areas are your responsibility, and the fact that these aren't easy areas to understand is not an excuse to ignore them. Who knows? You might find that your insurance guy is a real hoot, and your accountant probably knows more IRS jokes than you ever thought possible.

Finding Hidden Money

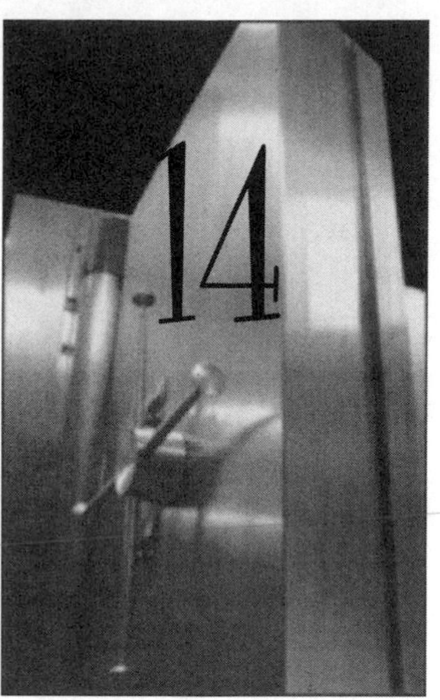

Degunking Checklist:

- √ Don't buy what you don't need.
- √ Spend money appropriately on things that you do need, and realize that you don't always have to trade off quality for a good price.
- √ Eliminate clutter from your life and make a profit along the way.
- √ If you can't sell it, donate it.
- √ Learn to make money with your hobbies.
- √ Find ways to spend less on entertainment.
- √ Use your special skills to increase your income.
- √ Use the barter system to trade goods and services.

If you've been following the advice in this book, by now you are probably in good shape with your records, your goals, and your spending. Perhaps there is still a bit of a shortfall in your budget, or maybe you just want to shore things up financially even more. Now is the time to find the hidden money in your life and in your budget. Unfortunately, it probably won't be hidden in a hollowed-out book or under your mattress, but there is money to be had in your life that can be yours by way of a bit of resourcefulness—or some better choices in what you're doing with it now. Let's go hunting!

Don't Buy Unless There Is a Need

Part of the degunking mindset is to watch your money more carefully, avoid impulse spending, and never forget your financial goals. Before you pull that item off the shelf and head for the register, stop for a moment and ask yourself if this purchase lines up with your goals. If you decide against buying, you may "find" a whole lot of cash produced by purchases you simply don't make. There can be so much money wasted on items that we don't need or don't think about before we buy: designer ice cream (even though the store brand tastes just the same), a high-priced latte at the local café, or premium gas when regular will do just fine. Added together, these expenses can represent a significant sum.

An easy way to find money is to look in your checkbook. Even though you have allocated $50 per month for clothing, it doesn't actually mean you have to spend it. The difference between needing an item and wanting it can be the difference between buying it and not. True, sometimes wanting it is enough. The question becomes, what is more important at this time—realizing your goals or buying another pair of boots? This is not to say you have to justify great need for every purchase. The point is that for this season, when you are dedicating yourself to paying off your debt (or whatever your main goal is), would that money be better spent on something temporary or something more permanent? What, for now, can you do without? It is very possible that next year, or in a couple of years, after following the degunking principles in this book, you will be in much better shape to succumb to a few more "wants" than you are now. If they are "wants" now and not "needs," put the money to better use by paying off debt or saving for that house. Put yourself in the position to be able to satisfy future "wants" without getting in the way of your very important goals.

So, look, there it is. Money. Right in your checkbook where you left it.

Spend Money Appropriately

There's a sentence that absolutely drives me crazy. I go nearly nuts when people say, "I never settle for anything but the best." Really? Why in the world not? In this life, there are so many choices for every possible purchase that immediately going to "the best" without checking out the second, third, and fifth options is like tearing up money into small pieces and using it as confetti. Businesses have become so competitive that there are now many shades of "really good" and "the best" is very often just a marketing hype.

TIP:* *Don't be suckered in by the power of a brand name. While you may think that the quality of the coffee beans you buy at your local café is absolutely the best (at $15 per pound), have you ever tasted the cheaper coffee beans sold in bulk at your local warehouse store? At a third of the price, you may think that you're buying poorer quality, but you may be surprised. It's worth giving it a try.

Shop for Price *and* Quality

When choosing something for yourself, your home, or your jewelry box, make certain you check out what is lower in price than what you would normally pick. Look at all the qualities of each item, look at the prices, and make decisions for purchases that have nothing to do with brand name, what it says on the bag it comes home in, or whether or not the store was a luxurious place to shop. Don't listen to the salesperson, who will always push the higher-priced item. Don't listen to the loud or seductive ads. Use your own judgment, think for yourself, and determine if what you're being offered is a good deal. And, it goes without saying, don't pay full price.

Shopping well doesn't mean buying junk. Just because the gas grill you're looking for at the specialty outdoor furniture store costs $450 doesn't mean you're relegated to the $129 model from Wal-Mart. Check around for a version with the same features as the fancy one that isn't being sold by someone in a nice shirt. A home improvement store (Home Depot, Menards, or Lowe's) may have a similar model with a different brand name—or a house brand name—for much less. There is a possibility of them having the very same model cheaper simply by virtue of being able to buy in bulk. If you just have to have a particular brand, go online and get the best price available within your budget, perhaps waiting until grills are out of season and you have a chance of getting a better deal.

I had a client who needed to outfit a professional office in a short time, on a strict budget. She first went to all the high-end stores and looked at office furniture, lighting, window coverings, and carpeting. When she decided on the look she wanted, she started scrounging for the things she craved at lower prices. At T.J. Maxx, she found lamps that were nearly identical to those she drooled over at Marshall Field's. She went to a used office furniture warehouse to get the snazzy, though used, furniture and found designer look-alike shades at Home Depot for a fraction of what they were at the ritzy shade store. Her window coverings came from Target, instead of Penneys, and she outfitted her desk and drawers with Wal-Mart merchandise instead of Office Depot's offerings. Her net savings? Setting up her office cost less than 40 percent of what it would have, and it is a beautiful and professional space.

Don't Forget Your Goals

The bottom line is that you can't have everything you want. If you want to reach your financial goals, you have to be willing to give up something, and often it can be as easy as lowering the bar of your expectations for what you buy. The feeling of entitlement that you "deserve the best" can go on the chopping block first. There will be great freedom that comes from being out from under that particular delusion, and it will open up a new world of shopping possibilities. If you're more used to making choices based on comparisons, make sure to check out all the possibilities before you buy. Learn to be a discriminating shopper, and never believe the hype.

If you really love a certain brand of designer clothing because it fits you well and is of good quality, look for it at outlet malls or consignment shops. High-end designer consignment stores have popped up all over and for good reason—you pay about a quarter of the price for the items they offer. Also, don't forget charity thrift shops. A client recently picked up 5 wool jackets in spring colors for $3 each, and she ended up trading me a scarf for the pink one, which I wear constantly. The moral is that it doesn't matter where you buy it and your friends certainly don't really care what bag it came in. Make it your little secret, and you can laugh all the way to the bank.

Also always look for quality over quantity. Buying a really well-made product that will last you for years is far better than buying 10 of a cheap shoddy product. Did you know that 80 percent of Americans wear only 20 percent of the clothing in their closets? It's because people gravitate to what fits well and looks good over time.

Eliminate the Gunk in Your Life. for Profit

I have 10 bucks right now that says that most of the people reading this book have enough extra, unneeded stuff in their home to have a fair to midlin' sized garage sale. Some of you have enough to have a mammoth one. Garage and estate sales are a terrific concept: someone gives you money for things you no longer want. It is amazing what people will buy from a garage sale, and it gives all the junk in your house a new lease on life.

eBay is another great way to sell your stuff, and you don't have to have a big mass of items to sell as you would for a garage sale. You can sell one or a hundred things on eBay; it doesn't matter. Local antique stores that sell on consignment represent another option, if you happen to have old furniture from Grandma that just doesn't fit with your Mid-Century Modern décor. If you can't bear to sell your stuff, you can always donate it, which will get you a receipt and a nice tax write-off.

Garage Sales

I am a big garage sale fan. I have them, I go to them, and I've found the most amazing treasures that other people were willing to give up for cheap, and they seem just as happy about the stuff they buy from me. Here's a truth of life. You are not always going to want to use those dishes you got when you were 19, and when it comes time to actually have some taste, you can sell them at your garage sale to another 19-year-old, who will thank you until they're 28. Young married couples can sell all of the guy's bachelor stuff (including the neon beer sign—sorry, honey) and end up with things they both like. I went to a sale in my town last fall and there was something there from a garage sale I'd had the previous summer. It didn't go with her couch, so she put it in her sale. This is recycling at its best.

We and our families grow out of things, we change colors in our homes, we get gifts we may not care for, and all the items left over need a new place to go. The garbage is a poor choice. At the very least, a garage sale is a place where people without much money can get some things they need for much less than they would spend to buy it new. I've outfitted many a college student's room with small appliances over the years, and there is a family in town that comes to my sales because their kids are a year or two younger than mine and they can pick up some jeans and shirts for a fraction of the original cost.

Lest you think this is small change, most of the garage sales I've had have netted around $600 to $700. That would usually include an item or two for $25.00 to $75.00, but mostly it's $.50, $1.00 or $5.00 at a time. It all adds up.

Community Sales

If you don't have enough gunk to have your own garage sale, consider putting together a community sale. This can be done if you and your neighbors don't each have enough to justify having your own sale but together you have more than enough to attract some attention. You can split the cost of the newspaper ad and appoint someone to keep all the finances organized so sales are attributed to the proper seller. It's fairly easy to orchestrate, and it can be a great community-building opportunity. You could get your neighborhood further involved by making it a benefit and donating, say, 10 percent of your earnings to your neighborhood association, a local church, or your kids' school.

A few years ago, my daughter was in cheerleading and she and her friends needed new uniforms. There was no money in the budget to buy them, so we organized a garage sale at my home (I had the best location), everyone dropped off stuff at my house and helped organize, price the goods, and work the sale. In a three-day period, we made over $1,800—nearly enough for all the uniforms. With another bake sale or two, the uniforms were purchased and are still in use. The girls who got to wear them helped with the sale as well and were taught a good lesson of working together to get something that benefits everyone.

eBay and Other Venues

Some things are too good for the garage sale. eBay has made it easy to list items on its site, and as long as you intend to be a good businessperson, it can work out very well. There are lots of books out there on how to start your eBay business, so look for one that suits your needs. Suffice it to say that there are millions of people who buy and sell on eBay every day and many thousands who make a living at it. If you don't have the inclination to barter with your local consignment shop or find an antique dealer who will give you a fair price for your grandmother's favorite pitcher, eBay is a terrific venue to find customers who know the value of such items. If you aren't technology savvy enough to do this, maybe your resident computer whiz can help you sell your unwanted items on eBay.

The alternatives to eBay include resale shops and antique dealers, many of which will take things on consignment. These may be less-satisfying alternatives because you may not get your money as quickly and the item may not sell. It will be important to establish a relationship with a local reseller. If you choose this option, make sure your property will be handled with care. If you have a number of items to sell, like a closet full of the clothes you wore before joining the health club, it would be a good idea to offer some of the items to one consignment shop and some of the other items to another. In this fashion, you can try out a few different shops to see which you like working with the most and develop a relationship with them for future business. Another great thing about clothing consignment stores is that many of them donate unsold items to charity and will give you a receipt for tax time at the end of the year.

Swap and Shop with Friends

Swapping items with friends is another great way to save money. I've heard of a group of families who have kids ranging in age from newborn to 5 or 6 who get together once a quarter to swap baby clothes and maternity clothes (as one of them is usually pregnant). With the high price of children's clothing and the limited use they get because babies grow like weeds, swapping out clothing is a great way for kids to be fashionably dressed and know that those great duds they've traded will have a new life. This can work for adult clothing as well. The same group also brings some of their own clothes and accessories that don't fit, were given as a gift, or they just never wore. They sit around, have a glass of wine (not the pregnant one), and try on each other's offerings. They get to go "shopping" and end up with something different that just might become their favorite new item. Anything not chosen gets sent off to charity, and they take turns on who gets the tax receipt. A night of free entertainment, and a new cool pair of capris to boot! If you don't have friends who want to part with clothing, what about household gadgets? That smoothie machine you never use might be a good trade for the camping lantern you desperately need, and a friend has two. You can either make the party an event unto itself or do it as a white elephant exchange at your next barbecue.

If You Can't Sell Your Stuff, Donate It

If you can't stand the thought of selling your things, at least get rid of what you don't want. Stuff clutters up our homes and uses up our time. If you don't want it and are never going to use it, get rid of it! If you won't have a sale, donate it to a worthy cause and get a tax write-off. You will rid yourself of gunk you no longer have to dust and free yourself from the obligation to hang onto that lamp base shaped like the Eiffel Tower that Aunt Rita got you. (Actually, save that for me. I'm looking for one.) Go through everything you own and ruthlessly extract what you no longer want or need. Have a sale, sell it in other places (such as eBay), or donate it somewhere. If you get a wad of money for it, do what you do with extra money: use it to further your goals. Wouldn't you just get a kick out of paying off a credit card with all the stuff that's been messing up your house? Talk about win-win.

TIP: There can be emotional issues related to being a packrat. When people have been raised in poverty or consider their possessions as extensions of themselves, they are sometimes unwilling or unable to part with them. If this feels familiar and your clutter problem is gunking up your house, irritating your spouse and family or creating a fire hazard, it's time to make some hard decisions. What is really essential in your life? A clutter-free house, a degunked budget, and a happy spouse—or that garage full of newspapers, old baby clothes, and hand-me-down furniture? If the gunk in your house is creating disagreements, it's time to listen to your family members and decide how to rid yourself of the unwanted mess. Check out www.clutterersanonymous.net if you feel your clutter problem may be more than just disorganization.

Make Your Hobby Pay

Hobbies are nice, but hobbies can also be very expensive. As part of your budget degunking process, it is very possible you have chosen to eliminate your hobby in order to achieve your financial goals.

There may be another option. Can you sell what you dabble in? There is an appreciation for the work of another's hands. If you paint, is there a market for your work? Perhaps there is a gift shop in town who would love to carry the work of a local artist. Do you do calligraphy? There is money to be made in addressing wedding and shower invitations. If you knit, make scarves to sell. So many people with hobbies give their work away and don't ever think of selling it—not because they don't want to, but because they don't think they're good enough. Take some of your things around to local shops. Ask if they would be interested in selling your items on consignment. Really listen to what they say, and be open to suggestions. If they're saying that it isn't right for their store, ask about other stores. Ask for an honest appraisal of your work and how you could change your product to sell better. Keep in mind, most shopkeepers will want to double the price of whatever comes in their store or take 50 percent commission, so your items must be priced so they will still sell after that bump. A couple words of advice:

√ *Make it profitable.* There needs to be a balance between the work you do and the money you make. It's not worth selling an item for $10 when it cost you $14 to make it. Chances are, if it is something worth selling, there will be people who will buy it at a reasonable price—*reasonable* meaning you get your money back for materials and make a decent hourly wage. If you're doing it for love, at least make back the money you spent to make it.

√ *Don't quit your day job.* The goal is, of course, to make money, not spend more. This venture isn't an excuse to go buy tons of materials pertaining to your hobby, quit your day job, and go into business. This may be a way to still do what you enjoy but not let it get in the way of your goals. And part of the profits can always go to buy more yarn.

√ *Consider eBay as a test.* There are hundreds of artists and crafters who sell their work on eBay and other sites. It's a huge store they don't have to pay rent for, and the price to list an item is far less than the chunk a store would receive for selling the same item. It takes time to get items listed on eBay, but the time invested is well worth it if you can find out whether there's a market for your product. This may be a good start to selling your handmade things. One issue with eBay, however, is that you are listed there with dozens of other people making, perhaps, much the same thing you are. The competition can be fierce. If eBay doesn't work for you, it doesn't mean you're out of business.

Spend Less on Entertainment

If we really stopped to examine our entertainment budget, we might well discover gunk there. It's rare to find truly inexpensive entertainment available. Sporting events are no longer cheap, even if you can tolerate the nosebleed seats. Theater tickets can be a budget-buster, and if you have kids, taking the entire family out might simply be impossible if you're on a tight budget.

It is a quick default to get to Friday night, go online to get movie times, and drag yourself off to the show. At upwards of $9 a pop, a movie no longer qualifies as cheap entertainment. Take someone with you, have some popcorn (costing more per pound than a nice piece of prime rib) and a drink, and now you're up in the $30–$40 range to see a movie you may or may not like. Add dinner and you've blown a big hole in a $100 bill. There goes most of your monthly entertainment budget.

Hit rewind and try again. Rent a recent movie and invite another couple to your house to watch it. Have them bring a salad and bread, make that great lasagna, pour a glass of wine if you like, and have popcorn for dessert. In fact, if you're feeling really wild, sprinkle M&M's on top of your popcorn. You've now had movie night at home, with better food, more comfortable surroundings, and good company. If you still miss the movie atmosphere, hire some neighborhood kids to sit in front of you and throw popcorn at each other. What did this night cost you? The price of a movie rental, perhaps some extra food, and a quick look at the bathroom to make sure it was fit for company. So far, even with the cost of food and wine, you've probably spent a total of $15.

There are hundreds of ways to entertain yourself for less money than you currently spend. Some of the changes you can make will involve some planning, and some involve taking more notice of your entertainment options. Be creative with your entertainment choices. Your previous entertainment habits may be one reason your finances got gunked up in the first place. Make it a challenge to cut your costs, increase your knowledge about what's happening in your area, and learn more about having fun for little, or no, money.

Go on, now. Have fun.

Explore Your City

Find out what is available in the city in which you live. Most cities have opportunities for entertainment that just take a little investigation to find. Our town runs a concert series in the summer months with different bands each geared toward different age groups. Take something to eat and drink, and now you have a picnic with live music. Every week in the local paper, there are columns of things to do in our village and neighboring towns. There are at least four community theater groups in our area. As smaller, more community-based theaters continue to spring up, they are presenting a better range of options to see both famous and obscure showings of everything from magic shows to dance companies and musical groups—all without the astronomical ticket prices and $20 parking fees of going downtown. Check out your local paper to see what's available.

Local Sports Teams

Is anything exciting happening with your sports teams? As I am from Chicago, this one has been tough for me in recent years, but having a gathering around a play-off game or championship can be a ton of fun and much cheaper than going to the local hangout to watch it there. I have a friend who dearly loves college basketball (especially Duke), and his home is a veritable open house throughout most of March Madness. And, while ticket prices are going through the roof for most professional sports venues, there are still opportunities such as spring training and foreign teams—where the prices aren't nearly as sky-high. Semiprofessional teams can be a ton of fun for less money. Also, if you're a fan of college sports, there are inevitably those games to attend throughout the year, and prices and availability tend to be less competitive than for professional teams.

Several years ago, I got the fine idea of taking my son to a Bulls game. This was when Michael Jordan was playing, and ticket prices were ridiculous. As Christmas got closer, it became clear that getting tickets through traditional methods was not going to work. My husband called some numbers in the paper and let me know that there were two types of tickets available. Two seats in the nosebleed section were going for $375 each, or there were two tickets in the front row for, hold your breath, $1,200 a pop. Obviously, neither was a good choice. Instead, we got my son and a friend tickets for the Chicago Wolves, the minor Chicago hockey team. For $90, they sat in the front row with their noses on the glass and had a fabulous time. When they got home, my husband said to me, "I think if I had given the team $1,200, they would have let the boys play."

Neighborhood Exploration

With the renaissance of many urban core neighborhoods, the idea of "going downtown" (here near Chicago, we call it "going to the City") has become a more attractive option for many people. Gentrification of many downtown urban neighborhoods has created new areas that encourage walking traffic and sightseeing. This may represent an opportunity to explore different parts of your area that you've never seen. Go for a walk in an interesting neighborhood and stop in the local coffee shop for a nice Chai. If you're lucky, there may be some local talent on the guitar, for color. Total cost—maybe $8, even with the fancy-shmancy drinks. A drive through your many downtown neighborhoods can be great fun. Chicago at any time of the year is interesting, but a drive along the lakeshore in the summer can net you music from the band shell and some fireworks from Navy Pier if you time it right. Gas is expensive, yes, but at even at 20 miles to the gallon, a drive downtown taking in the sights and smells might cost us $5, or maybe $10 if I make my husband stop for ice cream. Compare that to an ordinary dinner at the not-so-great place up the street for $35 and the drive will win out for entertainment value, new experiences, and money in the bank.

Local Parks and Recreation

There are numerous recreational opportunities scattered throughout most areas of the country. Even in most urban areas, there is usually a network of parks and publicly funded recreation areas that everyone can use. All it takes is a little investigation, a few phone calls, or a search for the websites of your local park service. Especially in the large western states, many parks departments have websites that list hiking trails and provide maps for your convenience. You might be surprised to find the range of opportunities just a 15-minute drive from your house. Take the dog and go for a hike—it will be healthy and the time spent with family or friends will probably strengthen your relationships.

Individual towns are working hard these days to get you to hang around near home. There may be a gallery walk, a house tour, or a downtown street fair that is right in your backyard, and though in some way it is certainly designed to make someone money, these events can be enjoyed for a minimum outlay of your entertainment dollar.

Do What You Do Well for Profit

Chances are there is something you do well that someone else would be happy to pay you for. This doesn't fall under the'"hobby" heading but could be more of a special talent. It could be doing oil changes and other repairs on the family car to save money or being especially good at cleaning out closets and reorganizing them in an orderly fashion. Perhaps you can rewire a light switch, fix a leaky toilet, replace broken windows, or repair a damaged roof.

What is your specialty, or what is something you don't mind doing that other people detest? Do you bake great cookies, paint children's furniture with bright colors and animals, or get a charge out of cleaning out your gutters? There are people in the world with more money than time who would be more than happy to pay you to make the cute snowman cookies for their child's classroom party or have you come and weed their flower beds one a week in the summer. This is not usually instant money, nor is it money you can always count on. This would more likely end up being a nice windfall now and again and a way to augment an income you are already receiving. It is possible to make this into a business that will pay real money over a long period of time, but that will take more effort and dedication.

Many people with this opportunity have a difficult time deciding what to charge for their services. Keep in mind, this is your time and expertise you're selling and it's worth good money. You don't want to price yourself out of a job, either. So, where do you start?

Set a Fair Price

Setting a price for your services is important to preserve short-term relationships as well as to obtain sufficient income to make the project worth your while. If you're working with time and materials, make a list of everything it costs you to produce your product. If you're making cookies, add up all your ingredients. Make a batch of your most requested cookies and see how long it took you, including licking the beaters and cleaning up. Give yourself an hourly wage, add the ingredients charge, and see where you come out. Can you sell your cookies for that amount? If it's too much, where can you cut? Can you use different ingredients or pay yourself less to get the price down? Is the price now so low that it's not worth it to spend the time? These are decisions you will have to make in relation to your own circumstances. Only you know what is worth your time and effort, but by making some small changes in your methods, you may be at a price that can pay you close to what you want and make use, for profit, of talents you know you have.

It you are selling just your time, it's a bit easier. Set an hourly wage for yourself based on what others are making. If you are a handyman, call around and find out what other handymen are earning for their services in your area. Do you have something that will make your services more attractive? Will you come at night or on the weekends? You can either charge more for that or make it a way to get business away from your competition by not upping your price. If you don't have to drive across town to do a job and can do it at your convenience because you're right down the street, this might allow you to underbid the competition. It's a deal for the homeowner, a convenience for you, and extra cash in your pocket. Be sure to consider all of the factors of a job, and then set an appropriate price.

Be Professional

Even though you may be doing a job for the woman next door that you've known since you were 10 or for a friend who owns a small construction business, you should always conduct yourself professionally. Even if what you're doing is fairly small-time, you must still act in a businesslike manner. In order to keep your customers happy and referring your services, you should do what you say you will do, when you say you will do it, at the price you've agreed upon. Every transaction will build your reputation in some way, be it positive or negative. You are putting your name and reputation on the line, so even if you do only two or three custom painting jobs a year, make sure they are work you are happy to autograph.

CAUTION: When accepting a job for freelance work, it is appropriate to have a written agreement with your customer. This is good business practice for even small jobs, and if you are working with someone who is unknown to you and their requirements seem to be specific and extensive, or if you have difficulties coming to a verbal agreement about what's to be done, a written agreement can help you hammer out the details and be certain you are both on the same page.

The Barter System

One way of saving money on a variety of jobs is to barter. This can be either an exercise in mutual trust and convenience or a minefield of potential disagreements. Bartering always sounds like such a great idea. "How about you refinishing this dresser for me, and I'll mow your lawn for a month?" Before money (just imagine), barter was the name of the game. Now, however, we can put a dollar amount on just about anything, be it a material item or our time. Bartering can still work very well, but both parties must go into the deal with their eyes wide open and be understanding of the fact that things may not work out in a perfectly equitable manner in the end.

Level Playing Field

Bartering works beautifully when you are trading apples for apples. An hour of babysitting for an hour of babysitting is a great deal and can be a breath of fresh air for single mothers or young couples. Neighbors trading lawn mowing while the other is on vacation is a good solution, and picking up mail for each other is another equitable job. Trading pet-sitting duties can be a welcome relief from paying the exorbitant fees to board Fido for the weekend at a kennel. When you have a level playing field in a barter situation, it is best for all parties. There is less chance of disagreement on the terms, and the obligations are clearly known ahead of time.

Unequal Situations

The barter situation where you're trading Service A for Product B, however, can be a little more problematic. For example, what if the dresser was found to need repair while the refinishing process was taking place: Who would be responsible for that extra time? Would the lawn mowing be extended then, as well? Suppose you were bartering for an hour of car repair and wanted to give an hour of housecleaning in return: Is that a fair trade? Mechanics usually make a lot more per hour than a cleaning person might, but an hour is an hour, right? These issues need to be thought through before the offer to barter takes place. You should also have a long discussion with your bartering partner before anything is decided and get something down on paper and signed by each participant when you decide what is to take place. That way, there is no room for "he said, she said" when it comes time for each party to do their part, and the terms are understood by everyone at the outset. If you are going to trade materials for time, or time for more expensive time, make really certain that both parties are aware of the inequities before entering into the agreement. These arrangements are more difficult to manage, and there is more of a chance of one party feeling cheated. Keep communication open, and make sure everyone discusses the process as it proceeds.

A friend of mine had a lovely china cabinet, which I admired, in her dining room. When she was ready to sell it, she called and let me know, as I had earlier requested. I didn't want to pay what she was asking for it, but a few days later, I asked her if she would like to barter for the stenciling I did on the side that she had admired. She was willing to discuss it, so I went to her house and we walked around and talked about what she had been thinking. She wanted extensive work done in several rooms, so I took notes, went home, and typed up an estimate of what it would cost, just as I would have done for any customer. The cost worked out to be within a hundred dollars over of what she was asking for the cabinet, so I did the work and got the cabinet. We both, happily, thought we got the better end of that deal. And, while I was doing her kitchen, she fixed me breakfast!

I do have an important caution for bartering of any kind. The parties need to be equals in the process. It can be detrimental to barter with someone if the system gives one person power over another. For instance, say a woman needs dental work and offers to clean the doctor's office in exchange. If, during the process, the doctor doesn't feel he's getting his time's worth, does he then stop the dental work or demand more from her than was originally contracted? She may agree at that point, as the work has already begun, but may end up feeling taken advantage of in the long run because the doctor held all the power in their bargaining.

Bartering can work, but it needs to start with good communication and the knowledge that what may sound fair to you could be a bit of a hit to someone else. Be open to the thoughts and feelings of who you are dealing with, and understand that yours is not the only important perspective. You may end up with a really nice china cabinet.

Summing Up

Sometimes, the money you need is either already in your grasp, or it's yours for a bit of extra effort and thought. From not buying what you don't need to cleaning someone else's house for money, your thoughtfulness and hard work will get you steps closer to achieving your goals without dramatically changing your circumstances. To make things even better, it may give you a way to continue doing something you really enjoy or give you the opportunity to use your talents and abilities to further your financial aims. Necessity is the mother of invention, after all, and the thought that the weaving you've always done for fun can now make money for you and make your life easier can be a freeing and very welcome thought. Use the talents that you have been given to their fullest extent and you can degunk your finances faster and smoother than you ever imagined.

15

Putting Your Computer and Other Technology to Work

Degunking Checklist:

√ Set up a basic personal computer system for recording and tracking your financial information.

√ Use electronic bill pay to better manage your budget.

√ Learn about the four ways to pay bills electronically.

√ Know what you're getting into before you set up automatic withdrawals to pay bills.

√ Develop a plan to pay bills electronically, paying some automatically and some manually.

√ Find out how you can keep track of your investments, research investment options, and manage your portfolio online.

There is no getting around that the fact that computers are here to stay, and they aren't just for solitaire or shopping on eBay. If you haven't yet used a personal computer (PC) to help you organize and track your personal finances, you'll be surprised at what they can do and how easy they are to use. If you have a PC at your disposal, you should consider using it for your financial good. Your PC can help make your money transactions faster, streamline your record-keeping and tracking, and increase the accuracy of your personal financial knowledge. Your PC can also help you balance your budget and set schedules to remind you to pay your bills on time. You can even use your PC and the Internet to track your investments. It's amazing how much useful financial information you can access on the Internet, and using this information to help you understand and watch the progress of your long-term money can be an even better use for your PC than getting theater show times.

For many people who want to degunk their finances, get their spending under control, and save valuable time in the process, their PC can help them reach that goal.

REALITY CHECK: It is important to state here that if you don't own a PC, this is not license to run out and get one. If your finances are gunked up and you don't have the cash sitting in an account to purchase a PC, the last thing you need is to go out and charge one to use it for this chapter. If you feel you need a computer, save up for one as part of your long-term goals, pay cash, and come back to this section of the book when you need it.

In this chapter, I'll first instruct you on how to get a PC system set up so that you can enter and track your financial data. If you already have a financial system functioning on your PC, you're ahead of the game. Your job will be to make sure that you have exactly what you need and that it is secure. You'll then learn how to degunk and streamline your finances by using your PC for electronic bill pay. I'll show you the different methods possible to help you decide which one fits your lifestyle. The trade-offs, as you'll learn, are that some systems are more manual but give you more control over which bills are paid and when and some are set up to be more automated (at your direction) and will do functions on a timed schedule.

Set Up a Basic PC System to Help Track Your Finances

If you've been into PCs since the beginning, good for you. If you're a relatively new PC user, it's time to study up. Get someone to teach you what they know, or take a class to get the knowledge you need to become proficient at using a computer. It's not brain surgery. Even with the bells and whistles that are constantly added to the financial programs that are always available, they aren't as difficult to use as you might first believe. You'll need to learn some new jargon and terminology, but the techniques required to enter and track your financial data using your computer isn't all that different from doing the work manually with paper and pencil.

If you don't have a PC set up in your home or office and you are prepared with cash in hand to purchase one, there has never been a better time than the present. Prices for PCs have come down so much that you can now buy one for almost less than a new suit at your favorite department store. For recording and tracking your finances, you don't need anything fancy. You need a basic PC, a monitor, and an Internet connection. If you have a friend who is knowledgeable about PCs, ask them to help you with the actual purchasing and be sure to look in *Consumer Reports* (or another informational offering) to check out different brands and units.

In addition to a PC, you'll need to purchase a software program so that you can input and track your finances. The two programs I recommend to my clients are Quicken and Microsoft Money. I'm partial to Quicken, myself, because I learned how to work with that system first. You'll find that people will stand by one or the other—like being a Ford man and not a Chevy man or only buying John Deere products. Both of these programs provide similar features, so you can't go wrong with either one. If you're lucky, you might be able to a purchase a PC that already includes one of these software programs as an incentive, but if not, you can easily purchase one for less than $50 at a discount electronics store (Best Buy or Circuit City) or at a warehouse club (Costco or Sam's). If you can't make up your mind about what software to purchase, consider purchasing one that your friends or family members use. That way, you'll have someone to call if you need help. It would be a good idea to call someone who knows more about this area than you do, so ask around and find your support system before you purchase software they aren't familiar with.

Financial Software

A program such as Quicken or Microsoft Money isn't difficult to use once you get your bearings. These programs basically provide you with a check register–like screen that you can use to input all of your checking account activity, as well as a myriad of other features.

It is vitally important that once you start using the software, you record all of your transactions. You'll also need to make sure to use your PC to balance your checkbook when you receive your monthly bank statement. I've worked with some clients who get all excited about having a new PC, but after inputting their checking account transactions for a few months, they lose motivation and quit. At that point, they don't get to wonder why their PC isn't really helping them like they thought it was going to.

Tips for Using Your PC

Because readers of this book will likely have different levels of experience using PCs, I won't spend a lot of time giving you specific instructions on how to set up and use your PC. There are, however, some general tips I can give you that will help you use your PC to better degunk your finances. If you need more help, there are many good books available that will show you how to set up and run programs like Quicken and Microsoft Money. If you prefer to learn in a classroom setting, take a class at your local community college or continuing education program. Many towns have senior programs teaching computer technology as well. However you go about getting started, keep these tips in mind:

√ *Plan for the transition.* When you decide to convert your record-keeping from a paper-based system to an electronic-based one, give yourself enough time to make the transition. If you try to do this one night after work, for example, you'll likely not have enough time to finish, and half of your information will now be in one place and half in another.

√ *Start slow.* Don't worry about using all of the advanced features of the software program that you've chosen. Keep in mind that your goal should be to get your important accounts set up, such as your checking account, credit card accounts, and any savings accounts that you might have. As you become more experienced in using your PC to record and track your finances, you can always start using the more advanced features.

√ *Control who uses your PC.* Try to set up your financial record-keeping system on a PC that you can access whenever needed. If you can't always use your PC, you might find it difficult to keep your information up-to-date, and you may not get the full benefits of using a computer.

- √ *Keep your PC secure.* Set up your PC in as secure a place as possible—out of the direct line of a window (computers are an attractive items for thieves) and preferably somewhere quiet and fairly private.
- √ *Keep paper records.* Make sure that you keep both printed and electronic records of your important financial data. Just because you're using your PC to record your financial transactions doesn't mean you should stop keeping good printed records. This is especially important in the early stages when you switch over to using your PC. Many a new PC user has lost years of records with one click of the mouse—and still doesn't know how it happened.
- √ *Back up your financial data.* Make sure that you back up your financial data files every time you change them. This is a very important habit to get into right off the bat. Fortunately, the popular financial tracking software makes backing up data very easy. You should also make sure that you keep copies of your backups in a safe place, such as a fireproof container. If your house caught on fire and you lost your PC, losing your backups would make putting your financial data back on your replacement computer a huge hassle.
- √ *Use passwords.* Use password protection to secure your financial data. The popular financial programs now allow you to password-protect the entire program or individual data files. This is an important safety precaution that you should definitely consider using—your financial data is a bonanza of information, both for identity thieves and for your nosy Aunt Edie.

Use Your Computer to Make Tracking Easier

Although this has been mentioned in previous chapters, it bears repeating here. Your computer can be a tremendous help in tracking the expenses you'll need to prepare your taxes. It can also help you update your budget whenever it needs upgrading. Your PC will make both of these functions easier by helping you track the perhaps less-dramatic but still important expenses that are present in nearly every life.

Depending on your tax situation, there are certain expenses that can make your tax load lighter. This was discussed in Chapter 13, so I won't reiterate it here, but tracking expenses like medical costs, child care, school expenses, and charitable giving will make either doing your own taxes or getting ready to have them done professionally much less painful. Imagine having these figures at your fingertips instead of going through your paper check register at tax time trying to find them.

***TIP:** For those of you who visit doctors frequently (due to chronic illness) or who have children, keep in mind that you will need to be more organized than those of us who just wander in to a doctor's office once a year. Dealing with a chronic illness is often a job unto itself, so it becomes increasingly necessary to make the record-keeping of medical expenses as easy as possible. Shuffling through several inches of paperwork at the end of the year looking for expenses is an exhausting and inefficient way to handle these types of medical records. If you have a lot of medical expenses, you know that this situation requires a great deal of time and energy from either the person with the illness or those supporting that person. Save that energy for more important things, and do it all on your PC as you go along.*

The same role of efficiency applies to all your expenses and can help you in the long run by making not only your tax-related expenses available but also other expenses you may not have known would be helpful to your tax situation. Tax laws change every year, and having everything categorized in your computer can be very helpful if you suddenly find out the food for your pet llama is now deductible.

Having good categories is important even in non-tax-related categories. Indeed, you can get as picky as you like when using categories and can use secondary categories to make your expenses even more accurate. Instead of a simple "Clothing" category, you can use secondary categories to name everyone in the household and track what it costs to clothe each. Under "Payroll" can be subcategories of the different ways you earn money. Your part-time pizza delivery job or the calligraphy you do on the side can be broken out from your full-time work. If you are in business for yourself, every business-related expense you incur needs to be carefully documented. Christmas gifts can be a secondary category to "Gifts," and if, like me, you are a tiny bit addicted to knitting, under "Hobbies" or even "Entertainment," there can be a "Yarn" subcategory. The reason for breaking out whatever categories you can is to give you more information on where your money is coming from, or going. You can't manage what you don't know.

***CAUTION:** Keeping secrets is rarely a good idea. There may be a part of you that doesn't want to know (or doesn't want your spouse to know) what is actually spent on golf or on scrapbooking. That is an issue that needs to be addressed within the relationship in which it's happening. Secrets can be detrimental to both budgets and relationships, and unless there is agreement to keep those numbers to yourself, try to find a way to discuss and come to some consensus on what is spent. Your finances and your relationship will both benefit. Immediately after writing this, I will tell my husband about the $189.22 I've spent on yarn in the last year.*

Use Electronic Bill Pay to Automate Your Transactions

Once you have a PC set up, you can streamline and automate some of your activities. Electronic bill pay is a good place to start. If you haven't done this before, it might sound scary, but it is becoming quite common, and after the first few times when you hold your breath before you click (as when you bungee jump), it becomes second nature and a huge time-saver. Consumers write fewer checks every year as more transactions are becoming electronic. The trick to taking advantage of electronic bill paying is to understand what options are available and what advantages and disadvantages the different options provide.

There are basically four ways that you can pay your bills electronically:

- √ *Use your bank's bill-paying service.* Most banks now have an online bill-paying service, which is usually available at little (or no) cost to established customers.
- √ *Pay the vendor directly.* Use a vendor's website to pay the bill directly by transferring money from your bank account.
- √ *Use a third-party Internet bill-paying service.* These are third-party operations, such as **www.checkfree.com**, that arrange for bill payment for you. There is a usually a fee for these services.
- √ *Set up an automated system.* The online services at your bank can be set up to automate your bill paying, taking the money from your account or charging it to a credit or debit card.

With each of these techniques, the goal is to write fewer checks and save time. Many clients I work with have developed a combination of the four techniques to fit their needs, but they can still control how funds are transferred out of their accounts. It is a sorry surprise to find out your system is automated to a point where you don't know what is coming in and what is leaving. In this section, I'll show you how the techniques work and compare the advantages and disadvantages of each.

TIP: If you are just entering into the foray of online services, electronic bill pay is a good place to start. Most banks offer it for a small, or no, fee, and it is an efficient way to pay your bills that may not involve using the postal service. Check with your local bank and ask what the terms are for this service. Some require that you use it at least once per month, and some require that you have a minimum balance in your accounts in order to get this service for no cost.

Use Your Bank's Bill-Paying Service

In my opinion, the best use of your time is using your bank's bill-paying system. This can help you pay multiple bills on a regular basis. Unlike paying through a vendor's website (next section), you don't have to find each vendor, remember your log-in name and password, and arrange for the bill to be paid. Your bank's electronic bill-paying service will enable you to make a payment to anyone you like, and as many payments at a time as you wish. Not only can you pay your electric bill, but you can send money to your favorite charity or to a family member who might be attending college. The bank will decide, within the scope of its particular program, if the money gets paid to the payee by electronic transfer or by a paper check, but that is transparent to you. (If the bank has to issue a paper check, it pays the postage—another bonus!)

Setting up a bill-pay system through your bank will take a little more work than simply paying a bill through a vendor's website. Your bank will likely give you a tutorial to follow, and you'll need to provide some key information, but you only have to do it once. You will need to provide data for every payee, including names, addresses, phone numbers, and account numbers (if applicable). You can continue to add payees as needed or change the information on the payees you already have. Then, when you go online to pay your bills, your personal list of payees will come up and you can check those you wish to pay at that time, along with the amount to be paid. You click on the mouse, and voila! The bills are paid. (See the Gunk Buster's Notebook later in this chapter on how to set up all your bills to be paid this way.)

The main advantage of using a system like this is that you can consolidate your electronic bill pay transactions to one source. You won't have to track down a vendor each time you want to pay a bill. Because everything is done through your bank, you can set up a regular time each month to go online and pay all of your pending bills.

The disadvantage is that your bank may charge you a monthly fee, but if you have a fair number of bills to pay each month, the time you save will make this fee money well spent. Part of your consideration can be the postage you'll save by not mailing your bills. Here are some other critical things that you need to consider when using a system like this:

√ *Bill due-dates.* You'll need to review all of your bills in advance and make sure that they are paid well before their due dates.

√ *Verification that the bank has made payment.* When you select a bill to be paid, it's up to you to make sure that your bank actually completes the transaction and pays the bill. I've heard of cases where the bank makes a mistake and fails to pay a bill and the vendor will charge a late fee. If the bank is at fault, it will usually contact the company to right the matter. Be sure to keep your transaction numbers whenever you make a payment.

√ *Additional bank fees.* If you encounter a problem with getting a transaction completed, some banks (not one I would ever do business with) may actually try to charge you a small service fee to speak with them on the phone (even if it is their mistake). If this happens to you, make it clear that the mistake is on their end and that you shouldn't have to pay a fee for them to correct their error. Again, have your transaction numbers handy.

REALITY CHECK: When using your bank's bill-pay system, you'll need to check your account numbers carefully as you don't want your money going to pay someone else's bill. If you have two accounts that are in the same name, find a way to nickname them so you can tell the difference. One year, my phone company and my cable company had the same name (they were part of the same conglomerate), and I paid the phone bill amount to my cable company on two separate occasions. As my phone bill is much higher than my cable bill, it created a large credit balance. It was quite a struggle to fix, and although both accounts were part of the same huge company, the company deemed it impossible to shift the money from one account to another. It became my problem to fix. Make sure your accounts are clearly named (some banks have a "nickname" feature) so this type of confusion doesn't happen to you.

CAUTION:* *If for any reason a payee changes its payment address, company name, or your account number, you will need to go into your bill-pay site and update this data. It's a good idea that whenever a credit card company sends you a replacement card, you double-check the account number and bill-paying address. On a regular basis, it's wise to double-check all your account information at least every six months. Even utility companies change mailing addresses (even though they're usually post office boxes), so keep an eye on these details to make sure your payments are credited properly and in a timely way.

Gunk Buster's Notebook: Set Up Your Bills on Your Bank's Bill-Pay System

All banks have slightly different software for their payment options. This Notebook is intended to provide you with guidelines for setting up your bank's bill-pay system. Here are the steps to follow:

- √ Get copies of all of the bills you intend to pay online.
- √ Look at each bill and circle or highlight the following information:
  - √ Payee name
  - √ Payee phone number
  - √ Payee address (where payments are sent)
  - √ Your account number
- √ For bills that don't have statements, such as regular transfers to checking or payments to your child at college, write down their names, addresses, and amounts to be paid.

Now you're ready to log onto your bank's bill-pay service, and you should have all the information needed to set up all your accounts online.

Pay a Bill Using a Vendor's Website

Here are the steps involved:

1. Select a bill that you want to pay, such as a credit card bill or utility bill.
2. Use your Web browser and go to the website that the vendor provides for electronic bill payment. You might be able to get this website address from your monthly bill. If you can't easily locate the website, call up the vendor. Make certain there is a padlock icon at the bottom of the page, denoting a secure website.
3. You'll likely be asked to set up an account for electronic bill paying. To do this, you'll need to enter some information about yourself, including your account number, user ID, and a password. (Once you have set up an account to pay bills with the vendor, you'll simply be able to log on with the user ID and password you created.)
4. Pay your bill by entering the amount to pay, your bank account number, and your bank's routing number. You can get your bank account number and routing number directly from one of your personal checks.

That's all there is to it. Once you approve the transaction, funds will be electronically transferred from your bank account to the vendor.

TIP: Keep records of your passwords! When setting up log-in names and passwords, try to use the same ones for all bill-paying accounts, though it may not be possible. Different entities require different combinations of letters and numbers (alphanumeric) to use in their systems. You'll need to keep a record of all these names and passwords, in any case. Make your passwords difficult to guess—your address or your anniversary can be easily guessed by someone trying to use your account.

The advantage of using this approach (paying the vendor directly) is that you'll have full control over when you pay the bill. You'll also know exactly how much money is paid, and then you can record this amount in your checkbook register. This is just like paying by check. The disadvantage is that you'll need to do this manually each time you want to pay a bill. If you forget to pay the bill on time, you can be charged a late fee.

***TIP:** If you pay some of your bills using this approach, you'll find that some vendors will allow you to have your bills sent to you electronically. You can even instruct the vendor to send you only electronic bills, which will cut down on the clutter you'll receive in the mail.*

Ask Your Bank What It Provides

Most banks have risen to the occasion of providing some online services to their customers. Larger nationwide or international banks may have more sophisticated programs, but most provide the basics, such as tracking transactions for various accounts, transferring money from one account to another, providing a debit card (if you choose to use one), and offering online bill-payment service. If you have loans with your bank, there will also be a way for you to track your loan and get up-to-date balances online. If you have an account with one of the larger banks and you have a credit card with it, you can download your balances, daily transactions, and statements at your convenience.

The point of all this is that technology has created conveniences for banking customers. These services can only enhance a bank's attractiveness to its customers, and it becomes your job to find out which of the offerings will make your life easier. Most of these conveniences come to you at no charge. The most common exception to this is some online bill-payment services, which may require monthly fees. You will need to decide if the charge is worth not having to have to write out checks and mail them or not having to pay the bills by using a vendor's website directly. These programs can still be quite worth the money in order to gain efficiency and speed and avoid late fees.

Whatever transactions you decide to perform online, they will carry with them the same limitations and advantages they would carry if you were at the teller window (but you don't get the sucker). Transferring money from one account to another will happen in real time, but other transactions are subject to the bank's policies. If you make a deposit after a certain time of day, it goes on the next day's date and may not clear for a day or two after that. Debit transactions will happen immediately, and if you are at an ATM other than your bank's, you may be assessed an additional charge. Bill pay (if the bank can do a wire transfer) can happen within 24 hours, but if the bank has to issue a check, it may be three to five days before your payee receives payment.

How Your Bank's System Operates

Most of your more common bills are paid by Electronic Funds Transfers (EFTs). Utility bills, credit card payments, and perhaps your mortgage will all be paid in this fashion. Some payments, to individuals or companies without an online relationship with the banks, will be paid by a printed check that is mailed by your bank. In these cases, the postal service is still involved, but at least you don't have to worry about mailing the bill. For the bulk of bills you need to pay, it's all done in cyberspace and quite efficiently.

It is, of course, imperative that you have the money in your account to pay what you are saying you want to pay. This is not credit and it doesn't work the same as sending a check today and depositing the funds you'll need to cover the check tomorrow because you know the electric company won't get it for a few days. It is coming straight from your checking account and should be considered a transaction in real time. Be absolutely certain, as well, to enter these transactions in whatever you are using to track your checking account. Many overdraft fees have been charged as the result of online transactions that never quite make it to the record-keeping system.

This is a very useful service and can make bill paying a faster, more efficient process. It will need management, along with any other financial doings, but can in the long run make the road smoother. In this area, smooth is good.

***CAUTION:** Even though you've automated your bill payments, it's important to regularly check that those payments are actually debited from your account. The best way to do this is (1) pay your bills on a certain day every month and (2) do a follow-up visit to your bill pay website a few days later to make sure all payments have been issued by the bank. If you have bills set on auto-pay, make sure to find out how much is debited every month. Utility, credit card, and other bills will vary every month, and it's important that you record these amounts in your checkbook.*

Paying Your Bills Using an Internet Bill-Paying Service

If your bank doesn't provide an online bill-paying service, you can still take advantage of online bill pay by using an Internet service. One site is **www.mycheckfree.com**, which offers its own bill-paying service and has millions of customers. Even if your bank does offer online bill pay (check with your bank to make sure), you can use this service, separate from the bank, to pay your bills online. Checkfree offers bill-paying services to hundreds of service providers, including most major banks, credit card companies, phone companies, utility companies, power companies, health clubs, cable providers, and newspapers and magazines. The following list includes some of the benefits of paying online:

- √ Save time while you manage bills and stay on top of your finances.
- √ Pay all your bills in minutes from your checking or savings account, all with just a click of your mouse.
- √ Set up recurring payments for bills that are the same each month.
- √ Receive e-mail reminders to pay bills that otherwise might be forgotten (unless you were paying attention in Chapter 3).
- √ Pay your bills whenever you like, 24/7.
- √ Schedule payments from multiple bank accounts.
- √ For Quicken or Microsoft Money users, data may be downloaded into either of these applications.
- √ Cut down on stacks of paper bills in your mailbox by switching to e-Bills, and have the ability to print a copy for your files.
- √ Track and view your payment history online.
- √ Payments are private, secure, and guaranteed to arrive on time.

This service is free (with a couple of exceptions—paying by credit card or needing a bill paid on the very day you initiate payment) to the consumer. The payees pay Checkfree. The company's thinking is that if you're paying a bill online, it's more likely to get its money on time and can avoid the "check was lost in the mail" excuse from its customers.

Other services, such as PayTrust, charge a monthly fee. AOL and Yahoo! also offer bill-paying services. Because you're trying to degunk your finances, keep your fee as low as possible, and if you pay one, make sure it gets on your Monthly Expenditures sheet as a reoccurring expense.

Set Up an Automated System for Bill Pay

If there are bills that you get regularly and whose amounts are consistent, you can take an additional step and automate payment to make sure they get to the payees on time every month. For example, if you get a phone bill each month for $49.99 or a water bill that ranges in cost from $14 to $25 per month, these bills might be ideal candidates for auto-payment. With this approach, you specify in advance the bills that you want paid automatically, and on what day, each month.

This function is for the benefit of anyone who would like money paid to them on a regular basis without having to wait on you. It gives a payee the right to reach into your account and take the money you owe them on a prescribed date. You can instruct your bank, through its online services, to pay any bills you like in this manner. There are positive and negative consequences that can happen as a result of these options, but there are steps you can take to avoid the negative ones and make these services work to your advantage.

You can automate the payment of your bills using either of the two methods:

- √ Set up an auto bill pay transaction through your bank or Internet bill-paying service. Here you can designate who gets the money, the amount you want paid, and on what date.
- √ Contact the vendor directly and have the vendor automatically deduct payment from your account. Many vendors provide a simple form that you can fill out and mail back to them to start this service. The form requires you to enter information such as your bank name, account number, and bank routing number. Once the service is set up, it remains in effect until you cancel it.

I have had so many clients who have gotten in huge trouble using automatic withdrawals that I usually don't recommend paying bills in this manner unless someone has a near-perfect monthly payment history. If not, do things the old-fashioned way: pay the bills when they come in the mail or online in whatever way you have decided works best for you, and make certain that the money is in the bank before you send them off in the mail or over cyberspace.

GunkBuster's Notebook: Be Very Cautious with Automatic Withdrawals

Most people sign up for automatic withdrawals to avoid forgetting to pay a bill that is due regularly. The problem with this reasoning is that they may also forget to note the withdrawal in their record-keeping, and although the payee gets paid, they may get hit with overdrafts as a result. Another way to rack up overdraft charges is to know that the payment is coming and still not have sufficient funds in the bank to cover it. If you have a history of not being able to pay your bills on time every month, this is not only likely to happen but very probable. The more automatic withdrawals are authorized, the more trouble you can get into.

This doesn't necessarily make automatic withdrawals a bad idea, but it does mean they need to be well managed. If you are unsure whether you should set up automatic withdrawals, follow these steps:

1. Pay your bills on time for six months before signing up for any automatic withdrawals. This will not guarantee a flawless transition, but it will get you accustomed to paying bills on time and on a certain date every month.
2. If you can pay all your bills on time for six months and you still want to venture into the land of automatic withdrawals, decide how you will track these transactions. How will you remember to enter them into your checkbook or computer register? Set up a system now.
3. If you are working in a computer program, you can program a reminder to come up as far in front of the payment being due as you like and it will appear when you log on to your computer and go to the account from which the payment is coming. This will hopefully give you enough time to get the money in place and avoid being caught short.
4. If you are working only in your check register, you will need to find a foolproof way to remind yourself the payment is about to be taken out of your account. You can mark the date on a calendar, in your Day-Timer, or in your PDA. If you are working off the budget you made in Chapter 4, you will have already scheduled which bills are to be paid with which check and you can continue to work off of this sheet to know how much to have in your account at which points of the month.

So, if automatic withdrawals look like an attractive way for you to pay bills due regularly, first get your ducks in a row by paying your bills on time, and then develop a way to remind yourself when they will be coming out of the account.

Keep Abreast of Your Investments Online

Depending on where you keep your investments, your account information is probably available online. All major brokerage houses and banks offer online access. The point of going online to check on your balances is not to encourage constant changes but to verify that transactions you are expecting have actually happened. Within a few days of making a request, deposits or purchases, or the sale of a part of your investment, it should be verified. If the transaction hasn't been handled, it should be reported to the company.

If your investments are with one of the larger investment houses, you will get much more than just a reporting of your account when you go to its website. There will also be a plethora of information you may or may not be interested in, as well as articles galore about your investment options and the wide world of finance. Smaller investment houses will have your account information and links to get you to more information, depending on which clearinghouse they use to store the money people invest with them. You can certainly pick and choose what to read, but it would be wise to read anything relating to your personal investments. At the very least, you should be reading a smattering of the general investment news items to stay informed. You may consider this to be right up there with reading the notices that come with your gas bill, but remember that a good consumer is an informed consumer. Stay informed about the company to whom you entrust your money.

TIP: If your account information is available online, you can probably conduct virtually any transaction you could do over the phone—buy, sell, get a check sent, or wire money to another entity. In addition, most brokerage houses offer extensive research capabilities, so you can check the status of your favorite stock (and their opinion of it) at any time. They also offer "portfolio analysis" tools, which can help you assess where your money is invested and whether that portfolio mix matches your goals and personal preferences. Use these online tools to become better informed about your investment options.

The usual point of investing is to focus on the long term and not make daily changes to your investments. Don't get in a cycle of checking your investments every day and making changes based on short time intervals of growth or loss. Micromanagement will not help in the long run because you can easily lose sight of the bigger picture. Check on your investments periodically, quarterly perhaps, and the rest of the time, let them be. (See Chapter 9 for more on savings and investments.)

Summing Up

In this chapter, we reviewed how a PC can help you manage your financial life. I showed you how a computer can record and track your financial information and how it can help you pay bills electronically. I reviewed the four ways of paying bills online, and I cautioned you on why automatic withdrawals aren't always a good way to pay bills. I also covered how using a PC can help you review and track your investments and how brokerage and banking sites can be a wealth of good information to help you degunk your personal finances.

Your computer can be a powerful ally in your financial life. It can make managing your resources, tracking your expenses, and planning for the future faster and more accurate. The key, as always, is to be aware of what your computer can and cannot do. Your own behavior will not change as a result of owning a PC, so you will still have to make decisions, plan, and execute steps, even though your computer makes conducting the transactions easy and fast. You will still need to be disciplined, and you will still need to do the actual management of your money. The computer won't keep you from overspending, and it won't enter the information it needs by osmosis. It is a tool, but only one that can streamline the procedures you have already learned into a smoother workable process. And, of course, if you don't already have one, this is not an excuse to run out and charge one. (Don't forget what you learned in Chapter 5 on degunking your credit cards!)

Improving Your Credit Security

Degunking Checklist:

√ Know which documents are important.

√ Organize and secure your key documents appropriately.

√ Find out why shredding old documents is an important practice.

√ Be aware of the threat of identity theft, and find out how credit reporting agencies can help you if you are the victim of this crime.

√ Beware of phishing (yes, this will be explained) scams, spam, and telephone solicitations.

√ Keep your Social Security number private.

√ Learn what to do if your credit cards are lost or stolen.

√ Keep on top of what is being spent by checking balances online.

Identity theft is on the rise in the U.S, and the easiest way to get into trouble is to not take proper care of the numbers, accounts, and information that make up your financial data. The Internet has created a host of opportunities for dishonest people to appropriate innocent consumers' personal information. Through various scams and outright theft, these crooks now know how to use your personal information for their own gain. If you use a computer to manage your finances, it is especially important that you read this chapter carefully, as I don't want all the hard work of degunking your finances to be undone by a crafty spammer or identity thief. There are a number of simple things you can do to keep your identity safe and make it much more difficult for a bad guy to use your credit to keep him comfortably in champagne or motorized scooters at your expense. We'll go through the most important aspects of safeguarding your key documents in this chapter, as well as give you some problem-solving tips to use in the event of becoming the victim of identity theft.

Identify Your Key Documents

The first thing to do, before you start thinking about electronic security systems and home safes, is to identity what you consider to be your key documents. I consider the following documents to be worthy of safekeeping:

- √ Birth certificates
- √ Passports and citizenship papers
- √ Credit card and other bill statements
- √ Any documents with passport, Social Security, or credit card numbers on them
- √ Loan documents, especially for home mortgages and lines of credit
- √ Credit reports
- √ Stock certificates
- √ Paycheck stubs
- √ Small business records
- √ Tax returns
- √ Bank and brokerage house statements
- √ Medical records

All these documents contain key pieces of information about you, including your Social Security number, your home address and phone number, your employer and employee identification number, names of clients or customers, account numbers, and the names of your parents and children. Any identity thief would relish the idea of obtaining this type of data. These documents, therefore, cannot be treated casually and must be guarded carefully.

Organize and Protect Important Documents

Do you have to keep all of your key documents locked up in a safe or filing cabinet? No. That's not always practical, especially if you're living in a small apartment with limited space. But, keeping these documents out of just anyone's hands is essential. Here are a few tips on keeping key documents organized and protected:

- √ *Create a filing system.* If you followed my advice in Chapter 3, you already have a dedicated work space and a filing system for all your paperwork. Make sure that everyone in your house knows the "hands off" policy when it comes to your files.
- √ *Keep citizenship and birth records separate and safe.* For documents such as birth certificates, citizenship papers, and passports, make a separate file and know where it is at all times. These are probably your most important documents, so you must keep them stored safely, out of harm's way. These documents should be kept in a fire-safe, locked container.
- √ *Save essential historical documents.* For essential historical documents—such as paperwork for old loans, old credit card statements, brokerage and bank statements, and mortgage files—dedicate a separate filing box. Store this box in a separate area, such as the top shelf of a closet, in the attic, or in a safe place in the garage.
- √ *Stock, bonds, and other investments.* Stocks, bonds, and other investment certificates should be stored in a safe-deposit box at the bank or in a personal safe in your home. These types of irreplaceable documents cannot be left sitting around.
- √ *Business records.* Keep all business records separate from your personal filing system.
- √ *Bank, brokerage, credit card, loan, and other statements.* Keep these filed within your paperwork system. Be sure to file all new paperwork at least monthly, when you pay your bills, so that this system stays up-to-date.

It's important for you to recognize that some documents are really important and must be organized well. The most important have been listed. It's up to you to decide if there are other documents that need safekeeping for your particular situation.

TIP: Make sure that your children and visitors (invited or uninvited) do not have access to your files. Only you and your spouse should be dealing with these key documents. This is all part of creating your private workspace and making sure that your financial records stay organized (see Chapter 3).

Document Disposal

I used to be very casual about disposing of my documents. I used to toss all white paper into the recycle bin without a second thought, even though some of those documents had important numbers on them, and I used to tear up old cancelled checks and toss them in the trash. Not anymore. With the increase of "dumpster diving" in this country, I have gotten much more concerned about people going through my trash, though it seems like a horrible way to make even a dishonest living. In some cities, there have been full-on alerts, as dumpster diving has resulted in thieves discovering companies' entire lists of customers, including credit card numbers and addresses. When it comes to key documents, you should make security a high priority.

I recommend that you shred the following documents when you no longer need them:

- √ Any documents with passport, Social Security, or credit card numbers on them
- √ Loan documents
- √ Credit reports
- √ Paycheck stubs
- √ Small business records
- √ Tax returns
- √ Bank, credit card, and brokerage house statements
- √ Bills of any kind that contain an account number or other personal information
- √ Medical records you no longer need

You should be mindful that some documents need a higher level of destruction than others. The inserts that come with your utility bills can obviously just be pitched. Your old utility bills, however, should be destroyed.

Identity Theft Precautions

It's difficult to overstate the concern I have about identity theft. This has become a huge problem, and you need to be aware of the most important threats and scams so you can protect your private information accordingly. Thieves are using the Internet, phone solicitations, and e-mail to grab your personal information. It's important that you be aware of all the major ways you can be conned out of important information and how to protect yourself against identity theft.

Internet Security

There are many aspects of ensuring that your personal information stays secure, especially if you are using a computer to maintain your finances. In the following sections, I'll go over the most important things to keep in mind when using your computer and the Internet to manage your personal financial data.

Secure Your PC

It's essential that you install security measures on your personal computer. At the very least, every PC user should have three things:

√ Internet firewall

√ Antivirus program

√ Password protection to get into your financial program

If you don't have these security measures on your PC, you are at great risk of being hacked and having personal information stolen off of your computer. A firewall and antivirus program are comparatively inexpensive (less than $50), and they're as important as locks on your front door. A password is just good sense. If you have children or other family members using your PC, you *must* have these security measures on your computer. A password alone is not enough—your password-protected Quicken file is not immune to hackers.

CAUTION:* *If you surf the Internet, install a firewall and antivirus program on every computer you have. Without these security items, the information on your PC is at risk of being hacked by an identity thief.

I am not being an alarmist by making these recommendations. There are lots of antivirus programs out there that are cheap or free. Norton is a leading brand. When it comes to firewalls, ZoneAlarm Pro is a reputable company and has a free version available to individual users. Get them both to protect the data on your PC.

Secure Internet Connections

When surfing the Internet, there are secure and nonsecure connections. Most Internet transactions—such as when you purchase a book on Amazon.com or view your bank statement online—are performed on a secure connection. These sites are "secure" because the vendor has provided security software to protect its customers' personal information, such as credit card numbers, account numbers, and passwords. Without this type of technology, no one would be doing business on the Internet.

The first thing to check for is the yellow padlock icon on the bottom line of the site, signifying the site has been secured. Although no system is 100 percent safe, as is evident from the fact that the Defense Department has been hacked into, there have been significant developments since the early days of the Internet to protect buyers from fraudulent use of their information. Even with these improvements, however, you need to hedge your bets for not being endangered. Read on.

The Phishing Scam

Phishing is a term that describes the practice of setting up a totally bogus website that looks *exactly* like the site of a well-known company, such as Citibank or eBay, right down to the privacy notice at the bottom of the page. The problem is that the actual Web address or link that you are prompted to click on—once you've entered in some key piece of personal information—leads you to a black hole. Where did your information go? To a phisher, someone who deliberately set up this bogus site to steal your password, account number, or other piece of personal information. This practice is *totally and completely illegal,* but phishing scams abound because enough people are vulnerable enough to provide this type of information over the Internet.

I got an e-mail some time ago from eBay requesting me to verify my sign-in and password. It stated that they were overhauling the program and needed to remove anyone from it that was no longer using it. The message said if I did not respond within 48 hours, my account would be deactivated. It was, of course, a phishing scam. Quickly following up on someone's report of the bogus e-mail, eBay sent one out saying they would never ask for personal information in an e-mail and to disregard any requests for such now and in the future.

No company or entity should ask you to verify confidential information in an e-mail. Most e-mail is interceptable, unless it is protected with third-party encryption software, which is rare. It would be tremendously unprofessional for a company to put its customers in such a vulnerable position. Similarly, you should never volunteer this type of information to anyone in e-mail form.

CAUTION: Never ever provide confidential information about yourself in an e-mail message. This includes your Social Security number, account numbers of any kind, passwords, passport number, or other key information. For example, if your spouse forgot the PIN for your new checking account, give it to them in a phone call—never in an e-mail or via text message on your cell phone!

Spam Isn't Breakfast Meat

If you're on the Internet and use e-mail, then you know about spam. That's the term for all those annoying e-mails you get offering you cheap prescriptions, pornography, and stolen icons from deposed Nigerian royalty. It's become, unfortunately, a staple in today's world and is the junk mail of the new millennium. There are a couple of points you should remember as far as your personal security is concerned:

- √ Never respond or "unsubscribe" to spammers. That just verifies to the spammer that yours is a "live" e-mail address, and you'll start getting tons more spam.
- √ Never provide personal information to spammers under any circumstances.
- √ Never click on any link in a spam message. This again just verifies to the spammer that yours is a "live" e-mail address.
- √ Never start an e-mail correspondence with a spammer. Check with your e-mail provider to see if it has a spam blocker, or check into third-party providers for spam protection. Some spam protection is list-based, meaning it will not let e-mails through from a list of unapproved sources, or it can be content-based. In content-based protection, the provider will actually scan the e-mail looking for key words or phrases (sexual content, advertisements, phishing) and block the e-mail according to that criteria.

For more on spam and how to reduce it, there's a great book called *Degunking Your Email, Spam, and Viruses* by Jeff Duntemann. It covers everything you need to know about e-mail, spam, viruses, worms, Trojan horses, hackers, and other security threats.

Phone Solicitations

Even though there's the national "Do Not Call" list, phone solicitations continue. You or someone you know probably still gets these calls, which usually come as you're putting dinner on the table. Do not, under any circumstances, give out your credit card number, Social Security number, or any other personal financial information when someone calls you and requests it over the phone. There have been dozens of cons involving cold-calling individuals using charitable causes as a way to get someone to give out their credit card number over the phone. You have no way of knowing who is getting this information, and once it's gone, it's gone. All someone needs from you is a credit card number, the expiration date, and the three-digit code off the back of your card to go shopping in any venue where they don't have to present the card to make a purchase. If you get a call for something that interests you, ask them to send you information in the mail or ask for their website address. You can then look it over and decide if they're legitimate or not. That will give you time to consider the gift or purchase and check out the caller at the same time. Don't let an emotional appeal relieve you of your financial sense.

This includes the Police or Fireman's Association, which is a common scam and works on your feeling of obligation for your local groups. These people call and give you the impression that the money you give them will go straight to your local public safety departments. My husband was a fireman for 25 years. At no time was his department ever given money gathered from these calls. He has no idea where it went, but it didn't come to them. When I mentioned this to the caller unlucky enough to pick my number in the lottery, he wasn't as anxious to talk to me anymore. If the caller is from a legitimate cause, they will still need and accept your money next week, after you have checked them out completely.

***TIP:** Even if a call sounds right, there are ways to check out who is calling you before giving them information. Recently, my family traveled to Mexico. A week after we returned, I got a call from someone who said they were representing my credit card company fraud division and that there had been foreign use on my credit card the previous day. They gave a toll free number to call, and when I did, the first thing they asked for was my credit card number. It occurred to me that I didn't really know who I was calling. Anyone can answer the phone with the name of my credit card company. I stated my concerns to the woman on the phone, who quite rightly advised me to call the phone number on the back of my card instead and have them transfer me to the fraud division. I did, and the call was legitimate. Someone in Mexico was using our credit card number, even though all of our cards were safely in our possession. At the end, I was grateful to my credit card company for keeping a close watch on my account (it denied the last charges attempted) but also glad I hadn't given away my number without being absolutely sure who was getting it. A normal exception to this rule is when you are calling a company to make a purchase and use your credit card to pay for it. Although there is still a chance that someone may get ahold of your number, the chances are much greater that it will be properly used to make your purchase, and nothing else.*

Keep Your Social Security Number Private

Your Social Security number is integral to your financial history. Don't use it for identification in any situation in which you are not absolutely required to do so. Most institutions have other options for you to use for identification, such as your mother's maiden name or the name of your favorite pet. Always ask for one of these choices, and keep your Social Security number off of as many documents and forms as possible. Some companies, such as the gas company, will put up a stink about not having your number, but there is almost always another option available. Social Security numbers are the most used pieces of information in identity theft and, as such, can be used to open accounts and get loans in your name.

Imagine the time and paperwork necessary if someone used your Social Security number to open a checking account in your name, used the overdraft protection to the tune of $1,500 or so, and disappeared. The bank will not be at all cheerful about losing that money, and it won't give up without a fight to get it back. Until the matter is cleared, it would show up on your credit report as a default, and you will need to be diligent in pursuing the matter to prove it wasn't you.

REALITY CHECK: Don't give out your Social Security number unless absolutely required to do so. Your local video store or supermarket doesn't need this number to enroll you in the membership program. Ask if another form of identification is acceptable. Even providing a driver's license or credit card is better than supplying them with your Social Security number.

Avoid the pain. Don't give out any of your pertinent information over the phone or on a nonsecure Internet connection, and use substitutions when asked for your Social Security number. If you are a business owner, make certain the numbers you are being given are for the person requesting the services and save yourself time, frustration, and monetary loss.

Know Where Your Credit Card Is

A common way to lose your feeling of security concerning your credit cards is to lose your credit card or have one stolen. In the days of having a dozen or more cards, it was easy to misplace one, either by leaving it at the store where you used it or by having a sneaky salesperson hold on to it when the transaction was finished. Significant damage can be done in a very short amount of time when a thief has use of your card, and you need to know what your responsibilities and liabilities are in that situation.

***TIP:** It's well known that credit card liability is limited in the event of loss or theft and is usually in the $50 to $100 range. Recently, banks have begun offering the same liability limits on debit cards, which is great news for those who use these cards frequently. Although you are usually not liable for more than $50 on your credit/debit cards if you can prove it wasn't you that made that charge to Tattoos R Us, it may take time to get the fraudulent charges taken off your bill. If there were huge charges and the thief exceeded your credit card limit, for example, it may take considerable effort to get the various black marks off your credit report and reestablish your good standing.*

Be diligent to make sure that this information is removed from your records as quickly as possible.

Lost Credit Cards

By using only one or two credit cards, you reduce the possibility of losing them. Having your one credit card in a visible place in your wallet day after day is a sure way to notice immediately if it's not there as opposed to having a card for every department store and boutique in the mall and needing to count them to be sure they're all in their proper slots. Keep one with you, and if you have others, leave them at home in a fireproof container or safe with the rest of your financial records.

In Chapter 3, you made out a list of your credit card account numbers and the phone numbers to call in case of a lost or stolen card. Now is a good time to call those numbers and find out what each company's policy is concerning liability if someone else uses your card. This is yet another way to decide which cards to keep and which to dump. If one company's policy is that you are liable for the first $50 of a fraudulent transaction and another's is the first $150, that is a good piece of information to use in the culling process. Is there a time limit after which you cannot dispute a transaction? Is there paperwork to fill out when one takes place? Get this information and keep it with the cards you are not carrying. If you do lose a card, that crucial contact information for the card issuer will be at your fingertips.

Here's what you should do if a credit card is lost:

√ Call the credit card issuer and notify it of the loss. Ask to cancel the card (not the account). The company will provide you with new cards (with a different number), usually within 24 hours.

√ Ask if any charges have been placed on that account in the last 24 hours or since you noticed the card was missing. If so, ask what those charges are. If they appear to be fraudulent, let the issuer know. Find out what kinds of paperwork are necessary to report this fraud.

Most credit card issuers will get you a new card quickly at no cost. Most credit card companies are also good at resolving fraud. Make sure you document your phone call to the company and jot down the name of the representative you spoke with. The issuer may give you a case number to use in following up on the call and will probably send you paperwork to fill out and an affidavit to sign stating the charges were not of your doing. As strange as it may seem, some crooks have used their own cards to make purchases and then called them fraudulent. The affidavit would be used for prosecution if this were the sorry case.

Stolen Credit Cards

A stolen credit card is usually a more serious situation because a thief doesn't usually steal just one credit card—your entire wallet is gone, along with your driver's license, medical insurance card, your cash for the week, and other essential information. As a result of this situation, you are a prime candidate for identity theft. What should you do now? Take action, and take it fast:

1. Get out the list of creditors (from Chapter 3) and call each one that would be affected by your missing wallet. This should be done immediately.
2. Just as if the card were lost, notify each credit card issuer that your wallet was stolen and ask to look at any transactions that have occurred on your card since it went missing. See if you can verify which transactions are fraudulent. Ask the card issuer about how it will resolve this issue. Ask for a new card to be sent to you.
3. Call all three credit reporting agencies and ask to be placed on the identity theft watch list.

GunkBuster's Notebook: Place Your Name on a Credit Reporting Agency's Watch List

If you fear that you've been the victim of identity theft, you can notify the credit reporting agencies to place your name on a "watch list" or an "initial security alert" list. What this does is to require the credit reporting agency to notify you *every time* someone requests credit in your name. Therefore, if someone has obtained your Social Security number or other key pieces of information and tries to obtain more credit illegally in your name, that credit will not be issued until you are notified and approve the transaction. If you're trying to rent an apartment and your potential new landlord inquires about your credit, a credit reporting agency will call (or write) you asking if you are aware of this inquiry.

If you have recently lost a wallet with your credit cards, or if you fear you've been the victim of identity thieves rummaging through your trash, you can simply call all three credit reporting agencies and they will place you on their watch list for 90 days, free of charge. They will also remove your name and address from the lists for prescreened credit offers for six months, which means that the number of offers for new credit cards should drop dramatically. Also, as a result of placing your name on the watch list, many credit reporting agencies will offer you a free credit report so that you can verify that no one has used your identity to obtain credit illegally.

TIP:* *A good way to make it tougher for a bad guy to use your card somewhere it must be presented is to write in big letters, in the space on the back where your signature goes, "Please Check ID." If the person doing the transaction even looks for the signature on the back, then they should also ask you for further identification. Though some clerks don't bother to check the signatures against each other when a sale takes place, it might discourage a would-be thief against attempting to use your stolen card in that fashion. It's certainly worth a try. I have noticed recently that more and more salespeople are checking signatures, especially during the Christmas rush. This speaks of good training by whomever they work for, but you can certainly help that process along by protecting yourself whenever you can.

The least likely place for this to be effective is a restaurant. In that situation, you hand over your credit card, and it is returned to you before you sign the slip. It would be very unusual and, in that setting, perhaps thought as rude, for the server to come back to the table and check your signatures against each other, since your credit card is probably already back in your wallet immediately after signing the slip. Even so, it can still be a deterrent for a thief and it is well worth you having to pull out your wallet once again if the server is especially good at what they do. If they request ID when they bring you the slip to sign, it might be worth another buck on their tip, with thanks for their observance and encouragement to do it again.

GunkBuster's Notebook: Warn Your Credit Card Companies Before You Travel

Your credit card companies look for charges that are different from your usual use. If they see activity coming from states or countries other than those in which you live, it raises red flags, especially if charges from both places are posting concurrently. It's a good thing for us as consumers that they monitor the activities of our cards. At that point, they will likely call your home phone to provide you with an'"early fraud detection alert." If you are traveling and using the credit card, you'll likely miss the call. Your credit card company will monitor your account closely if it doesn't hear back from you. If its representatives see hotels, restaurants, and gift shops being charged on your card, they will assume you are traveling. If this pattern continues for more than seven days, they may put flags on your account necessitating a merchant to call them before accepting more charges and requesting information from you to complete the transaction. If you find your card is blocked for any reason, there is a toll-free number (or a number to call collect if you are out of the country) on the back of your credit card to call in order to get the situation (and your hotel bill) straightened out. These numbers are manned (or womanned) 24 hours per day.

To avoid any problems while traveling, call your credit card companies before you leave and let them know where you will be traveling and for how long. They will put a note in their database and wish you a happy trip (and hope for increased spending on their card!).

When you're packing to travel, write down the telephone numbers for the companies whose credit cards you plan to use. If you are taking an international trip, you'll need a number that you can call from outside the U.S. Again, check the back of your cards for these numbers, and keep them in a separate location from your credit cards in the unfortunate case of your cards being lost or taken during your travels.

Know What's Being Spent

An easy way to lose track of your credit security is to not know what is happening in real time. Because most of us have instant access to our bank and credit card statements, we can easily monitor what's being spent on a day-to-day or week-to-week basis. If you're trying to degunk your financial life, you can use the Internet to monitor your expenditures more closely.

Watch Credit Card Statements throughout the Month

It isn't enough anymore to wait for your credit card bill to come in and simply pay it (not that doing that was ever really enough). If you're trying to degunk your finances, it's probably necessary now to keep track during the month of your expenditures and understand where you sit with all of your accounts as the month progresses. It is a quick job to go online to your credit card statements and take note of your recent activity. It's much better to do it as you go along rather than waiting until you have dozens of transactions to check in your credit card checkbook. You are keeping that record in your checkbook, right? (This was discussed in Chapter 4, in case your memory is failing.) That way, if a phantom $1,000 towing charge shows up on your account (which happened to me—another result of the Labor Day weekend I spent in Kalamazoo), you can call the company immediately and question first what would cost $1,000 to tow and then inform them that the charge is incorrect and have it removed from your bill.

Watch Your Bank Balance Like a Hawk

The same is true of your bank accounts. It is a quick check-in to get your balances online and, even if you don't do a full-scale balancing, to know during the month whether you are on track with your budget. Many an overdraft charge can be avoided by getting the news that there is $35 left in the account on which you just wrote a check for $120, and transferring some money from savings to cover your check can buy you time to find out where the confusion occurred. Remember, debit charges are posted in real time on bank websites, so your online statement probably has charges on it that you made just an hour ago. It's a great way to give yourself a reality check and keep on top of the changes you, and anyone else with access, are making to your account.

Summing Up

In this chapter, we looked at how you can improve your credit security. The first step is to know which documents are important and how to organize and secure them appropriately. Safeguarding your financial records is extremely important, as the threat of loss or theft of these papers can result in identity theft, a crime that's of growing concern to everyone. If you are the victim of this crime, you now know how to report it and how credit reporting agencies can actually help you in this stressful time.

So many people keep their financial records on their computers that it's very important to learn the proper security measures you should deploy if you have a PC. Having a firewall, antivirus programs, and a password are essential (not optional!) in this day and age; both pieces of the software can be easily purchased for less than $50, and your financial program has a password option built in. The Internet represents a tremendous convenience for PC users, as it allows us to keep on top of what is being spent in our credit card and bank accounts, but it also can present threats in the form of phishing scams, spam, and telephone solicitations. In this chapter, I also mentioned some actions you can take if your credit cards are lost or stolen.

You've worked so hard to degunk your finances, set up a good financial plan, and improve your credit score. Don't let thieves and scammers steal your identity and wreck havoc to your hard work. Be careful to protect your personal information against people who may have ulterior motives. They will, unfortunately, find someone else to pick on, but it won't be you.

Backup and Emergency Planning

Degunking Checklist:

√ Know how to back up your financial records on your PC.

√ Keep your receipts and other important documents.

√ Protect your statements, documents, and key personal data.

√ Investigate home security options, such as purchasing a safe.

√ Get to know your banking institution and the people who work there.

√ Know what to do if a catastrophe hits your home and everything is destroyed.

The final stage of degunking your personal finances involves setting up a backup and emergency plan. Unless you live in Tornado Alley or on a flood plain along the Mississippi River, most of you probably don't have a plan for how to reconstruct your financial records in the event of a catastrophe. It is not a common occurrence, after all, to have your house burn down. It is wise, however, to plan for the unlikely event in case it occurs.

When it comes to your financial records, a good rule of thumb is to wonder what would be lost if you came home and found the place in flames and to guard against that loss. If you've gotten this far in this book, you've gone to great lengths to organize your financial life. Now it's time to protect your documents against not only life's small accidents—such as computer crashes, spilled coffee, or theft—but also larger and potentially devastating catastrophes.

Backing Up Your Records

If you use a computer to maintain your budget and records, then it's imperative that you have a backup strategy. What if your system crashes? What if you get hacked? What if you (or someone you love) spills Gatorade on the keyboard or your killer poodle chews through a power cord? If you have an active household filled with children and pets, these kinds of accidents are not uncommon. Even if you live alone and are extremely organized, it's important to have a backup plan for your computer files. Like it or not, you don't have control over everything.

If you ask a computer person, they will tell you that there is one thing you can count on concerning your computer. At some point, probably when you least expect it, your hard drive will crash. If you have your financial records on the computer, it is necessary to back them up frequently. That means that every time you go in and record a transaction, pay a bill, reconcile your accounts, or add a category, you must back up. If you use your computer for business, it is even more important. Getting into this habit is the only way to ensure that your records will be up-to-date and accurate if the computer crashes or if some other computer catastrophe occurs.

There are two places to store your data: back up to your hard drive or use a detachable backup device that contains all your information. I'll show you how to do both of these activities in the next sections.

Back Up to Your Hard Drive

The first backup you do should be to your hard drive. The way to accomplish this is to go to the help section of your particular financial program and look under, surprisingly, "backup." It will tell what buttons to click and will help you determine where on your hard drive this backup file will be stored. It's great to back up, but it can be disconcerting if you can't find the backup file when you need it. You can also, within most financial software, set the system to back up to the hard drive every time you exit the program. That will take away some of what you need to remember and keep your first backup as automatic as possible.

You should also consider doing a system backup. Your operating system, whether it's Windows or Mac or some other technology, should provide you with a way of partitioning and backing up your entire hard drive. Again, go to your operating system's help files and follow the instructions. If you're really confused about how and why to do a system backup, I recommend that you consult the following books: *Degunking Windows* by Joli Ballew and Jeff Duntemann or *Degunking Your Mac* by Joli Ballew.

Backup Storage Devices

While doing a system backup is a great way of ensuring that your data is saved securely on your hard drive, it is important to save your information on a removable storage device as well. The next backup should be on something you remove from the computer and keep in a locked waterproof and fireproof box. That is the backup that will get you out of the weeds if the computer is taken, crashes, gets destroyed, or gets a killer virus and you need to reinstall all of your information.

You have several choices when considering a backup system separate from your hard drive:

- √ Floppy disk
- √ Zip drive
- √ External hard drive
- √ CDs
- √ Other storage technologies

Floppy Disk

The first, and most common until recently, is a floppy disk drive. Although in its first inception, the floppy disk was actually floppy, it is now a stiff and hard $3^1/_2$" plastic square. The problem with floppy disks is that they don't hold much information. Your financial files can get quite large, and if you intend to keep all of your data in one place, a floppy disk is not going to have enough space long term. I don't recommend them as a complete backup solution. They are better used transferring a file from one computer to another or keeping small amounts of information remote from the computer.

Zip Drive

A second choice is a Zip drive. A Zip drive is a floppy disk on steroids. It can hold between 75 and 500 times more information than a floppy disk, and it is much more suitable for storing years of financial information in one place. Go again to the help section of your program for specific directions on how to back up to your Zip drive. If you have a Zip drive, consider using it as a backup device to save each day's work in between full backups. Zip drives are Plug and Play, which means your operating system will recognize them as soon as you plug them in the USB port. Most Zip drives have drag-and-drop capabilities, which means you can just highlight files and copy them from your main hard disk to the Zip drive. This is a good option for households using Quicken or Microsoft Money, as backing up is a 30-second action and can easily be worked into your computer routine. After you back up, drop the disk in your handy fireproof container and sleep well.

External Hard Drive

The external hard drive is becoming more popular as a backup device. You can connect it to one computer, do a backup, connect it to another computer, do another backup, and then unplug it and store it in a safe place until the next full backup is needed. External hard drives can be purchased from almost any computer store and are usually Plug and Play. With this device, you can also drag and drop folders onto the external hard drive from your main menu. Again, these represent an easy and cost-effective way of doing a backup.

CDs

Saving data on a CD is getting to be a more common way to keep information. For this to work, you need a CD burner on your computer and you need to purchase special CDs on which to save your information. Most CDs cannot be changed once written on (CD-R), so more expensive, specialty CDs (CD-R+W) are necessary. Information that has already been saved can be changed on rewriteable CDs. Transactions and entries can be modified and then saved again, as opposed to making the change and having to save the entire file on a new CD. How to save data to a CD will depend on your operating system, but it's a fairly painless process.

TIP:* *In acronyms such as CD-R, CD-RW, DVD-R, DVD-RW, R means that the disk can be written to, meaning information can be stored on it. RW means the disk is rewriteable, meaning it can be written to again and again.

Other Storage Technologies

The tape drive is a technology traditionally used by businesses to save their information, but they never really caught on for the private user. If you have this option on your computer, however, it is a possible method you can use to back up your data. Tape drives tend to be expensive and unwieldy for most home users. Another option is a portable USB drive that also doubles as an MP3 player. Creative Nomad fits in the palm of your hand or a pants pocket, can store 128 MG of data (about the same as 88 floppy disks), and plug directly into a USB port. A memory stick is yet another option; it is a device about the size of a stick of gum (hence the name) that plugs into the back of any computer. Memory sticks can store up to 512 MG of data.

Storing Your Storage Devices

Whatever backup device you decide to use, after backing up your financial material, place the floppy, Zip, CD, tape, or other removeable media in a fireproof and preferably locked container. Make the location for this container as convenient for yourself as possible, but make sure it's inconvenient for thieves. It's fine to keep the container in the same room as the computer, but don't leave it out in the open. A locked container can be something a thief takes just for fun, so keep it out of sight but close enough so you will actually use it for its designed purpose. Although deciding to keep the backup container in a different room, on a different floor, or even in a different building is probably a good idea, unless you are tremendously disciplined, you may not use it because it's not convenient. Design a plan you will actually use.

TIP:* *The most important thing about a storage device is to actually use it. Make your backup system easy and understandable. Then, every time you change your financial data, back up. Think of changing your data and backing it up as being like peanut butter and jelly—you don't often see one without the other.

GunkBuster's Notebook: Educate Yourself or Check with a Computer Expert

One of the best ways to use technology more effectively is to educate yourself on its various applications. Almost all software has built-in tutorials, and most of them are well designed and easy to follow. There are also many inexpensive books that can help you learn about the software and hardware that you already have. Depending on your level of computer expertise, you may require a bit of professional help to get your financial system in place. If you've done a lot of reading and research and are still having trouble, ask your 12-year-old. It's amazing what kids pick up in school from just being around computers most of their lives.

Your computer professional may have even more options for you to consider. The computer industry is notoriously prolific concerning new hardware and software, and new programs and systems are being introduced every day. I'm not recommending that you go out and find a $100-per-hour consultant, but at least try to talk with someone who has a talent for computers or works with them regularly. You can also take classes at your community college, continuing education program, or senior center; the classes are inexpensive and geared for all user levels. Regardless of the path you take to learn about the technology, it will be worth your time and effort. Remember to keep it simple. Make sure you understand how to work whatever program you end up choosing. And, always, keep learning!

If You Don't Have a PC

For those of you who don't have a computer, a lot of the preceding material may sound like bad Hungarian. Keep in mind that the principle of safeguarding your key documents still applies to you. Here are some actions to consider:

- √ Keep photocopies of all key citizenship documents, such as passports and birth certificates, in a separate place from the original documents.
- √ Separate "current" from "historical" financial documents; make a decision about the best place to store old documents (options are discussed later in this chapter).

If you don't have a PC, I'd urge you to consider saving for one. I realize it's a big chunk out of a (probably) stretched budget, but this technology is here to stay. If you make a computer a budget item to purchase in the next year or two, it will be accessible and could be tremendously beneficial for you and your family in the long run.

Important Documentation to Keep

Documentation of key transactions is part of degunking your finances—not to mention making tax preparation that much easier. In this section, I'll talk about what kinds of documents you need to keep, how to keep them safe, and what kinds of data need to be safeguarded from thieves.

Verify That Transactions Have Occurred

Paper is proof. What happens if you make a deposit and the bank misplaces your money? Granted, it doesn't happen often, but perfection isn't a reality in people or machines, and mistakes will happen. The only way you have to prove you actually went to the drive-through and handed over the cash from the garage sale is to produce the receipt you were given when the transaction was finished. On it will be important information, such as the amount of hard-earned money you deposited, the account number to which it was credited, and the date. That way, if a mistake has been made, it can quickly be corrected and the money returned safely to your account, where it belongs.

If you can get to your bank accounts online, it would be wise to check a day or two after every transaction to be sure it happened the way you intended. Comparing what is on the receipt against the online information can either confirm your transaction or alert you to fix a mistake that may have been made. It can also help ensure that money has been deposited into the correct account so you don't write checks on money that isn't there. Fixing the problem before checks are returned can make your life much easier and keep you from having to tell the companies to whom you bounced checks that, no, really, it was the bank's fault. They've actually heard that excuse before. Keep your reputation and your payment history safe. Check the receipt against the online information, and if it matches, make a check mark on it and file it.

***TIP:** Keeping your key documents safe is very important. (See Chapter 16, "Improving Your Credit Security," for more on this.) I am big on fireproof containers, but you will have the house lined with them if you're not selective. If you check your transactions during the month, the receipts you receive can just be filed and not kept in a hermetically sealed container. Retain them all through the year, but they don't need to be vaulted.*

If you are making transactions online that affect your bank balances, you don't get a paper receipt. Transferring money, for instance, and having the transaction go cyber-haywire will mess you up as badly as a misdirected check. The way to effectively make sure of your balances in this case is to treat your work online as if it were the drive-through. With every online transaction, there will be a reference number given. Write it down, along with the date and what you were attempting to do, in your checkbook. You have now made yourself your very own receipt, and it can be used if something goes wrong and the money doesn't end up where it should. (If you don't receive this reference number, it is your first clue that something has gone astray and that the transaction probably did not go through.)

Once you have the number, do what you would have done with a paper receipt: The day after the online transaction has taken place, go back online and check the recent changes in your account, making sure the money you transferred to your son's checking account to pay for college tuition actually made it there. Make your check mark on it, and file it.

Protect Your Numbers

It's unlikely that your house will burn down. More likely is that someone will drop in and leave with things that don't belong to them. Thieves steal stuff that can help get them money quickly, or even keep it for the long term. Identity theft can be much more profitable than selling your trinkets for immediate cash.

Protecting your personal data and the numbers that appear on your financial records is an important task. Keep all paperwork with numbers on it in a locked cabinet or drawer. Although most things can be broken into somehow, keeping your financial documentation as protected as possible will be a deterrent to thieves. Thieves are usually in a bit of a rush, so these precautions can sometimes make the difference between them getting or not getting that information. As I mentioned before, having access to these important numbers can allow someone to open accounts in your name, get credit, spend your money, and generally mess up your life.

Also of great interest to thieves are your passport, citizenship papers, and birth certificates. When I talked to the police about identity theft, they told me it is popular to steal birth certificates and use them for the same illegal purposes stolen account numbers are used for, which is to get credit by using someone else's identity. These documents can also help someone establish U.S. citizenship. The police said it was not uncommon for a thief to sell these papers to someone who would use them to get a job and a driver's license, all in the original person's name. Some people have been found out after comfortably living that way for years, paying into another person's Social Security account but not caring about that if the document at least got them the job they needed. People doing this don't want to attract attention to themselves and may never borrow money that might end up noted on a credit report, let alone cash in on Social Security benefits. This activity is still illegal, however, and highly profitable, and citizenship should still not be for sale.

To avoid these issues, keep your important paperwork locked up. It's not hard, and it's not inconvenient. Okay, maybe it's a little inconvenient, but it's worth the trouble not to have to replace government documents and take the chance of someone not nearly as attractive as you are getting a driver's license with your name and their picture. What a tragedy that would be.

Home Security Options

There are many ways to secure your home. Security companies make lots of money offering home security systems, for as little or as much as you want to pay. Luckily for those of you on a tight budget, there are a few affordable options.

Get a Safe

Buying a safe is the same as purchasing insurance: it's a waste of money until something happens, and then you give yourself a big pat on the back for being smart enough to think ahead. A safe is a one-time investment than can keep you from losing whatever money, jewelry, or other saleable trinkets you have lying around. It will also keep your insurance company from getting annoyed with you. It gets so darn touchy when it has to pay out large settlements.

A safe is the perfect storage place for worthwhile items that are easy to steal. Think about your home right now and consider how easy or difficult it would be for a thief to find your stash of extra cash, your inherited diamond ring, and your car titles. Cash may be kept in a drawer or hidden under a desk mat. Women usually keep jewelry where they can try it on with whatever they're wearing and find it inconvenient to have to go and get it out of a safe, so it's usually in the bedroom, close to the closet. Car titles usually sit in the file marked "Car Titles."

Thieves are familiar with the standard hiding places for these items, and they can probably find yours. As most of us hide things where we can easily access them, the first place to look is your bedroom and bathroom. To add insult to injury, thieves often use your own pillowcase to carry all these things from your home. Now you've lost your jewelry, your money, and essential paperwork, and you're left with an incomplete set of sheets to boot. That would constitute a bad day.

Depending on where you have decided to keep your important paperwork, a safe can be used for that purpose as well. Safes come in a variety of sizes to fit every possible living space. Chances are you don't need a vault, but your jewelry, the family silver, and your emergency $150 in cash would probably fit in a safe costing between $150 and $200. Like anything else, it can have bells and whistles on it that make it more expensive. Keep in mind that simply deciding you need a safe is not an excuse to go out and charge one. If you need one, you can save up money from your household category and then choose the right safe for your needs, the same as any other purchase.

Home Security Systems

Home security systems come in various levels of complexity and price. Depending on what you have in your house, you may or may not want one. Most people don't really need one, but if you live in an area that is known to have a consistent number of uninvited guests or if you own a lot of quickly saleable items, you should consider getting a affordable system. The first place to ask about home security providers is through your insurance company. Your insurance company has a vested interest in not getting a theft claim from you, so it can probably recommend a reasonably priced home security system or provider with a "special rate" for its clients. If you get this kind of a deal, they may waive the initial installation fee, which can be substantial. If you're not happy with the company your insurance company recommends, and to get competitive pricing, check with friends and neighbors about what system they use. Remember that home security systems do require monthly monitoring fees, which will need to be figured into your budget.

Off-Site Storage

Another option is to have off-site storage for your valuable items. I've already mentioned that certain irreplaceable documents, such as stock and bond notes and possibly birth and citizenship papers, should be stored in a bank safe-deposit box. If you have one, use it. They are inexpensive and very safe. For all the movies you've seen of people robbing banks and safety deposit boxes laid open with their contents gone or strewn about the room, it happens very seldom—much more seldom than these important documents being taken from someone's home.

Some people rent a storage unit for old financial records and unused household items. If that is the case, you didn't pay enough attention to Chapter 14, when getting rid of your extra "stuff" was discussed. Paying for a storage unit to keep stuff you should get rid of...but, I digress. Concerning storage units, I don't recommend this option for financial documents because security in some storage places may not be great. Most rented storage spaces are secured only with a combination lock, which can be easily chopped. It's best to keep old financial records in your home or somewhere that is safe from strangers.

***CAUTION:** Don't store valuable personal documents in your office. Remember that anything on your employer's property is technically your employer's. If your place of employment should shut down unexpectedly , you could have no claim on any personal property left on the premises. Furthermore, even though your desk or file cabinet at work may be locked, that's no guarantee that people won't break the lock or have duplicate keys to open it. Don't store anything at work that you can't afford to lose.*

Get to Know Your Bank

Another way to gain security for your financial information is to make sure someone is watching your back. For all the work you may put into storing your financial information, things still go wrong, and there still remains a chance, albeit small, that you can lose what you've worked hard to maintain.

Time to give your bank a call. What is its method of backing up, and how secure are your records? Making that call to my bank netted me the information that it backs up in four different places, three of which are outside the walls of the bank. I was also told that if I lose my records, they could be replaced in seven days for a minimal cost. My records, I was told, are permanent, which means the bank doesn't get rid of them after a certain number of years but keeps them forever. The technological options for backing up have made the storing of millions of transactions much more efficient than it used to be, and as some backup choices can hold the equivalent of hundreds of file boxes of information, keeping records forever is a feasible promise for banks.

Within the banking world, it can be very helpful to have a real person to talk to, preferably one who knows your name. In this age of incredible competition, customer service has become a litmus test by which to judge not only how to spend our money but where to keep it. Personal service goes much further than a getting a toaster, so when deciding where to bank, pay attention to how you are treated when enquiring about an account, and after you have accounts open, make sure you show your face in the bank occasionally to get the employees familiar with you. There is usually more help available from people whom you have met face-to-face than from those who see you as a blur when leaving the ATM.

***TIP:* One of the ways to establish a face-to-face relationship with a bank is to make sure that your main banking facility is as close to your home (or office) as possible. That way, visiting the bank will not involve a drive across town. If it's easy for you to pop into your bank and ask a question or get an issue resolved, you will be less inclined to delay taking care of business. This will also let the staff get to know you, and vice versa. If you develop a relationship with the bank's staff, chances are you'll get more personalized treatment than someone just coming in to cash a payroll check. You need to find out how safe your records are with your banking institution. If you lose your records, how can they be replaced? How long are they kept, and what is the procedure on getting them back?**

***TIP:* With most banks and most checking accounts, you have the option of having your cancelled checks sent to you while the bank keeps the originals. This is a great option for cutting down on the gunk you keep in your house. If I find I need a full-sized copy of a cancelled check, my bank can get it to me in a day or so. This saves a ton of storage space and reduces the amount of papers I need to save.**

Businesses that rely on detailed records to conduct their work are usually extremely careful about how their records are stored. Consider how much your life would be disrupted by losing your financial records, and then imagine the havoc if the bank lost the records of the thousands of people who do business with it. It is not enough, however, to just blindly believe the bank is doing a good job. Make a phone call, or stop in, and find out what the procedures are if your records are lost (and you haven't taken my advice in the previous sections to back up this information).

REALITY CHECK: If you lose your records, they won't be immediately reconstructed by your bank. It can only provide you with the information it has, which is a record of the transactions it has handled for you. The bank won't put them back into the register for you and won't categorize them for tax time, so don't be thinking it's not important to back up because your bank will bail you out. It can probably provide you with all the statements and copies of the checks you need, but you will still have to classify every transaction.

Another plus to being known at your bank is the care it provides when something out of the ordinary happens.

My son wrote a check recently that seemed a bit strange to the folks at the bank, so instead of cashing it and finding out later it was bogus, they called him and asked before putting the check through. The check was authentic, but I called to thank them for looking into something that seemed out of place. What a great feeling it is to have a financial guardian angel, and it comes from the bank knowing who you are, knowing when something seems a bit hinky, and taking the time to investigate the situation.

The world is big, and banks continue to get bigger, but there are still people who work there with whom you can develop a relationship. Not only is it friendly and a more pleasant way to do business but it can help you in the long run to have someone at your institution know who you are and know enough about your habits to recognize when something is amiss in your accounts.

When Catastrophe Strikes

This is the ultimate gunk—a catastrophe strikes and you need to rebuild your financial records. What if your house was flooded by a foot of water and your computer, as well as all the documents you had in boxes on the floor, was completely destroyed? Where to begin? Aside from contacting the Red Cross and wailing, I'd recommend the following:

- √ Contact your main bank and explain the situation. If your debit card has been lost, it can usually issue a replacement debit card within hours so that you can get to your money.
- √ If your credit cards and other identification have been lost or destroyed, notify those agencies as quickly as you can. Even if all you know is that you had a BankOne Visa card, you can call the main BankOne number, explain the situation, and the bank will get you on the right track.
- √ Call your insurance companies. They may assist in arranging for temporary housing, as well as restoring your home, vehicles, and property.
- √ Replace your bills. At your convenience (though nothing may be convenient at this point), you will need to contact your other creditors and notify them of the situation. They should have records or assistance they can provide. This is a project that can be put off a bit if you have other, more pressing matters to deal with, depending on the severity of the catastrophe.
- √ Rebuild your financial history. Once you have resettled, it will be important to begin reconstructing your financial history. Your creditors should be able to provide you with a paper trail of recent bills. Your banks and savings institutions should be able to provide past statements. And, if you have backups in a safe, flood-proof container, it could be as easy as plugging in the new computer, and reinstalling the programs.

The worst news is that if you have nothing backed up, it will be up to you to rebuild your financial records to whatever degree you can. More important things—such as housing, food, transportation, and clothing—may be your priority for a while, but once the crisis is past, you'll have to get back to your degunking plan, which now may be more difficult, and try again.

Summing Up

It is certainly the hope of all of us that our homes remain standing and that the fire insurance premiums we pay will be money wasted. The sad truth is that houses burn down every day, and catastrophes happen.

In this chapter, we looked at how to back up your financial records on your PC and what kinds of storage devices are available to do this. I reminded you that it's important to keep your receipts and other important documents, but also to know what level of security is required to protect your statements, documents, and key personal data. I mentioned a few home security options, and I recommended that, if nothing else, you purchase a home safe. Another way to ensure that your bank will get your back if you need help with your records is to get to know your banking institution and the people who work there. Finally, I looked at some key actions to take in the event that a catastrophe hits your home and everything is destroyed.

The people that lose the least in catastrophic situations are those who planned for the remote chance that something like this might happen, while hoping that it would not. Be one of those people, and if the unthinkable happens, you're already on the road to system recovery.

Now that you've finished the book, I hope that you've incorporated some of the teachings, strategies, and actions presented. This can be a reference you return to again and again, and as your finances change and grow with the principles you put in place, you can come back and brush up on what you may have glossed over the first time through. This is one of those books you'll never outgrow.

You couldn't have read this entire book without realizing that the single most important thing you can do for your finances is something you have now done—you have paid attention to them. You have unearthed the problems, have worked toward a solution, and are on your way to degunking your finances (and some of the rest of your life) and becoming infinitely less stressed.

Appendix A

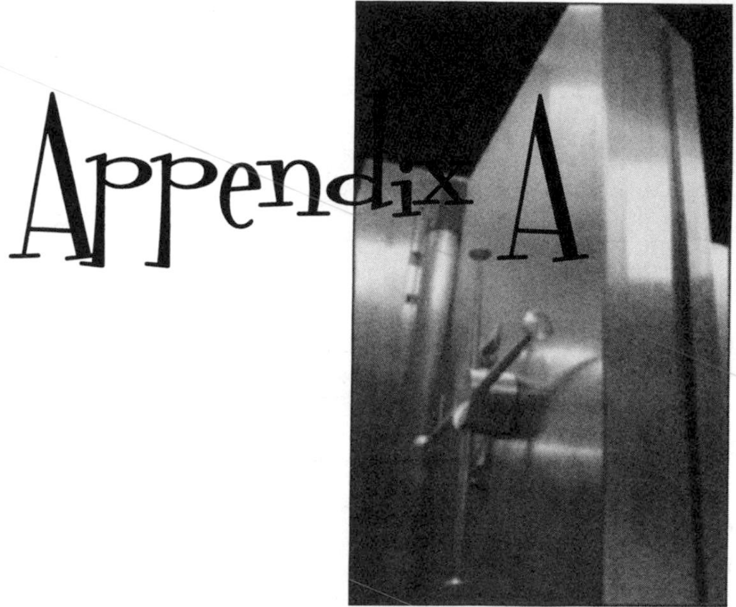

Forms for Tracking Your Expenses

This appendix provides the three main forms to help you gather and track your finances: the Income and Assets form, the Big D (Debt) form, and the Monthly Expenditures form. For more information about how to fill out and use these forms, review Chapter 4.

Income and Assets Form

Income

Job # 1____________________ every____________________

voluntary contributions____________________________

Job # 2____________________ every____________________

voluntary contributions____________________________

Job # 1____________________ every____________________

voluntary contributions____________________________

Job # 2____________________ every____________________

voluntary contributions____________________________

Assets

Checking Accounts________________________________

Saving Accounts________________________________

Money Market Funds______________________________

Home (market value)______________________________

Car(s)____

Investments, CDs________________________________

IRAs, Retirement Funds____________________________

Other Property__________________________________

Other____

The Big D (Debt) Form

Mortgage (current balance) ____________ ______%

Home Equity Loan ____________ ______%

Car Loans:

____________ ______%

____________ ______%

Credit Cards (current balances):

____________ ______%

____________ ______%

____________ ______%

____________ ______%

____________ ______%

____________ ______%

____________ ______%

____________ ______%

Friends and Family ____________ ______%

Education Loans ____________ ______%

IRS ____________ ______%

Other ____________ ______%

Monthly Expenditures Form

Total Income ________
Saving ________
Giving ________
Spendable Income ________

Housing ________
Mortgage/Rent ________
Association Fees ________
Electric ________
Gas ________
Water ________
Trash ________
Phone/Internet ________
Cell Phone(s) ________
Repairs ________
Other ________
Total Housing ________

Auto/Transportation
Car Payments ________
Gas ________
Train/Parking ________
Maintenance ________
License/Stickers ________
Other ________
Total Auto ________

Household/Personal
Groceries ________
Clothes ________
Dry Cleaning ________
Gifts ________
Household Items ________
Personal Maintenance ________
Books/Magazines ________
Activities/Lessons ________
Education ________
Other ________
Total Household ________

Insurance
Auto ________
Homeowners ________
Life ________
Medical/Dental ________
Total Insurance ________

Loan Payments
Credit Cards
________ ________
________ ________
________ ________
________ ________
________ ________
________ ________
Education Loans ________
Friends/Family ________
Bank Loans ________
Other ________
Total Loan Payments ________

Pets
Food ________
Shots/Medications ________
Vet Visits ________
Grooming ________
Other ________
Total Pets ________

Professional Services
Child Care ________
Medical/Dental/Presc ________
Legal ________
Counseling ________
Other ________
Total Professional ________

Entertainment
Dinners Out ________
Lunches Out ________
Movies/Events ________
Babysitting ________
Travel/Vacation ________
Cable TV ________
Fitness/Sports ________
Hobbies ________
Media Rental ________
Other ________
Total Entertainment ________

Total Expenses ________

Total Income ________

Over/Under ________

Index

C

D

E

L

T